TRAVELLING THE AMERICAS.

TRAVELLING THE AMERICAS.

A 70,000 KM BACKPACKING ADVENTURE FROM NOVA SCOTIA TO PATAGONIA

TIM CARTER

Follow Us2travelling on Instagram to view the posts and photos of our journey

www.instagram.com/us2travelling

FOR HELEN

Table of Contents

CHAPTER 1 - THE BEFORE

"Do you know what Helen? I'm tempted to hand my notice in and then we can both go travelling."

I remember saying those words even now and where we were when I spoke them.

It was sometime in August 2015. We were at home having our tea and the TV was on in the background.

I can also still vividly remember Helen turning her head and looking at me.

"Really? Are you serious?"

"Well yeah, why not, we could just do it."

A couple of days before, Helen had mentioned she was tempted to go to Asia to help out with some volunteering at a dog charity. Helen was soon to be unemployed after redundancy and had an opportunity for some down time before starting work again. Yes it would have been amazing for her to do something like that, but from a selfish point of view I wanted to be with her.

But we were in our forties. This is not the sort of thing you do at our age. Going travelling is something you normally do after University or when you are retired. But if you think about it, when you are young, you probably don't have the money to really get the best out of travelling, you may miss out on things as a result but you have your health, you are fitter. When you are retired, you may have the money, but how much can you really see and enjoy if your health isn't as good as it used to be? So our way, in our forties would hopefully be the best of both worlds. We have a bit of money after working for 20 years and we are still relatively fit, enjoying hiking and running. Therefore it actually seems the ideal age to travel if you have no kids. The only downside is that you have to re-start your career when you return, but we'd worry about that when we got back.

1

I really don't know what sort of reaction I was expecting from Helen, but I sensed she was up for it and to me that was all I needed to know. It looked like this could be on.

Of course this is a book about our travels but I want this book to also explain the before and after, not just the travelling itself. The range of emotions, the highs and lows we have gone through. Hopefully it might inspire some of you to do the same or help in your own preparation with some useful tips. Not at all are we claiming to be experts on travelling but we did pick a few things up along the way, and we visited some pretty amazing places. Also I'll be the first to admit that I'm no Michael Palin or Bill Bryson so sadly you may be disappointed if you are expecting a book of their high standards.

The world now though is a different place to the one back then. Covid-19 has affected us all. Lockdowns and quarantines have restricted worldwide travel. Most of us did not go abroad in 2020 resulting in staycations. Winter and a second wave are sweeping through Europe. The travel and tourism industry will never be the same until the vaccines are rolled out. The decision to release a book about travelling maybe not the wisest one, but with restrictions as they are, hopefully this book may provide an escape from your current situation. It may stir up an impulse to travel once this nightmare is over and wanderlust will be high on the agenda for a lot of people after suffering from cabin fever over the past year.

To be absolutely sure that we would be able to go travelling, we had to make sure Helen's health would not be at risk or an issue as she is a type 1 diabetic.

We had no idea about buying insulin abroad or how much it would cost depending on where we are going. Insulin also needs to be kept chilled, so how would that work if we are on the move a lot? These were important things to consider and would need looking into. Helen has been a diabetic since she was 30 which is unusual as you don't normally get diagnosed with Type 1 as an adult. And credit to Helen, it has never stopped her doing anything and she has never used it as an excuse.

For those who don't know about Type1 diabetes here is an explanation.

Type 1 diabetes is a serious, lifelong condition where your blood glucose level is too high because your body is unable to make a hormone called insulin. Your body attacks the cells in your pancreas that make insulin, so they just can't produce any. The problem is we need insulin; it does an amazing job of allowing the glucose in our blood to enter our cells and fuel our bodies. But when the glucose enters the bloodstream, there is no insulin to allow it into the body's cells. This causes a build-up of glucose in the bloodstream. Type 1 diabetics like Helen get insulin into their bodies by injecting it, calculating how much insulin is required for the meal they are about to consume. Helen injects every time she eats, so about four times a day, directly into either her abdomen or thigh. Also during the day she has to check her blood glucose levels to see that they are not too high or too low. This is done by using a finger prick test and placing a droplet of blood into a small handheld machine. The blood is then measured and gives a digital reading of the blood sugar level. For a non-diabetic person, the display will show anywhere between 4 and 7 depending on what they have recently consumed. When Helen was first diagnosed at the doctors, her blood sugar level was in the high 20's. Helen had a strong suspicion that she was going to be told she was diabetic; she had all the symptoms, needing to wee a lot, extreme thirst and feeling incredibly tired. She had also lost some weight recently which can also be attributed to diabetes. With such a high reading at the doctors, Helen was given insulin immediately as over a long period of time if blood sugar levels are too high this can lead to serious complications with the heart, eyes, feet and kidneys. At the other end of scale there are more immediate problems if the blood sugar levels drop too low, these are called hypos or hypoglycaemia. These usually happen quickly, so understanding the symptoms is vitally important in order to be prepared for what to do. Everyone has different symptoms but the most common and which Helen suffers from are trembling and feeling shaky, sweating, anxiety or irritability. The scary thing about hypos is that if you don't react quickly enough and get some sugar inside you to raise your sugar levels, one outcome is that you can pass out. For this reason we make sure she never goes anywhere without her dextrose sweets. There is always a can of full sugar coke in each of our

3

cars and both upstairs and downstairs in the house. In our 20 years together she has had to endure lots of hypos. She has explained the insatiable need for sugar that overwhelms you when you have a hypo and the hours of feeling awful afterwards, therefore the day is a write off.

Even if we thought Helen's health was not going to be at risk whilst travelling we needed to know how we could obtain insulin and also how to transport it and keep it chilled along the way. At an appointment with her consultant and diabetic nurse they confirmed that insulin should be available to buy either from a pharmacy, doctor or hospital, although costs may vary depending on which country you are in. In terms of transporting the insulin, we were advised to buy a medical bag. This is similar to a little cool box, but made of a softer material rather than hard plastic and with packs of frozen gels inside, the insulin can be kept chilled for up to 24 hours, a lot longer than a normal cool box. Helen was also advised to buy a Frio insulin wallet. These are more portable than the medical bag and can be used when out and about for the day and be carried in a day pack. The wallet has a part which you soak in cool water for about 20 mins and this activates whatever is inside and keeps the insulin cool for hours in hotter temperatures.

Safe in the knowledge we should always be able to buy insulin and keep it chilled, we were now convinced we were doing this. When I first suggested to Helen about going travelling, she had just been told she would be made redundant and was due to finish work at the end of November, so I needed to get on and hand my notice in at my work. Starting our travels in January seemed like the ideal time. That would allow us to sort out the house and have a good Xmas and New Year with family and friends before setting off. I always find January to Easter depressing anyway. I'm just wishing for spring with warmer days and longer evenings. We are definitely summer people, there is nothing worse than going to work and coming home in the dark.

I can't remember exactly when I told my parents, but I know it was a sunny weekend, and they were sat out in the back garden. I told them what we were planning, that we had thought about it for a few weeks and we were confident Helen would be fine with her diabetes. They were happy for us, however I wondered how both sets of parents must have really felt. Both my brother and Helen's brother are married with children and have secure jobs. So to then have your middle aged son and daughter announce something like we were planning, it would have been a surprise. They must have thought their days of worrying about us were over! Any parent would surely feel the same, but they knew that it was something we really wanted to do so they supported our decision.

With our friends the response was the same, some said we were brave to do this, however the hardest thing we found was actually making the decision itself. Once that was made, the planning began. Ahead of us I needed to quit my job, empty the house, find tenants and plan a route.

So with a rough leaving date of sometime in January 2016, initially we thought of starting towards the bottom of the West coast of the US, in San Diego. Although it would be January, the weather would be pretty good. From there we would head north, aiming to get to Vancouver Island, Canada for the spring, as I think we would only be allowed a three month visa for the US anyway. Canada was always a place we wanted to visit. We are both outdoors type of people; we love hiking and just being outside. One of the reasons we were able to go travelling is because we have no commitments, we have no children to keep us here. We also unfortunately no longer had any pets. When Helen and I became a couple we went through the phases of going out, getting serious, first holiday together, then buying a house together. We never had kids, we started off with a couple of rabbits, then decided to get a dog. We chose a Weimaraner and called her Macy. She was a fantastic dog and we had lots of great walking holidays in Wales every year with her. When she was just five we noticed a few lumps on her body and thought we had better get them checked out. It turned out she had mast cell tumours and would need the lumps removing. Over the years she had the odd extra lump removed, underwent three rounds of chemotherapy and took steroid pills. We were blessed that she lived to age of 11 and had a fully active life all the way until the end. It wasn't actually the skin cancer that sadly took her away from us. She also developed bladder cancer and it was that which eventually led to us having her put to sleep. Those decisions are horrible to make but it was the right thing to do. That morning, the three of us went for walk around the local nature reserve, one of her favourites. It took a long time for pain of missing Macy to subside but everyone knows time is a healer. It was the end of Sept 2014 when we lost Macy and now a year on without her, we were looking at potential travelling routes.

A couple of years earlier, Helen had bought me the Lonely Planet guide to Canada and it just looked amazing, and huge. From the rugged West coast and mountains of British Columbia, to the Rockies in Alberta, the flats of Saskatchewan and Manitoba. Ontario, the Great Lakes and Niagara Falls to the Maritimes in the East. Canada is massive and with so much to see there is no way a couple of weeks holiday would ever do it justice. This was a country we always wanted to visit and it looked like we would get the opportunity in spring. Canada is known for a few things. The stereotypes are bears, ice hockey, and maple syrup to name a few but it is also known for being cold, very cold. If we arrived at the start of spring then that would allow us until the end of summer to make our way across the country before it got too cold. When I say too cold, I mean our backpacks have limited room so we might not have the right clothes to deal with minus 30 degrees. In very rough terms we had a bit of a plan, which would take us to about September, after that who knows, we could head down the east coast of the US, fly on to somewhere else or just head home?

I needed to hand my notice in at my work if I was to finish around the same time as Helen, maybe a little later in December. I had been with my current employer for four years. Those years had been great and I really liked my job and the people I worked with. However they were owned by a Private Equity company and in the time I had worked there they had already sold three other businesses, all larger than the one I was working at, leaving it as the only company left. You didn't need to be a genius to work out what was going to happen, they were going to be looking at selling us as well at some point. So early November, the day I was going to hand my notice in to my boss, I was asked to attend a meeting and told what I had expected, the business was going to be put up for sale and they wanted it done as soon as possible. Sometimes when a company is sold things go smoothly but more often than not there are casualties. If I didn't go travelling the company would be sold and I would probably be made redundant, with a small pay out for four years of service. I was asked to play a role in the sale of the business and would receive a bonus should the company be sold. I couldn't believe the timing of this and at the end of the meeting I asked my boss if we could have a chat. I then told him that it was unfortunate timing based on the meeting we had just sat in, but I was going to be handing my notice in soon and wanted to give them the heads up so it allowed extra time to hire someone new and allow a smooth handover. I then told him what our plans were and he was genuinely happy for us, he knew that Helen was going to be made redundant and I got on really well with my boss

And then came the "but."

He then asked me to reconsider when I would be leaving and asked me for an extra six months, so sometime in June. In return I would still receive my bonus when I left, regardless whether the business had been sold. The bonus was very appealing. It would help with our travelling funds. I needed to speak with Helen and see what she thought about the situation. I told my boss I'd have a think, talk it through with Helen and give him a response by the end of the week.

I spoke with Helen about it that night. She was obviously gutted about the fact that something we had been looking forward to would potentially be put on hold for six months, but she definitely saw the appeal of extra funds. For a number of months we had a date in our minds and even a vague planned route of where we were heading and then all of a sudden it is put on hold. You mentally prepare yourself that you are leaving on a certain date, but we had to look at the positives, the six months would soon pass and our travelling funds would be better as a result. We decided we would wait. Fortunately at this stage we hadn't announced our plans to everyone we knew, I think only our families and a few friends knew that we were going travelling. Later that week I told my boss I would stay on for the six months until June 12th 2016.

Now we would have to revise our itinerary as we were due to head up the west coast of the US and arrive in Canada in the spring. We now wouldn't be leaving England until the end of June or early July so if we continued on the same path, we would reach Canada late summer rather than in the spring. That could wait for now as we had extra time to prepare but Canada would still be definitely in our travel plans.

Christmas was soon on the horizon; Helen had finished work on the 30th November and was officially unemployed. However this only lasted a few days and she quickly found the ideal short term job. It was a part time job share role as maternity cover, working three days a week for six months. Absolutely perfect.

Xmas was good and spent with both families. Presents for us both consisted of things we would use for travelling. Helen already had a Kindle and I received one for Xmas. They are ideal for travelling compared to taking loads of books. As a joke Xmas present I bought Helen a washing line. But looking back now, they were one of most prized possessions in our backpacks. It was a travel pegless washing line which is basically two pieces of intertwined elastic with hooks on either end. You don't need pegs as you can simply push your washing between the two bits of elastic and it stays in place. We ended up buying two, one of the best things £10 can buy for travellers, they don't weigh a lot and take up very little room in your backpack.

The 28th was a landmark birthday for me, my 40th, and it is also the birthday of my brother's youngest daughter Emma. She was celebrating her 9th Birthday. Both our families went out for lunch and my brother's family gave me some really nice presents. One did bring a tear to my eye. It was a travel journal, but inside were handwritten messages with some photos taped to the first few pages to remember them whilst we were away. It was such a heart-warming present. I had never considered keeping a diary or journal of our travels but I would now. We had a lovely meal then we went home and chilled out for the afternoon in preparation for the evening. I really wasn't sure what I wanted to do for my 40th, but we had decided I should have some sort of party. I hired out one side of a pub, arranged a buffet and we were just planning to play our own music through the pub's sound system.

When Helen and I arrived at the pub just after 7pm, my mates had surprised me by hiring a live band. We all love live music and the band was great. It might be because I was drunk but everybody seemed to be having a good time as there was lots of dancing and I was really grateful as about 30 people came out to celebrate my birthday. Having your birthday on the 28th December is not ideal as it's hard to expect people to make it with other commitments around the festive period.

Over the next couple of months it was just business as usual, working, trying to save a bit more money and planning for our trip. By March we had decided on an initial destination. We were now going to start in Canada, it seemed an easy country to start our first backpacking experience. For starters they speak English; they are also incredibly friendly and mock themselves about how apologetic and unthreatening they are. We also decided to start on the Eastern side. The main reason for this was cost. It would have been so much more expensive to fly to Vancouver so it made sense to start in Nova Scotia and head west. So we booked the flights. On the 12th July, Helen and I were flying one way to Halifax in Nova Scotia, via a six hour layover in St Johns, Newfoundland. This was it, we were actually doing this.

At work, in early April we started to present to prospective buyers down in London. Straight after one presentation I made a hasty exit to catch a flight. I was heading to Galway in Ireland to see an old friend as otherwise it could be a long time until I might see him again. As you get older it's easy to lose touch, and in terms of seeing each other face to face, the moments become more seldom. So I really needed a good catch up with Hamish and spent a good weekend with him drinking, watching sport, hiking in the hills and catching up with his family.

At the end of April I was due for my first appointment at the doctors to start having all my necessary jabs for travelling. I was given a new vaccination card and at my first appointment was vaccinated for Tetanus, Diphtheria and Polio. I retuned three weeks later to have my first Rabies vaccination. I then went back for the following two weeks for my second and third rabies shots. At that final session, I also had a Yellow Fever vaccination.

By now the spare room had started to become our packing room. We had started to make packing lists and one thing we both agreed on was that we didn't want a backpack that just had top access, meaning it was difficult to reach things which were located towards the bottom. We had read about some backpacks that opened with a large zip going nearly all the way around, so it opened up like a suitcase. I bought a Lifeventure one, it was a 60 litre pack. Helen bought a 60 litre Vango backpack that also had a 20 litre day pack that could zip onto the main backpack. A lot of time was spent researching what we should and shouldn't take and there are a lot of websites and travel blogs to help with this. They all said one thing. You will take more than you need, start questioning why you packed it and then eventually get rid of it. I can confirm we were "those people". There were travel bloggers and writers who were saying that you should basically be able to fit everything you need into a rucksack small enough to be allowed as carry on so as avoiding baggage charges. For us that seemed to be a bit extreme. We wanted to be careful about stretching our money as best we could but there was no way I was going to persuade Helen that two t-shirts is enough and do you really need three pairs of socks and knickers? I accepted we would be paying baggage charges if required and Helen would take as many knickers and socks as she wanted.

As well as preparing what to pack for the trip, we also had to pack away our home belongings. We decided that we would rent out our house whilst we were away and used an agency to find suitable tenants. In the meantime we started to box things away. By now the to-do-list was getting quite large.

As the days and weeks went by, we kept adding to the packing room and ticking things off the to-do-list. For only £5, and valid for a year, we picked up our International Driving licences from the post office. Subscriptions such as Sky TV and the internet were given their notice. We also made photocopies and scans of passports, medical insurance, driving licences and medical cards in case we lost them or had our bags stolen.

By now Helen had finished her temporary role and did a fantastic job of sorting and boxing things up. We had decided to rent a storage container with a company about a 45 minute drive away but it was the best price and it looked safe and secure. The weekend before our Tuesday flight was when we would move everything into the container. Our families also stored some of our possessions. Both my parents and brother stored some things for us but the vast majority was stored in Helen's parents' attic.

My time at work was coming to an end. It looked very positive from a buyer point of view that the company would be sold soon. The plan therefore was not to replace me as things would change under new ownership so a colleague would cover my role for a very short time.

When travelling we decided that we didn't want to be constantly on the move. I know this is essentially travelling, but what I mean is staying in places for a little while by volunteering. It also helped on the funds as by volunteering, food and accommodation would also be included. I found a website called workaway.info. On here you could find voluntary work almost anywhere in the world and the range of work available was so varied. You basically filter on a country, then region and look for a volunteer position that suits you. Helen and I found a workaway on an organic farm needing help. The general rule on Workaway is that for four hours work a day the volunteers are provided with food and accommodation. We created our online profile and tried to sell ourselves as best we could against other workawayers who are most likely to be younger than us. Experience and trustworthy were two words I'm sure we emphasised in our profile. Our message was sent to the farm and a couple of days later we were pleased to find out they had asked us to stay with them for three weeks. So now we had an initial plan. Within three days of landing in Nova Scotia we would be working on a farm. About as far away from office work as you can get, but just what we wanted. After that we had no further plans, we had three weeks at the farm to decide where we were going next.

Leading up to our leaving date the UK was in the process of voting in a referendum on our future in Europe. The Conservative Prime Minister, David Cameron, had pledged during the 2015 Election campaign to hold a referendum. The vote was to take place on the 23rd of June and the country was to vote whether we should stay part of the European Union or leave. Brexit, as it became known was everywhere and everyone had an opinion.

The problem for Helen and I, and it seemed for everyone else, was who to believe? Politicians from both Remain and Leave were quoting all types of figures and scare stories should we stay or leave. I don't mind a bit of politics but to be honest my main concern was how this was going to affect the Pound Sterling whilst we were travelling. In January we could have exchanged just over 2 Canadian Dollars to the Pound. By February and March it was hovering at about 1.85 - 1.90. All the talk in the media was that the Remain vote would win. That creates a bit more stability and confidence and therefore the Pound should strengthen. We decided to wait before exchanging some Canadian Dollars. Everyone knows what happens next. The Leave vote won, no one really expected it, the Prime Minister resigned and everyone was left wondering what happens next. Well the first thing that did happen was that the Pound dropped. Overnight the Pound went from 1.90 to 1.77, by the 7th of July it was down to 1.67.

Ok, so we lost a bit straight away by not exchanging some before the Brexit vote but this would have an impact on our travels. The Pound was now weaker against other world currencies and it might continue to weaken during our time away. Overnight our travels just got a bit more expensive as a result of the Brexit vote. Hopefully all of this Brexit business wouldn't drag on and be sorted by the time we returned.

My last day at work was on the 24th of June. It was quite emotional. I really liked my job, but more importantly I really liked the people I worked with. They kindly bought me some gifts, mainly to be used for our travels including some Amazon vouchers that came in very handy for last minute purchases, and a lovely card full of kind messages.

From finishing work, this left me with about three weeks before we set off to Canada. Fortunately, or unfortunately for Helen, this coincided with the European Football Championships so I took full advantage and made sure I watched as much as possible. Selling both of our cars also became a priority; luckily Helen managed to sell hers quite quickly. Mine was taking a bit longer to sell. It is a fine line between aiming to get a decent price for your car against not actually selling it, it came to the point where I tried one of those "we will buy your car" companies but was amazed at the ridiculously low price they were offering. Luckily I sold it a week later for a respectable price. With no cars in the household we relied on pedal power and parents to help transport us around.

In the short time before leaving we wanted to spend as much time as we could with family and friends and the question of how could they keep up to date with our travels kept popping up. Some asked if we were going to write a travel blog. No, we had no interest in blogging about our travels. I have a Facebook account but very rarely post anything, Helen never even had one. I didn't believe Facebook would be the right platform where people could follow our travels. No one would want to see me bombarding their feed with my travel exploits. We both had Instagram accounts and thought this would be the best way. We therefore created an account called us2travelling. That way if people wanted to follow us, it was their choice. We also wanted another way to share more with our families. Both Helen's and my parents are retired and we knew they'd be happy seeing more than the odd Instagram post, so we signed up to Flickr. On here we were able to create a private group where we could upload as many photos as we liked and only those in the group, our close family, could see them. It was also a really convenient way of not worrying about space for photos. Again, compared to years ago when you had a roll of camera film which you had to then send away to get developed and not even have a clue what the photos would turn out like. Quite soon after we decided we were going travelling we went for a drink with Helen's brother Steve and his wife Karen. They went travelling themselves and it is how they met. They were younger than us when they went and it was before the days of the internet, old school travelling. Steve was telling us how it must be so much easier to travel these days compared to when he went. Aside from books instead of Kindles and camera film instead of digital, these were the days of traveller's cheques, so it was more hassle just to get money. Finding a room for a night, we take that for granted now that you can search and book online in advance, but 30 years ago you could arrive somewhere and not have a clue where to stay, or if and when you do find somewhere, how much it is or whether they have any rooms? You can read reviews of hostels and hotels now, but not then, you didn't have a clue what you were walking into. Google maps and translate were two things we relied on so much when we travelled but these were just not available back then. Has it taken the sense of adventure out of travelling? Yes, it definitely has. Has it made it easier for more people to travel though? Yes as well.

Our flight to Canada was on Tuesday July 12th. The Sunday before, my brother and his family had a BBQ as a sort of farewell party for us. My parents and uncles were there and so were Helen's parents and her brother's family. Luckily the weather was great and it was a really nice way for us all to get together before we left.

The next day we finished emptying the house and putting things in storage, then returned the hire van. Our house was completely empty apart from the things we were taking obviously and a blow up camping mattress and sleeping bags for us to sleep on for our last night. Helen's mum was going to come round in the morning and give the house a final clean as our tenants were moving in that day. We finished packing, the allowance was 25kg and we used it all. When we returned from travelling I was sorting out some paperwork and came across my packing list. It was as follows:

T Shirts x 3

Shirts x 3

Long sleeved top

Summer vests x 2

Zipped Micro Fleece

Comfy Joggers

Lightweight Down Jacket

Walking Zip off Trousers x 3

Underwear x 5

Socks (pairs of) x5

Shower / Beach Sandals

Trainers

Buff, neck warmer

Xero Shoes

Travel Belt with hidden zip

Running Vest

Running Shorts

Swimming Shorts

Walking / Working boots

Baseball Cap

Microfibre Large Travel Towel

Microfibre Small Travel Towel

Rain Poncho

JagBag Silk Sleeping Bag liner

First Aid Kit

Sea to Summit X Plate

Sea to Summit X Bowl

Travel Cutlery Set

Wash Bag

Ear Plugs and Eye mask

Travel Washing Lines x 2

Torch

Multitool

Penknife

Howsar Quick Twin Lock

Travel Umbrella

Portable Charger

Ipad and ipod

Chargers and cables

Kindle

Digital Camera

Travel Journal

Waterproof bags for electronics

PacSafe

Sunglasses

Frio Bag for insulin

Spare blood testing kit

Spare day insulin injection pen

Spare night insulin injection pen

Gardening gloves (I know, but we knew we were working on a farm for the first three weeks!)

There may be some things on here that you've not heard of so I'll explain and also mention other things we found useful.

Howsar quick twin lock. This is a really clever little device that allows you to lock a door from the inside. If you are staying somewhere that doesn't have a lock on the door, such as a bedroom or bathroom this handy little device allows you to lock the door for peace of mind. We used this a few times during our travels, takes up very little space and weight in your backpack.

Waterproof bags, of course you would have heard of these but they are very important. They again are a real lightweight item and if you are stuck in the middle of nowhere, say hiking, and it starts raining, these are ideal for keeping things dry. We kept a waterproof bag of important documents permanently in our day packs.

PacSafe. This is a large exomesh steel cage that completely covers your backpack and can then be locked. Ideal for public transport, Helen and I had one each. Before we left we weighed every item that we were taking. These PacSafes were the heaviest items in our entire rucksacks but we never used them once in all of our travels. As you read the book you will understand why but I really think it depends whereabouts in the world you go whether you should have one of these. I carried both mine and Helen's throughout our journey, stored at the bottom of the backpack. But, you never know if you are going to need it. That's why we (I) carried them all the way with us.

Cables. If like us you have a few gadgets, we took ipods, Ipad, Kindles, phones and Fitbits, you will have a few cables. I ended up taking a small pencil case where you could just fold all of them up inside.

Portable charger. Does what it says on the tin, but very handy. We relied on ours a number of times when battery levels were low. They can be quite heavy but certainly worth taking.

We did wonder whether it was worth taking a small travel umbrella and a poncho. The thing is you normally wait for it to rain before you buy one anyway and as we already had them we figured they could sit in the backpack until needed. They don't weigh a great deal or take up to much room.

Multitools, Penknife, Torch etc. Again I had a little pencil case type bag where I kept these sorts of things and it would also carry spare batteries later on. As a leaving present from work I was given a tiny little metal case which was essentially a mini survival kit. It contained everything you would need in an emergency but in a box no larger than 5x3 cm. These were always in my daypack when we went out hiking.

Ear plugs and Eye masks. These are probably the lightest items in the backpack but so important. Travel is cheaper at night and there are always going to be times when you need to catch up on forty winks or have a long bus journey and will need to have a sleep. Hostels are not quiet places either. These items are invaluable for getting a better night's sleep.

X Plate and X Bowl. These are quite expensive but ideal for travelling. Made of a flexible silicone material they press flat for easier storage.

First aid kit. We didn't go stupid here, it was more a case of pain killers, plasters, diarrhoea tablets, a couple of small bandages, some dressing and surgical tape.

Silk sleeping bag liner. Expensive but worth it, costing nearly £50. Made from 100% silk, these are used inside sleeping bags for extra insulation or alone in hotter climates. Also just handy to use when the place you arrive at looks pretty grotty.

Microfibre Towels. Ours were by Lifeventure but they are made by numerous brands. What is great about these towels is how small they fold up. Also they doubled up as a beach towel for me whilst Helen used a sarong.

It goes without saying that a decent pair of boots is essential. I didn't want to go for a pair of standard hiking boots as they can be heavy. Instead I stumbled across a brand called Ridgemont, the Outback model, they were really comfy, great for walking but actually looked really good as well, good enough to go out in as they didn't look like normal walking boots. Helen did the same, but I forget the brand she used. Basically there is a lot more choice for travelling gear these days. One of the shirts I took was a green / olive colour, as were a pair of walking trousers, and sometimes due to dirty clothing they were worn together and perhaps should not have been, so I looked a bit like Ray Mears, not that looking like Ray Mears is a bad thing.

Travel belts are handy as they have a hidden zipped pocket on the inside. Wherever we were I would always have a stash of the local currency in case we lost our bags or were mugged and our money was stolen.

Xero shoes. Seemed like a good idea at the time, minimalist lightweight sandals, these seemed ideal for travelling. Actually, if it wasn't a nice paved road it was really painful to walk in them. I should have just bought a normal pair of walking sandals instead.

Buffs. Very versatile, lightweight, also double up as eye masks.

Our first actual Instagram post was a picture of our clean new backpacks in our empty front room, the night before we left. INSTAGRAM POST 1. At the time of writing it has one like, from Matt, an old University friend, thanks Matt. It would really help if you have Instagram for this book, as I will mention each post so you can look at our feed, that way it's a little bit different to just reading a normal book; as you can also see the pictures we took at the time. Our Instagram name is us2travelling. Unfortunately Instagram runs posts from newest to oldest so you always have to scroll down to the bottom for the start. Don't blame me, blame Mark Zuckerberg. Hopefully you like our idea as it is more personal.

The above list included some of what we carried in our day packs. Helen additionally carried a testing kit, insulin pens, emergency sweets or can of coke. Things we usually had in day packs were;

Important documents, (copies of travel insurance, passports, driving licences, medical cards etc.)

Guide book, we had an actual book for Canada, thereafter we downloaded them onto our Kindles.

Kindle

Ipad

Ipod

Charging cables

Snacks and drinks

Toilet Roll and Hand sanitizer

Ear Plugs and Eye Mask

Travel Journal

On my person I had a travel wallet, Lifeventure again that had two zipped pockets for change, useful for when you are carrying different currencies. I also had a security wallet that is worn under your top but never used it after the first day. And a phone obviously, we kept our existing ones and decided to each use an international SIM card. This had a UK +44 number but it meant we were able to keep the same number all the way through our travels. The alternative was to buy a Pay as You Go SIM every time you entered a new country. I'm still not sure if we would have been better off. Our way was convenient in that as soon as you landed or crossed the border you could use data or make a call in an emergency. The reality was we never needed to and as there is so much free Wi-Fi around these days you can use emails and WhatsApp to communicate anyway.

The only thing left before our early start was to say our goodbyes. My parents called round first. I have never seen my dad cry before now. I wasn't expecting it and it made me really emotional as well. He said he was really proud of us and what we were doing. After lots of hugs and tears we said goodbye and waved them off as they drove away. It felt really strange not knowing when we would see them again in person. I don't normally have long periods when I don't see my parents as they live so close. We didn't know how long we would be away for but assumed it would be somewhere between six months to a year. Helen's mum actually wanted to wave us off, so we headed to bed before setting our alarm for 3am. Our flight was at 9am and we were leaving at 4am. A good friend of mine, Merv, or Nick to use his real name was on gardening leave between jobs and offered to be our taxi to the airport. I had chatted to Merv quite a bit about travelling; he had travelled a bit in his younger days, mainly Asia and Australasia. Before Merv arrived, Helen's mum came round to say her goodbyes. Again it was very emotional. I can still remember as I hugged her she said "Please look after Helen". I assured her I absolutely would. When Merv arrived we loaded our bags in the boot and then it was time. Last goodbyes to Helen's mum and we pulled out of our estate.

The roads were empty at 4am heading down the A1 and around the M25 so we made it in good time. Merv took our photo for INSTAGRAM POST 2. We had just arrived at Gatwick airport and we were at the back of the car with our backpacks looking clean and short haired. We said our goodbyes, Merv wished us well and we headed into the airport. Bags checked in, into departures for a decent breakfast, it really started to hit home what we were doing. All around us, everyone else was going away for a week or two, maybe three if they were lucky. We didn't know, and that was the great part of travelling, the unknown. We knew we were going away for a while but where and when wasn't set in stone. This was really exciting; we were actually doing this, something we both wanted to do for some time was actually becoming a reality. It wasn't long before we were boarding our flights and saying our goodbyes to each other. As we didn't want to pay extra to pre book our seats, it was inevitable that we would be starting our adventure of a lifetime sat 20 rows from each other. It didn't matter too much. We were going to be pretty much inseparable for the foreseeable future. Time to catch up on a bit of sleep and then we would be waking up at our stopover destination, St Johns in Newfoundland. Day 1 of our travels, July 12th 2016.

Chapter 2 - The During

Part 1 - Canada

We landed in St John's around midday. St John's is the largest city and capital of Newfoundland and Labrador, the most easterly province of Canada. Province is the same as County in the UK or State in the US. Newfoundland itself is a rugged Island but Labrador is part of the mainland. The strangest thing about Newfoundland is that it has a time zone half an hour ahead of the mainland, which for us when we had been awake since 3am GMT was a little bit confusing. Unfortunately we were not going to see any more of this beautiful part of Canada. We were here for a six hour stopover, but as it was raining and blowing an absolute gale outside we were not leaving the airport. INSTAGRAM POST 3, I took a photo of Helen having a nap, you can see how full our backpacks are and Helen's cool bag for carrying her insulin is sat on top of our backpacks. You can also see how inexperienced we are as travellers as I have left my security wallet, which is supposed to be discreetly hidden on my person, left out and clearly visible for anyone to steal. The six hours went by soon enough considering it was a pretty small airport. It wasn't long before we were ready to board our Westjet flight to Halifax in Nova Scotia. Walking out to our plane, the weather was miserable. INSTAGRAM POST 4, See, look how bad it is, July according to the Lonely Planet is when the province is at its sunniest. Well not today it wasn't.

Nor was it when we arrived in Halifax. It was torrential rain, thunder and lightning and to think we had left the UK in glorious sunshine to come here to this weather. We landed late in Halifax, there was nothing to do apart from a catching a taxi to a motel for our first night of accommodation. One thing Helen and I had both agreed on from the start was that we wouldn't be staying in dorms in hostels. We weren't skint teenagers, we had a bit more money than that so if we ended up going home three months earlier just because we stayed in motels and hotels then so be it. In Canada, we hardly came across any hostels anyway. Hostels though in the end were actually fine, but that's for further on in the book.

We woke on our second day to find that Halifax was bathed in glorious sunshine, a complete contrast after what we witnessed the previous night. After grabbing some breakfast we went for a long walk along the waterfront and then back through the city. INSTAGRAM POST 5. One thing that made me chuckle was walking past a McDonalds and seeing an advertisement for a McLobster. I am sure it is quite trivial to citizens of Nova Scotia but it tickled me nonetheless.

When the famous Titanic ship sank on its maiden voyage across the Atlantic, the bodies not lost at sea were brought to Halifax to be buried. There are 150 graves across three cemeteries in Halifax with 40 graves still unidentified. The most famous attraction though in Halifax is the Citadel, it is actually Canada's most visited national historic site. It is a huge star shaped fort that sits atop a hill. We went for a look around and it was an interesting visit.

We returned to the motel early afternoon in time to catch the bus to Truro at 3pm. INSTAGRAM POST 6 is me sitting on the steps of our first motel, I admit it's not a great picture, nor flattering but we were new to the photo and social media game. It's not flattering for the motel either as those steps could do with a lick of paint. It was on our first day that we realised how useless it was to have a digital camera. We didn't have a laptop, only an Ipad so any photos we took on our digital camera, we would then have to spend time in internet cafes uploading them to Flickr. We realised you could take decent photos on the Ipad anyway and upload them via the app, the same as Instagram. So for the foreseeable future, the digital camera was going to join the two PacSafe's at the bottom of my rucksack. We considered walking to the bus stop which was a couple of miles away but we were new to this, we didn't want injure our backs on the first day, so we took a cab instead. INSTAGRAM POST 7, was taken on the bus looking back to Halifax as we headed to our next destination. Halifax sits on the southern coast of Nova Scotia. We were now heading north to Truro, a stopover before we meet our Workaway hosts in two days.

The bus journey didn't take that long, just long enough for me to read my Kindle, feel sleepy, put the Kindle down, sleep, wake up, get off the bus in Truro and not realise I had left my Kindle in the seat pocket of the bus.

What. An. Idiot. I had been travelling for two days and I had already lost my Kindle. My thoughts went back to Helen's mum asking me to look after Helen, I needed someone to be looking after me more like! Yes I was gutted, I would try the bus company in the morning and see if was handed in but I was pretty sure I wouldn't see it again. One thing for certain though, whenever we travelled on a bus or a plane after that I double and triple checked the pockets in front of me. That was a mistake I certainly learnt from!

Truro is famous for its tidal bore. A tidal bore is a tidal phenomenon in which the leading edge of the incoming tide forms a standing wave of water that travels upstream, against the current of a river or a narrow bay. They take place in very few locations in the world, and are normally found where incoming tides are funnelled into a shallow narrowing river or bay. Sometimes the Tidal Bore at Truro can be over a metre high. Unfortunately our time in Truro coincided with a period between moon cycles therefore the wave was more like a ripple. It must have been poor, as we didn't even take a photo. In the afternoon we went on a long walk along the Cobequid trail to Victoria Park. The sun was shining, it was a great walk. This is what Helen and I love doing. Just getting out and walking, finding somewhere on a map and heading for it. Back in July 2016, you could still only post one photo per post on Instagram, I can't remember when it changed and increased to ten photos. So the next four Instagram posts were all of the same walk and visit to the park, when one post of four photos would have been fine. So apologies, blame Zuckerberg again. The first post showed the trail to the park, INSTAGRAM POST 8, then the rather unimpressive waterfall, INSTAGRAM POST 9, the never ending steps of Jacobs Ladder, INSTAGRAM POST 10 and the walk back when we saw our first ever chipmunk, INSTAGRAM POST 11. On the way back we dropped into the bus depot to see if my Kindle had been handed in but there was no such luck. Early evening we had our first go at washing some clothes in the sink and trying out our pegless washing line. We sat outside playing cards whilst they dried. For the remainder of our trip the cards remained at the bottom of my rucksack with the two PacSafe's, the digital camera and my security wallet.

The next day was when we would finally meet our Workaway hosts. We arrived at the bus depot early, so as an excuse for commiseration in losing my Kindle, and the fact that Helen thought we could potentially be meeting our murderers, we decided to have a beer at 11.30am. At the bus station I took a photo of Helen leaning against the wall. INSTAGRAM POST 12. Although it looks like it is staged, it isn't, she had no idea I was taking her photo. The bus left at 1pm and took us to Sackville where we were going to be meeting our hosts. Sackville was in New Brunswick, the neighbouring Province to Nova Scotia. New Brunswick, along with Nova Scotia and Prince Edward Island make up a region of Canada called the Maritimes.

Mary was the daughter of our hosts and she had arranged to pick us up. As the bus pulled in and we saw her waiting in her truck, Helen quickly texted the license plate number to her mum just in case she never heard from us again. There was no need to worry, Mary was lovely, she was a teacher, not a serial killer. We drove back to her parents farm and met her father, called Norman. His wife was called June but we didn't meet her until she returned home from work. The house was on two levels but from the outside it would look like a bungalow. We would soon discover virtually all houses in Canada have an underground basement level. This is where our bedroom and bathroom were located. Norman hand built the whole house himself and also Mary's house which is about a quarter of a mile away. My journal entry for that day said "This is a big culture shock for us and a bit overwhelming really but we'll see how it goes." It was our first day, we were here for three weeks, if it didn't suit us, well we could just leave, say sorry this isn't for us, thank you but goodbye. We didn't have to do anything we didn't like. Helen and I agreed on this straightaway, we said on a scale of 1-10 of happiness if either of us are feeling below a 5 because of what we are doing or where we are staying we should consider moving on. It was just the fact this was so alien to us, just staying with strangers in the middle of nowhere, in Canada. We were out of our comfort zone but that's why we were doing this, I'm sure we'll be fine.

In the morning after breakfast we were shown what we would be doing. We also met the dogs, Shady, Cindy and Santa and also Mary's dog called

Billy, they were great and just followed us around. At 8am we started by picking strawberries, then we dug some carrots, and finally we picked peas to finish off our first mornings work. Pretty easy really. For lunch, Mary cooked a large hot meal, and we all sat around and ate together, apart from June who was at work. The conversation flowed as we tried to get to know each other. After lunch Mary took us for a drive to Confederation Bridge. The farm we are staying at is very remote, the nearest place would be called Cape Jourmain and this is where Confederation Bridge is located. It really is a sight to behold. INSTAGRAM POST 13 and INSTAGRAM POST 14. The bridge is 12.8 km long and it links the mainland province of New Brunswick to the island Province of Prince Edward Island. It took nearly four years to build opening in 1997 and cost $1.3bn Canadian Dollars. It really is a surreal sight as this bridge just goes on and on into the distance. On the New Brunswick side of the bridge there is a sort of services stop before you cross the bridge. There is also an information centre on everything about the bridge, a restaurant and some gift shops. In the evening at the farm it seems a sandwich, cold eat affair is the norm and you help yourself. After cleaning up Helen and I headed down to our basement room and listened to the radio. For our first day it was fine, the thing we were always going to struggle with is living under the same roof as someone else but it just takes time to adjust. Even just helping yourself to things in cupboards and the fridge seems strange but it will be become normal over time. At least we had our own bathroom.

By the end of our second morning we basically knew our list of chores. Norman is always up and about early, so he has already collected the eggs from the chicken pens, and he leaves them in a bowl near the back door for us. Helen then washes and cleans the eggs and puts them into egg boxes. Whilst she is doing that I go and fill up the drinking water for the cows. Then we fill up the Hummingbird feeders. INSTAGRAM POST 15. We had never seen Hummingbirds before and they are fascinating to watch, they are so fast. We filled up the bottles with some sugar water twice a day. INSTAGRAM POST 16, Strawberry picking is always the first job we have outside on the farm. There are about six long lines of strawberry plants we go up and down every day, filling up our punnets. Norman sets up a stall at the front of the house and all of our punnets go on the table ready for sale. This becomes the farm shop and where all of the selling takes place. The area around New Brunswick is a popular holiday destination for Canadians. "Cottagers" is the term as they come here to spend their vacation time in small holiday cottages. Due to its remoteness there is nowhere to buy fresh produce. This is where Norman and his farm cash in. For the short holiday season, Norman sets up a stall and every day "cottagers" drop in and buy his produce, depending what is in season and available. We added carrots to the table; two price tiers were available for carrots, a $1 bunch or $2 bunch. Picking peas, INSTAGRAM POST 17 was another job we had, which we then shelled INSTAGRAM POST 18 and bagged up and put straight into the freezer. It seemed none of the cottagers were getting their hands on the precious peas. Nothing goes to waste on the farm, all the food scraps go to the chickens and the pea shells go to the cows, and they love them. INSTAGRAM POST 19. It is difficult to share them out as they are all so desperate to eat them. And that is pretty much what we did in the time we were here. The second week saw the much anticipated arrival of the potatoes. Everyone in the first week was asking when the potatoes would be ready. We also picked raspberries when the strawberries had run out.

With finishing at midday, lunch eaten and cleaned up by 1pm we then had the whole afternoon to ourselves. Most of the time we went for a walk. We were only a few hundred metres away from the sea but around the farm is marshland rather than beach. This was the reason for the ridiculous number of mosquitos that were always around. Mosquitos love Helen and she was becoming a feast to them, we didn't know whether it was because of her diabetes and they could sense something different in her blood. The mosquitos were not so much a pain for me as the horseflies. They are jokingly called the National Bird of New Brunswick and I can see why. You know when you have been bitten by these as it feels as though they are taking a chunk of flesh out of you. Turning right at the end of the drive onto the main, but quiet road, we could find access roads to the actual beach after either a 20 minute, 40 minute or an hour's walk. At the hours access there was a tiny little store. This was usually our incentive to walk the hour, buy an ice cream, lie on the beach all afternoon and walk another hour back to the farm. Most of our afternoons were at the 40 minute access, INSTAGRAM POST 20 and we would head home for about 6pm to have a sandwich, retire downstairs and listen to the radio. Sometimes if the mosquitos weren't too bad we would sit out on the porch and brush the dogs and watch the hummingbirds, INSTAGRAM POST 21. It all seemed a world away from the life we had at home but we were really enjoying ourselves now and getting on well with our hosts.

Norman was a character, he was constantly moaning at the news on the TV and asking us about Brexit. Norman found it amazing that we didn't make our own bread, grow our own food, brew our own beer, or make our own cookies like he did. We explained to him that our lives are completely different and that we shop at large supermarkets back home and sometimes buy convenience food. Our lives are worlds apart but that is why we are doing what we are doing, so we can see and learn from other people's lives. There is no doubt they live in a very worthy and sustainable way which makes me jealous and slightly ashamed that I can't do a quarter of the things that Norman could do but that's why we are different. If there was an apocalypse, Norman's farm is the place I would want to be as you could continue living off grid for a long time. INSTAGRAM POST 22 shows the front of the farm house. If you look closely in the picture you can just make out the table shop on the right hand side at the end of the drive. Norman showed us some photos of previous winters where the snow levels had reached the roof of his house.

So all in all life on the farm was pretty easy, I remember Helen and I were picking some green beans one Monday morning in the glorious sunshine knowing that we only had a couple of hours before we were done and probably beach bound. Helen turned to me and said "I've had worse Monday mornings than this" She was certainly right, it was great to be out in the fresh air on a sunny day in a field picking vegetables compared to being in an office back home. The next few posts showed our life on the farm during our stay. From hanging out with the dogs and the cows INSTAGRAM POST 23, INSTAGRAM POST 24, INSTAGRAM POST 25, and INSTAGRAM POST 26. Also more hummingbird videos, INSTAGRAM POST 27. On July 22nd, we announced to the world via Facebook that potatoes were now ready and available on the farm, thanks

28

to my brilliant photography, INSTAGRAM POST 28. There is also a video of the chickens when Norman lets them out every morning. INSTAGRAM POST 29

By now we had also sorted some plans for post farm life. We were going to cross the bridge to the promised land of Prince Edward Island. This is how we viewed it. Every day for the last couple of weeks we would just see this huge bridge stretching out into the distance. We used to compare it to the yellow brick road or a rainbow that had a pot of gold waiting for us on other side. I also posted far too many photos, INSTAGRAM POST 30, INSTAGRAM POST 31, INSTAGRAM POST 32, INSTAGRAM POST 33 and INSTAGRAM POST 34. We had found another workaway with a man who lived on his own in Charlottetown, the capital of Prince Edward Island and he just needed some help doing some jobs on the house only requiring two hours work per day.

It is amazing how we as humans settle into routines and this is exactly how life on the farm was. Each day we worked in the morning and walked to the beach in the afternoon, we always used to pass a street sign called Stormin Normin Lane. I found it quite quirky and obviously tried to take an arty photo and make it look all moody by choosing a black and white filter for INSTAGRAM POST 35. Same with INSTAGRAM POST 37, don't worry I'll come back to 36. We used to walk past this old battered truck every day and I liked the number plate LAD. Anyway back to INSTAGRAM POST 36, we were very lucky with the hot, sunny weather in our time on the farm. I say we, meaning Helen and I as it made the afternoons on the beach much more enjoyable. Norman on the other hand wanted rain for his crops. The photo showed the thermometer reading 42 degrees, now I'm not sure if that was right or not. It was hot but I don't think it was that hot. Anyway, there were a couple of days when Norman declared it too hot to work and all we downed tools, so we weren't complaining. Other photos we posted included a Red Squirrel INSTAGRAM POST 38 and a bowl of eggs collected and ready for cleaning, INSTAGRAM POST 39. Even more random was the hand painted road sign warning of "MOOSE" INSTAGRAM POST 40

Obviously Canada is famous for Moose, we hadn't seen one yet but hoped we would sometime during our stay in Canada.

One night whilst we were sat in our basement room just browsing the internet, I stumbled across something that was to change the rest of our travels. I discovered the concept of house sitting. This is where there are websites with people asking for help to look after their homes and pets whilst they are away. I showed Helen this revelation and she was onto it in a flash. This would be an amazing way to continue our travels. We enjoyed our first workaway experience but wouldn't it be great to just look after someone else's home and their pets. We started creating our profile immediately and then looked to see if there were any over this side of the country. Our time at the farm was supposed to finish on the 5th of August but we had decided to stay and help out until the 8th as there was still a lot to do. The host of our next workaway was fine with the change of dates and we were only staying with him for five days anyway. On July 28th we Skyped our parents for the first time since we had been away. It was great to talk to them and turn the Ipad around and show them how the farm looks. When I Skyped my parents, Lucy and Emma were there so it was a bonus to say hello to them. One Saturday evening, June and Mary took us out to a pizza restaurant. Norman didn't come but they brought him back a takeaway. It was a really nice evening with them away from the farm. We never used to see as much of June obviously as she worked during the day but she was a lovely lady. The last week rolled through and bought a new arrival, a calf called Wendy. We weren't present at the birth because it was a bit complicated, but Norman sorted it out and we met Wendy when she was just a couple of minutes old. Again another experience we would have never had at home, INSTAGRAM POST 41.

On our final morning we said our goodbyes to Norman and June. June gave us both a big hug and a little pin badge which I kept on my rucksack for the duration of our travels. Mary took us to Confederation Bridge to catch the public bus over to Prince Edward Island, or PEI as everyone calls it. We only spent three weeks on the farm but it seemed so much longer. By the end of it we were really enjoying ourselves and the company. It was a very simple laid back life. I'm sure it is more stressful for Norman but for us it was a great start to our trip, it couldn't have been further away than sitting in an office staring at a computer.

We loaded our bags on the public bus and headed over the huge bridge that spanned the Northumberland Strait, to the capital Charlottetown where we met our host called Jim. We quickly grabbed a few groceries before heading back to Jim's house in a great central location. As it was still early afternoon Jim asked if we would do a couple of hours work today. We did, then Jim poured us a glass of wine and we got to know each other. He was quite open about his personal life which surprised us. To be honest we didn't know what to make of him. My journal entry on that day said, "Not sure about our host, he's a bit strange" It was early days, hopefully things would improve. In the evening Jim said he would drive us to the other side of the island to Brackley Beach. INSTAGRAM POST 42 and INSTAGRAM POST 43. It was a stunning beach, but Jim pointed in one direction and said "You go that way; I'm going this way and headed off in the other direction. Obviously Helen was having the same doubts as me, we talked about it as we walked our designated way along the beach. We talked about our 5 out of 10 rule, we were both below 5 at the moment. Some of that was due to our bed being a single so it was a bit of a squeeze and there was no door to our room, it was sectioned off by a curtain. There wasn't any Wi-Fi either. Despite this we were prepared to stick it out and see how things developed; we were only here for five days after all.

The next morning we were awoken by loud banging on the side of the house at 7am. Jim had started work. We therefore started at 8am. My job was to strip the entire side of Jim's two storey house of the wooden shingles. Shingles to those who don't know are thin tapered pieces of wood to cover roofs and walls of buildings to protect them from the weather. Basically the way to remove them was to force a crowbar up and lever them off. Helen's job was to sand down an old table for re-varnishing. At 10am we finished, made ourselves a packed lunch and went to explore Charlottetown for the day. It was ok, full of holiday makers but nothing special.

Again in the night we were woken up by a loud noise, this time about 4am with Jim cleaning out his aquarium! Just three more days we kept saying to ourselves. Things didn't improve with our chores. I was still ripping off shingles with dust flying everywhere to discover there was a load of asbestos behind some shingles. After work we made our way to the bike shop as we decided to hire some bikes and explore the Island as it was a beautiful sunny day. INSTAGRAM POST 44 and INSTAGRAM POST 45. Cutting across the island we ended up at Stanhope beach and lazed around for a couple of hours. On our way back we cycled along the Confederation trail. INSTAGRAM POST 46. It is a 470 km trail system on what used to be old railway lines on PEI, so at least it was flat most of the time. The bikes were due back at 6pm and we made it with about five minutes to spare. It was a really enjoyable way to see PEI and get us away from the house for most of the day.

For the penultimate day of work Jim had us painting a shed. Again we didn't have luck on our side as there was a wasp nest under the roof and Helen was stung. After work, we were at a loss of what to do. Jim asked us to be vacant as he had a lady friend visiting in the afternoon. We had already explored Charlottetown so we sat in a park for most of the day. Helen read her Kindle, and I read the Lonely Planet guide to Canada to see where we were heading next. On our last day, even though we didn't have to, we did a couple more hours work and finished the painting. We finished and said goodbye to Jim. It wasn't an enjoyable workaway but at least it was short. Accommodation for the evening was in an Airbnb just around the corner. It rained all afternoon so we stayed in our room and watched the Olympics on the TV and signed up to another house sitting website. That afternoon we had a Skype chat lined up with a lady called Rebecca who lived in Montréal wanted someone to look after her cat and her house for three weeks whilst she was away. We planned what we would say in a posh British accent and smartened ourselves up as much as possible. The chat went really well, Rebecca was lovely and after about five minutes she said she would like us for the housesit. Afterwards we went to the pub for fish and chips to celebrate as we were so happy that we had landed our first house sitting assignment. It was just the news we needed after a weird week with our latest workaway host. It would be interesting to see how house sits compare to workaways,

Next morning we were up early to catch the bus back across the bridge. PEI had not quite lived up to our high expectations, it certainly wasn't the pot of gold at the end of the rainbow for those three weeks looking across at it from the farm. Mary met us, it was nice to see her friendly face again after the week we had. Whilst we were on PEI, my new Kindle had been delivered. It also seemed I left my fleece at the farm as well. Must stop forgetting things! Mary kindly drove us to Moncton, where we said goodbye for the last time.

Today was the 13th of August, we were due to be at the house sit in Montréal on the 16th and it was over 1,000 km away. For some of the journey we would be using a hire car. The problem was neither of us had driven on the right hand side of the road before or driven an automatic. Helen drove first and did a great job. One law we soon discovered was turning right on a red light, mainly because the person behind let us know. In the UK, at a junction with traffic lights, if we wanted to turn left, the law is that you wait for the lights to turn green. In both the US and Canada this is not the case in some provinces or states. Obviously they drive on the other side of the road, but the same principle applies. If you are waiting at traffic lights and want to turn right, you do not have to wait for the lights to turn green, you are allowed to turn right on a red light, if safe to do so.

We were going to drive along the coast of the Bay of Fundy. With the unique geography causing some of the most extreme tides in the world, it stirs up some serious whale food. Therefore there are lots of opportunities for whale watching along the coast. Today we were heading to Hopewell Rocks, New Brunswick's top tourist attraction. The rocks are bizarre sandstone erosion formations that look like mushrooms. INSTAGRAM POST 47, INSTAGRAM POST 48, INSTAGRAM POST 49, INSTAGRAM POST 50, INSTAGRAM POST 51, INSTAGRAM POST 52, INSTAGRAM POST 53 and INSTAGRAM POST 54, I know, I definitely took too many photos again. During low tide you can get a closer view by walking on the beach. This area has the largest tide differentials in the world, with sometimes 40 feet between low and high tide. The next day, after a night in an Airbnb we returned at high tide. The tide wasn't as high as we hoped but you get the idea, INSTAGRAM POST 55,

INSTAGRAM POST 56, INSTAGRAM POST 57 and INSTAGRAM POST 58.

The next destination was St Andrews, four hours away; this was supposed to be prime whale spotting territory. It had rained constantly and we wondered if there were going to be any tours going out today. The tour operator said it should be ok, why wouldn't he? We headed out and it was pretty misty, we only saw one minke whale, some seals and a golden eagle, pretty disappointing really for what we paid. A bit down hearted at not seeing more whales, we drove to St John for the night. In the morning we took the rental car back to the airport. INSTAGRAM POST 59. For the last three days I had been panicking that we were going to be charged for a scratch at the back of the car I found and they would assume it was my fault. When we picked up the car, it cost so much more because of the extra things they sell you for peace of mind. Luckily no one even checked it. With the car dropped off at the airport we just needed to catch the bus into town to then wait for our overnight bus to Montréal. It turned out we had missed the last bus, even though it was lunchtime. A guy who worked security at the airport tried his best to help but it seemed the only way we were going to be able to get into town was paying for a taxi. Then living up to their friendly reputation as a nation, Ryan the security guard told me he was shortly finishing his shift and would give us a lift to town. After dropping our bags at the bus station we stretched our legs for a walk around St John before boarding for a 12 hour bus ride to Montréal. If you look on a map of where Montréal is compared to St John, it is virtually direct west. However the US state of Maine is in between, therefore you have to drive up and around it. If you cut straight through the US, it is a 730 km journey, but the detour around Maine adds an extra 190 km. One hour into our journey the bus had a blow out so we sat on the side of the highway before we were able to transfer to another bus. The overnight bus was not as bad as we expected for our first experience and we pulled into Montréal station at 7am, having checked the seat pockets way too many times.

Montréal is in Québec, another new province for us, where the official language is French. We could speak a bit of French so it was ok, especially when it came to ordering a café au lait and pain au chocolat at the bus terminal for our breakfast. Montréal has a population of 3.4 million people and Rebecca lived in an outer lying predominantly English speaking suburb called Dollard-Des Ormeaux. Navigating the bus timetables we arrived at Rebecca's condo at a respectable 10.30am, we didn't think we should arrive any earlier. Rebecca was really nice, very friendly and helpful. Her cat was called Ocean, she was less friendly and pretty much ignored us and stayed in Rebecca's room. The place was a nice little two bedroomed condo with a small garden. We went for a walk in the afternoon, it was close to a busy boulevard and there was a huge Maxi supermarket not too far away. Rebecca worked remotely and she was going to Sweden to house sit, doing the same as us, cat sitting. It must be amazing to be able to work remotely and be able to house sit anywhere in the world. Having not really slept on the overnight bus we decided to have an early night. We said our goodbyes to Rebecca as she was leaving at 5am and she handed over her house and car keys.

The next morning, I was sure this wasn't real. I thought it was a joke and we were secretly being filmed for a TV show or something. Someone we only had a ten minute Skype call with, had just left us with their house, car and cat for three weeks. It just felt strange that people can be so trusting. It was a new concept to us but judging by the amount of listings, not just on the site we used but others as well, there is certainly a demand for house and pet sitters.

For the first week we didn't really do much, we explored the immediate neighbourhood and found a nice park, so mapped out a 5 km run. A lot of the time we just lazed in the sun in the back garden. Rebecca had left us her car to use so one day we went to a famous area in Québec called the Laurentians which is a renowned ski area. It is only an hour's drive from Montréal. We went to Ville de Mont Tremblant. INSTAGRAM POST 60, INSTAGRAM POST 61 and INSTAGRAM POST 62. By coincidence it was hosting the North American Ironman Championships so the place was overrun with people wearing lycra looking knackered, whilst their friends and families cheered them on. The town itself was gorgeous with loads of activities to choose from, unfortunately it was raining a lot on the day we visited so we vowed to come back and do a hike in the area. That week we signed up to Netflix, Rebecca didn't own a TV and as we were not working we had more time to ourselves and needed some additional entertainment. Helen's birthday was on the 24th of August so we decided we would return to Ville de Mont-Tremblant. Before we set off, I handed over the Birthday cards I had been storing in my backpack for the past few weeks. I didn't get Helen a card or a present and felt really guilty about it but even prior to setting off we agreed that it was pointless, and this was going to be the same for Xmas as well. Arriving at the town, typical us, we decided to attempt the longest and most difficult route up Mt Tremblant. We set off at 1pm, the walk itself was lovely, difficult and steep in parts, especially as we are from a flat part of the UK. INSTAGRAM POST 63, INSTAGRAM POST 64, INSTAGRAM POST 65, INSTAGRAM POST 66. We arrived at the summit at 5.20pm. INSTAGRAM POST 67, INSTAGRAM POST 68 and INSTAGRAM POST 69. However, Helen wasn't feeling great as she was having a hypo. Another problem was that we missed the last cable car back down to the town. I managed to find a ranger and in my best French explain that Helen wasn't very well. Fortunately we managed to get a lift all the way back down in his jeep, picking up other stragglers on the way. On the drive home we had a birthday meal at McDonalds and eventually walked through the front door at 9pm, shattered.

The next day we were discussing how that in order to see the best parts of Canada we really needed a car, so initially we visited a number of car hire places to see how much it would cost for a long term rental. The cost was unbelievable, they were all quoting around $4,000 CAD for just three months hire, which was about £2,500. It would be cheaper to buy an old car, so that is what we started looking into. Finding a car was tricky, we didn't want to spend too much but the only ones we had viewed looked like they would fall apart after a few miles. We went to a car dealership which was selling hundreds of flash new cars and at the back of their car lot, they had a car which we had come to view. The car dealer, Sebastian, took us over to the car, Helen and I looked at each other and straight away knew we wouldn't be buying it, it was another pile of junk. But then, out of nowhere Sebastian told me he was selling his own car, well his wife's, and did we want to have a look? I thought we might as well but thought it's going to be well out of our price bracket. The car was a Mazda 6 Estate and we went for a test drive and really liked it, it was only about ten years old. So we were absolutely gobsmacked when he said we could have it for $700 CAD, about £400. Sebastian knew we were travellers, and he mentioned his nephew was travelling around Europe at the moment so I guess he just wanted to help us out, and he did say he'd been trying to sell his wife's car for ages with no success. It was a done deal as far as we were concerned, we just needed to sort out insurance, and then we could contact him and let him know we would definitely be buying. Trying to sort out motor insurance as a foreigner is tricky, especially in the French speaking part of Canada. This is when we should have swapped to a local sim card, as we spent a small fortune phoning around insurance companies to see if they would insure us. As soon as we mentioned we were not Canadians, they weren't interested. This was now getting really frustrating, we had a car we wanted to buy at a ridiculously good price but no one would insure us. Helen kept persisting and investigating and it paid off massively. She found an ombudsman stating that absolutely everyone including foreigners and visitors are entitled to car insurance in Québec. We called them. The kind lady on the phone asked us to provide her with a list of ten companies, and a contact name at each, who all declined us car insurance. After phoning a few back just to get a contact name we had our list and emailed it to the lady. She called us back not long after. She said she had spoken to one of the companies on the list, we should phone them again, ask for the contact and they will sell us car insurance. It was as simple as that. And amazingly, it was. We re-phoned, we spoke to the same person who previously didn't want to help us and yet they were now able to. We relied on a lot of luck, and a bit of persistence, but we were now able to buy the car we wanted. Calls were made and we would pick it up at the end of the week.

During our time in Montréal, we hadn't actually visited the City centre itself as we were out in the suburbs, so we made sure we did. Montréal is a nice city and it helped that it was another glorious day. To start with we hiked up to the top of the Parc du Mont Royal which gave fantastic panoramic views of the city below, INSTAGRAM POST 70. We did a lot of walking that day, through downtown to buy a satnav for the car, Old

Montréal which looks out onto the St Lawrence River and past the Olympic Park. Montréal hosted the 1976 Olympics, INSTAGRAM POST 71.

Rebecca was due home the day after we picked up our car and I realise I've hardly mentioned Ocean, the one reason why we were in Montréal. That's because she was so easy to look after. I have never owned a cat before, Helen has, but I couldn't believe how little they actually do, especially house cats. Ocean was such low maintenance, she seemed to either sleep or eat, and occasionally if she could be bothered, she would play with the toys we dangled in front of her. We were in constant contact with Rebecca about Ocean and the house, and she kindly allowed us to use her address to register the car for insurance.

Buying a car in Québec is also a different process compared to the UK. Both the seller and the buyer must go to a Société de l'assurance du Québec (SAAQ). This is basically like a walk in office. Sebastian drove us there, we then had to pay tax on the price we paid for the car. This is where Sebastian excelled in his generosity. He stated we purchased the car for just 1 dollar, so that was all we had to pay tax on. Papers were read and signed and we were given a new registration plate. Unlike in the UK, where the plate stays with the car during its lifetime, in Québec and probably elsewhere in Canada, the registration plate stays with the owner. Out in the car park, we swapped the plates over and said a huge thank you to Sebastian. He had no reason to be as kind and generous as he was to us, we were so grateful to him. I might be cursing him in a week when the car breaks down in the middle of nowhere, but for now he was an absolute legend to us. The first thing we did when we got the car back to Rebecca's was to order breakdown cover, well you know, just in case.

But we were now the owners of our own car in Canada! INSTAGRAM PHOTO 72.

Rebecca arrived home the next day and we exchanged stories of our house sitting experiences, it seemed like she really enjoyed her time in Sweden on her house sit. As Rebecca arrived later in the evening we stayed the night and set off the next morning. It felt great to have the independence of our own transport. Our first destination in our new car was across the border into the next province of Ontario and to the capital of Canada, Ottawa. The province of Ontario holds nearly 40% of Canada's population, quite a lot considering there are 13 Provinces in total. As it was only a couple of hours drive we arrived at our Airbnb around lunchtime and after dropping off our bags we walked into the city. Ottawa is a really great city, it seemed to be really green with lots of space. Running right through the middle is Rideau Canal, INSTAGRAM POST 73, and INSTAGRAM POST 76. All along the paths alongside the canal there were people jogging, rollerblading, cycling or simply going for a stroll as we did. On my post I stated the fun fact that in the winter the Canal freezes and at 7.8 km long, it becomes the world's largest ice skating rink as people use it as a way to commute to and from work. Another recommendation from our guide book said we should try a Beavertail whilst in Ottawa. INSTAGRAM POST 74. BeaverTails is a chain of pastry stands and its products are fried dough pastries stretched out to resemble a beaver's tail. We ended up staying in Ottawa city centre well into the evening as we had heard about the lightshow. One of the big tourist attractions in Ottawa is the Parliament building with its turrets and gargoyles as well as the centrepiece, the iconic Peace Tower. In the summer there is a lightshow displayed against the parliament building, it is an amazing spectacle and lasts about 45 mins culminating in the National Anthem. INSTAGRAM POST 75. We may have only spent one day in Ottawa but it was a really enjoyable one.

The next day was a day we would term a driving day, we would have a few of these. It was a day with nothing apart from the intention of getting from A to B, namely our accommodation for the night. We were skirting around Lake Ontario past Thousand Islands heading for Toronto but the place we stayed at overnight, Bowmanville was completely forgettable. I had managed to contact an old University friend in the meantime. I hadn't seen Cameron for over 20 years but knew he now lived in Canada, in the province of Ontario. We arranged to meet up, the plan was to head up and see him after visiting Niagara, he lived in Algonquin Provincial Park, a few hours north of Toronto and I was really looking forward to seeing him again.

Continuing on towards Toronto from Bowmanville, our intention was to spend a day or two exploring Canada's largest city with it's famous CN tower. That was until we hit the outskirts on the infamous Highway 401. Highway 401 is North America's busiest highway and one of the widest. At one point I counted 15 lanes. After a very short discussion we decided that we would skip Toronto and continue on and around towards Niagara Falls. Helen and I aren't really city people anyway, we prefer the open air to crowded cities. Give us a mountain hike over a museum, cathedral or art gallery every time. Besides, we had visited Montréal and Ottawa city centres within the space of ten days anyway. Inevitably when you are travelling, you cannot visit everywhere, so on this occasion we carried on, much to the relief of Helen who was actually driving at the time.

It was early afternoon when we arrived in Niagara and booked into our cheap but particularly nice motel. The Falls were about a 20 minute walk from the motel but you can see the cloud of mist in the distance. As you get closer you can then start to hear it. Jaw dropping was how I would describe our first sight of Niagara Falls. It really doesn't matter how many times you have seen pictures of the Falls or seen them on TV, nothing prepares you for when you actually see them in person, they are amazing. So the following posts do not really do the Falls justice but here they are; INSTAGRAM POST 77, INSTAGRAM POST 78, INSTAGRAM POST 79, INSTAGRAM POST 80, INSTAGRAM POST 81, INSTAGRAM POST 82, INSTAGRAM POST 83, INSTAGRAM POST 84, INSTAGRAM POST 85, INSTAGRAM POST 86, INSTAGRAM POST 87. Especially INSTAGRAM POST 88, which is just a photo of me with a rainbow protruding from my head. On the Canadian side you can get a lot closer to the Falls, you can see across to the US where they have the Bridal Veil Falls, but the famous Horseshoe Falls are best seen from the Canadian side where you can get right up close to where the water tumbles over the edge. The spray coming from the bottom also creates a permanent rainbow. There are lots of ways to view the falls, by boat on the famous Maid of the Mist, by air in a helicopter or walking down the side. We didn't choose any of these, we felt we didn't need to. You can honestly just stare at the falls for ages without even knowing how long you've been looking. We returned again in the evening as there was a large firework display. A word of warning about Niagara itself, it is tacky, a bit like an outdated seaside amusement park, which is in complete contrast to the natural wonder that the town is built upon.

Deciding to stay an extra night in Niagara we were up really early the next day. We wanted to see the Falls at sunrise. We walked through the quiet dark streets, but the roar of the falls could be heard in the distance. There wasn't a cloud in the sky apart from the mist cloud formed by the falls. We walked up to the part at Horseshoe Falls where the water tumbles over the edge. There were only three other people there, the day before all along the path there were hundreds, maybe thousands of people, but right now it was just us and three people with really big expensive looking cameras. We just had our Ipad. It was well worth getting up early for, INSTAGRAM POST 89. McDonalds was our breakfast stop before heading back to the motel, there was no chance of getting back to sleep so we jumped in the car and headed about 20 km to a park where we enjoyed a nice 7 km looped walk in the morning sun. The scene at the falls in the afternoon was completely different to when we were there at sunrise hours earlier. The huge numbers of tourists were back, taking selfies. We just sat there for a couple of hours watching the falls.

Back at the motel in the evening we had confirmation of our second house sitting assignment. It was right over the other side of Canada in the Alberta province at a place called Cochrane which is just outside Calgary. It didn't start for another three weeks but the distance was 3,300 km away if we took the most direct route. We had some serious road tripping ahead of us. So far we had been travelling for two months.

Leaving Niagara Falls to head back up towards Toronto we took a circular detour. Rather than going back along the same stretch of road we used three days earlier we headed west and anti-clockwise to Port Elgin, and through the Blue Mountains, INSTAGRAM POST 90. Toronto was going to be our place to stay for one night but we just wanted to stay on the outskirts as we were heading North to Algonquin Park to see Cameron. We had arranged an Airbnb, from the listing it looked like it was student accommodation. When we turned up it was more like a fraternity house and we felt really old all of a sudden. He showed us the room, it was a

41

complete mess and stank of weed. He looked pretty embarrassed, we told him we weren't staying here, and what else did he have? By now it was getting quite late and we needed somewhere to stay. He offered us another place, again University accommodation. He gave us a key and the address and told us to head there. When we turned up the lights were on and it seemed to be occupied but he never mentioned that anyone else was there. I didn't want to walk straight into a house and have the people there not know who we are. I called him, he assured me it was empty and told us which was our room. By now it was late, so we just went in, straight up to the room and fitted the Howsar quick twin lock, as there wasn't one on the door. We didn't sleep very well that well night and made a hasty exit in the morning. It was a driving day as we needed to get up to see Cameron, the overnight stop was Orillia, and I took a photo of Lake Simcoe, INSTAGRAM POST 91.

As there was no room to stay at Cameron's, the nearest place we could find was about an hour away, it was a really nice huge cabin motel in the middle of a forest. We arrived at Cameron's place at 6.30pm, Helen drove so I could have a drink. It was great to see Cameron, he had hardly changed, a bit greyer like me, but still the same laid back Cameron. His accent had changed though; it was now a mixture of Scottish and Canadian. We met his partner Tiff, she is lovely and an artist. They showed us the studio they had built next to the house full of Tiff's gorgeous creations. They lived in a stunning cottage with a river running right next to the garden. It was a great evening, they cooked us a superb meal, we had a few drinks and just chatted about everything. Cameron worked in Haliburton Forest, in the winter he ran the dog sledding and in the summer he ran some climbing courses called "Walk the Cloud" where you walk on planks suspended high up in the trees. As any adopted Canadian should be, he is also handy with an axe and chainsaw when it comes to forestry maintenance. We stayed there until quite late but we were aware we had an hour's drive back to the hotel. Unfortunately Cameron was working the next day but he wasn't due to start until the afternoon. So he suggested that we call back in the morning and he would show us around Haliburton Forest. Haliburton Forest is privately owned woodland covering 240 square km. Cameron drove us around some of the forest in his truck. There are lots of things to do there as it operates recreational, tourism and education programs all year round. Canopy walks, snowmobiling, dogsledding and mountain biking are just some of the activities. Cameron then took us to meet Hershe the moose. So far on our travels we hadn't seen a moose, so this would be a first. Hershe was orphaned at just three weeks old when his mother was killed in a vehicle accident. Now he lives in a safe 4 acre enclosure within the forest and loves the company of horses, dogs and humans. Seeing him up close, you get a real sense of how big they actually are. After seeing Hershe, next on the tour was the Wolf Centre. Here, in a 15 acre enclosure it is possible to observe a pack of wolves, from an observation room. It was really interesting watching the pack interact with each other, there was a person in the observation room explaining all the dynamics of the pack and pointing out the alpha and beta males and females. Sadly lunchtime arrived and it was time to say goodbye to Cameron. It had only been a short catch up but really enjoyable and I was really pleased for him that he had made a life for himself here in such a gorgeous part of Canada.

The weather had been miserable all morning and it rained all afternoon, and as we still had a night at the hotel, there wasn't a lot we could do so we just relaxed in our room. Over 3,000 km still remained between us and our house sit, and that was just over two weeks away, we had nothing planned in between. Just to put the distance into perspective, London to Edinburgh is about 640 km. Our route now was following the Trans-Canada Highway. This is the world's longest highway and stretches from St John's in Newfoundland, where we originally landed over two months ago all the way across the bottom of the country until it reached the Pacific coast in Victoria on Vancouver Island. In total it is 7,800 km long and is technically a patchwork of provincial roads. There were to be some big driving days coming up soon, but first we wanted to explore some more of Algonquin Park. Luckily the weather improved the next day so we set off towards the park. Two months and we don't see a moose, but then we see two in two days. Today we spotted a wild one in Algonquin park just next to the road. INSTAGRAM POST 92. Typical eh? Well it got even better when we also saw our first black bear INSTAGRAM POST 93. A moose and a bear on the same day, we were doing well on Canadian stereotype bingo.

Algonquin Provincial Park is Ontario's oldest and largest park, 7800 square km in size and is exactly what you imagine Canada to be like, lakes, forests, streams and cliffs. We enjoyed two walks in the park, INSTAGRAM POST 94 and INSTAGRAM POST 95, before we hit the road and pressed onwards west towards our overnight destination of Sudbury. Waking up the next day we typed our next destination into the car's satnav, Waha. That meant 500 km of driving today. We didn't want to rush our road trip west so we decided we would wait until check out time each morning and we should still reach Waha before the sun went down and we were not driving in the dark. There were two reasons we never wished to drive in the dark, firstly the scenery. Since we bought our own car in Montréal and had our own independence you get a great appreciation for the beauty and the scenery of Canada. Basically Canada was too pretty to be missed; everywhere you drive could be considered a scenic drive. Secondly, safety was our other concern. In Ontario alone there are more than 14,000 collisions between cars and wildlife per year. Moose are especially dangerous because the car knocks out their long legs and their bodies' barrel right though the windscreen. Not wanting to add to those sorts of statistics, we had a rule that we would stick to driving during daylight hours whenever possible. Halfway into our journey from Sudbury to Waha, at Sault Ste-Marie, the Trans Canadian highway starts to hug the shoreline of Lake Superior. The journey from here to Waha is considered by many as the most picturesque of the whole highway as it passes directly through Lake Superior Provincial Park. It didn't disappoint, we had now been in Canada nearly two and a half months but were still in awe of the beauty and ruggedness of it all. Driving 500 km would normally be considered a chore, not for us though.

Therefore, the thought of repeating this distance again the next day did not fill us with dread, we were actually looking forward to it. Today we were heading to Thunder Bay, 511 km away, INSTAGRAM POST 96. All of the day's journey would be along the shores of Lake Superior. Lake Superior on our left hand side was superior in size and beauty. It is the largest of the Great Lakes in North America. It covers a surface area of 82,100 square km and is the largest freshwater lake on the planet with its own ecosystem and micro climate. In INSTAGRAM POST 97, there is a clever picture I found that shows a map of Lake Superior over a map of England, this is when you get a perspective of just how large the lake is. When driving long distances as we had, it is necessary to take toilet breaks and switch drivers, and at our convenience was something as Canadian as maple syrup, but we had never even heard of it before we arrived in Canada. I'm talking about the famous Tim Horton's. Tim Hortons is Canada's McDonalds, it is a fast food restaurant chain specialising in coffee and donuts. They are everywhere and they are great. There are over 3,800 chains across Canada, worldwide there nearly 5,000. The coffee is good and the prices are cheap. It is also very difficult not to have a pit stop and pick up a donut or a muffin with your coffee. They are clean and there is free Wi-Fi, which was really handy for checking our emails on our latest house sitting applications. Travelling along the Trans-Canada Highway, you come across a "Timmy's" fairly frequently. Tim Horton is a real person or was, a famous Canadian Ice Hockey player (of course!) who partnered with investor Ron Joyce and opened their first chain in 1964 in Hamilton, Ontario. Sadly Tim Horton died in a car crash in 1974 and Joyce expanded the chain and the rest is history. In 2014, Burger King purchased Tim Hortons for $11.4 billion. In addition to muffins and donuts there are burgers, wraps and soups which we tried along our road trip. After a while when you've visited a few Timmy's and stood in a queue, you start to pick up on some of lingo used when ordering your coffee. A "regular" is 1 cream and 1 sugar. "Double Double" is 2 creams and 2 sugars. "Triple Triple (you get the pattern) or 4x4. The other Canadian words we learnt along the way were Loonies and Toonies. A loonie is a dollar coin, and obviously a toonie is a two-dollar coin. Another famous Canadian dish that originated in Québec, but one we never tried ourselves is poutine, it is basically French fries and cheese curds, topped with gravy.

Both the views and the weather that day driving alongside Lake Superior were stunning, we pulled over numerous times just to stop and admire the sheer beauty. INSTAGRAM POST 98, INSTAGRAM POST 99, INSTAGRAM POST 100, INSTAGRAM POST 101, INSTAGRAM POST 102, INSTAGRAM POST 103 and INSTAGRAM POST 104. If you zoom in on INSTAGRAM POST 99, you can just make out the train snaking its way around the shores of the lake, what an amazing train journey that must be! We felt great and realised how lucky we were. When we had chatted to any Canadians and told them we were just heading west, most of them said we were doing something that most Canadians themselves have never done but would love to do, a long road trip across their vast country. We eventually arrived at Thunder Bay late in the afternoon. INSTAGRAM POST 105. The guidebook says this about Thunder Bay. "Thunder Bay is about as comfortably isolated as you can get, it is 692 km west of Sault Ste-Marie and 703 km east of Winnipeg (in Manitoba). if you're arriving by road it's a welcome and obligatory return to civilisation: no matter how beautiful those forests and that shoreline are, it starts to blur together after a while." We disagreed, we thought the whole two day journey around Lake Superior was fantastic. Maybe the trip had taken a bit of toll on the car though, there were a couple of things not quite right with it so we decided spend an extra day in Thunder Bay whilst the car went into the garage. Fixing the car cost us $500 dollars and we also decided it was worthwhile changing our tyres to winter tyres. Although not law apart from in Québec, it is recommended that drivers switch over to winter tyres for increased safety when the conditions worsen. Thunder Bay was also the place where I had my first and only "run in" with a Canadian. We were walking from our motel to pick up the car from the garage and someone called me from a house on the side of the street. They asked me if I would help them with manoeuvring someone who was in a wheelchair out of the house. I had no problem in helping so walked in. The person in the wheelchair though sounded as though she was having a bad day and was quite vocal about it. Anyway her friend told me to grab the front of the wheelchair to lift her outside. I did, assuming that they were also going to be lifting the back of the wheelchair at the same time, but they didn't. So I ended up nearly tipping the woman backwards out of her wheelchair. This caused her anger to escalate even further and the swearing this time was aimed at me. I lowered her back down, walked away and left them to it. With the car collected we still had most of the afternoon to spare. Luckily there was somewhere we wanted to visit.

Since we left Montréal, we drove through dozens of towns and kept seeing signs for the Terry Fox memorial run. The first few towns I didn't think anything of it, but then to still see signs for the memorial run 1,500 miles further on, I thought I should find out more. I admit we had never heard of Terry Fox before we arrived in Canada but it turns out he is one of the most famous Canadians ever. Terry Fox wasn't a professional athlete; he played baseball, rugby and soccer as a youngster and was a very good basketball player and distance runner. At the age of 19, in 1977, he was diagnosed with cancer and this resulted in amputation of his right leg above the knee. With a prosthetic leg, Terry was able to walk again and also joined a wheelchair basketball team. But he aspired to do more, especially witnessing the pain and suffering of other fellow patients as he himself underwent chemotherapy. He took up distance running inspired by Dick Traum who was the first amputee to complete the New York Marathon, and completed his first marathon in 1979. Terry's overall bigger aim was to run across the breadth of Canada raising money and awareness for Cancer research, it was called the Marathon of Hope. He started on the 12th April 1980, in St Johns, Newfoundland (where we had our first layover). Initially his run did not gain much attention or money but then it grew and grew as he was running every day. Soon he became a media sensation and a national hero as he passed through the towns and provinces. Sadly Terry was forced to stop running at Thunder Bay on Sept 1st 1980 due to exhaustion and chest pains as the cancer had returned and spread to his lungs. At this point he had already covered 3,339 miles over the course of 143 days, equivalent to a marathon a day and he had raised over $1.7m dollars. Sadly Terry died on the 28th June 1981 aged just 22, however he had secured over $24m in donations. Prior to his death he was awarded the Companion of the Order of Canada, the youngest person ever to receive the award and was twice named Canadian of the year. His legacy continues through the Terry Fox Foundation when memorial runs are organised all across Canada. That afternoon we visited the Terry Fox Memorial, close to where he ended his great Marathon of Hope. We had taken virtually the same route ourselves in our journey across Canada, but we had used public transport and our own car, Terry did it running with a prosthetic leg and suffering with cancer. It was only right that we should go and pay our respects to the great man. INSTAGRAM POST 106 and INSTAGRAM POST 107.

With new tyres and our car issues now sorted we continued our journey west and also entered a new time zone, Central Standard, so we were now five hours behind Greenwich Mean Time instead of 4. INSTAGRAM POST 108. Today's destination was Kenora, 485 km away. On the way we took the opportunity to see Kakabeka Falls. Any waterfall was going to have to really sell itself having seen Niagara Falls so recently. As far as waterfalls go, we were impressed, not Niagara impressed, but still impressed. INSTAGRAM POST 109, INSTAGRAM POST 110, INSTAGRAM POST 111 and INSTAGRAM POST 112. Kenora was to be our last stop in Ontario before entering Manitoba. It had taken us two weeks to travel through this enormous province. Ontario covers an area of 1.4 million square km. By comparison, the United Kingdom is 245,000 square km, nearly six times smaller. Kenora was nothing special, another one of those towns that sits on the Trans Canada Highway with a Tim Hortons. When we booked our accommodation, we used Booking.com and usually sorted it by cheapest first and invariably stay in one of those. The one we chose in Kenora looked pretty good for the price. Upon arrival we realised the motel was 50m from a prison entrance. I think I was more surprised that Canada has prisons than the fact our motel was right next to one, as all but one Canadian so far had come across as very friendly. I looked into the prisoner statistics though and they are slightly better when compared to Britain; 139 per population of 100,000 as opposed to 149.

Manitoba is a very different landscape compared to Ontario, at least it is along the southern area on the Trans-Canada Highway. Flat is the first word that springs to mind, and it gets a bit of stick as it is assumed there is not a lot here. The two main cities in Manitoba are Churchill and Winnipeg. Churchill is way up north, about 500 miles on the shores of Hudson Bay. This is a destination for wildlife watching. Polar bears, 200 species of birds and beluga whales can all be seen from Churchill. With it being so far north it is also a good place to see the Northern Lights. Churchill was not on our list as we were still pushing west, Winnipeg was going to be our stopover, the gateway to the West. After booking into our motel and having a walk around the city we weren't impressed, it just seemed a bit edgy. The weather was awful and maybe that didn't help or it could have been the remoteness of driving around Lake Superior and then arriving in a city with a population of 663,000. Whatever it was, we just didn't like the place on our first impressions, but we would sleep on it and see if it improved tomorrow. It didn't so we headed to an Airbnb just outside Winnipeg. The host of our Airbnb was deaf, she was really nice and we communicated by writing on note pads. Another thing that Canada is famous for is the Canadian Goose and Fortwhyte which sits just outside Winnipeg is the ideal place to see them. I had read that this particular time of year, thousands and thousands of migrating geese are heading south for winter and Fortwhyte is in their path as a rest stop. Arriving at the centre we listened to an interesting presentation on the geese and were then told to make our way to the lake just before sunset. As sunset arrived so too did the geese, thousands of them flying in to rest on the lake. You could see clouds of them in the distance heading to the lake and then landing until the lake looked completely full. It was an amazing spectacle and we were really pleased we witnessed it. Also at Fortwhyte we saw a herd of buffalo, but we particularly liked the prairie dogs that had set up home in and around the car park. It was now dark, but to our surprise, only one of the car's four front lights was working so it made for a bit of a scary trip back to our Airbnb but fortunately we made it with no problems. Driving during daytime was now essential until we were able to get our lights fixed, so we were gutted when we set off the next day, the weather was so bad it might as well have been night time. Driving through thunder, lightning and torrential rain we eventually arrived at our Airbnb, on the side of the Trans-Canada highway in the middle of nowhere. The weather had improved since leaving Winnipeg so we went for a walk. The middle prairie provinces are also well known for their strong winds. That walk was one of windiest we have ever had! INSTAGRAM POST 113, INSTAGRAM POST 114 and INSTAGRAM POST 115. Our time in Manitoba was short and sweet as we crossed into Saskatchewan, the "Land of the living skies". Similar to Manitoba, in the southern part of the province it was very flat and on a clear day the sky just seems huge above the flat prairies. The first large city on our drive through the province was Regina. This was to be our pit stop to fix the lights on the car. Another concern though, the engine warning light came on about 25 km from Regina.

It took about four hours to fix the car, a bit longer than expected, so we ended up staying the night in Regina. So far, we had spent $700 on fixing the car, the same amount we bought it for three weeks ago. Let's hope this trend doesn't continue. On a more positive note, we found out today we were accepted on another workaway. We applied for it a couple of days ago. It was near Watrous which is north of Regina, on the way to the Provincial capital Saskatoon. Progress has been really good on our drive west and we still had just over a week before our house sit started. Aside from Churchill which was too much of a detour, there wasn't really much to do between here and Calgary, so we looked into workaways to see if there was anywhere we could help. A sheep farm in the middle of nowhere looked like just our sort of thing, it was completely out of our comfort zone so we thought we'd apply and offer assistance and luckily we were accepted, so that was our plan for the next week.

The drive the next day was surreal. Our hosts had sent us directions as their farm was in the middle of nowhere. Like really in the middle of nowhere, it was unbelievable. On one long straight dusty road we were driving along, just in the distance we saw something big cross the road, we sped up to see what it was and it was an enormous moose. This one was much bigger than the one we saw in Algonquin Provincial Park. Arriving at our host's farm we were greeted by a number of dogs. Our hosts came out to meet us and we immediately noticed a familiar British accent. To our disbelief we discovered our hosts, Alan and Nikki were originally from England, not only that, but from a town about 45 mins away from where we live back home. Immediately we warmed to Alan and Nikki, Nikki loved to chat and we knew we were in for a good few days here. The farm is huge, hundreds of acres in size accommodating around 300 sheep, 10 dogs and 10 horses. A covered riding paddock is at the back of the house as Nikki also teaches horse riding when she isn't working on the farm. That first afternoon we didn't do any work, we all just sat outside chatting in the sun, stroking the dogs. The dogs are as follows: Firstly Shep, he is Alan's trusty companion and goes with him everywhere, in the tractor and on the quadbike where he likes to sit up front. The other dogs are Jax, Bear and Saska. These are house dogs, so pets that live in the house. The other dogs are proper working livestock guardian dogs, they are Andrex, Chandra, Smiler,

Major, Toffee and Floss. We spent the first night listening to how these dogs, Great Pyrenees, all work together to look after the sheep. They tend to work at night and each has their own roles. There are the perimeter dogs, such as Smiler and Chandra who patrol the fence line of the farm where the sheep are kept. Floss, who only had three legs was the watch dog, always vigilant and alerting the others to any potential danger, and then there were the dogs that mingled with the sheep, carefully disguised with their fleece like fur, always guarding and watching their flock. Major as to be expected was the leader. He was a distinguished old chap who kept his troops in line and ready for duty, but he was nearing retirement and seemed to understand this, as he appeared to be passing his skills onto the new young apprentice Andrex. When Alan and Nikki bought the farm and the sheep, Toffee was also part of the deal. Toffee was introduced to the sheep at an early age, imprinted on the livestock, and spends her entire life with the flock out in the fields. Nikki and Alan cannot get within 100 metres of her so they have to leave food out for her on the edge of the field. Toffee only then feeds when she knows Nikki and Alan are far enough away. These types of guardian dogs form an amazing bond with the sheep and will confront and fight predators in order to protect the flock. Alan and Nikki shared some fascinating stories about guardian dogs giving us a great insight into an area of gaurdian dogs we had previously never known about.

That evening Nikki cooked a fantastic meal and we stayed up chatting until midnight. Next morning we were up and ready to go to work, but after we had breakfast and stopped chatting, it was 11am. Alan had already left to do some work, so we all went to join him over in one of the barns. Today we were separating ewes from lambs, counting, clipping and tagging. Helen helped Nikki at one end with the counting and I helped Alan (and Shep) at the other end by sending sheep though and tagging them. Due to our late start, it wasn't that long before it was lunchtime. Nikki showed us a caravan, it was very basic but this was where she spent her long cold nights during the lambing season, rather than over in the comfort of the house. We had only been here one morning but had a lot of respect for what Alan and Nikki had here and the work involved. It was amazingly remote and tough work when it was busy. Alan and Nikki were planning to sell their sheep soon. They have done it for a number of years and they have decided to rent their land out for pasture. After lunch we carried on counting and tagging the sheep. It seemed since their last count they were missing a few sheep, probably as a result of coyotes, which is what the dogs help deter. There then followed another evening of great food, company, beer and wine.

We felt like slackers the next day as we hardly did any work. We filled up the water for the horses, picked up dog poo and did some house cleaning. I also helped Alan load a ram into a trailer as he had been sold to another local farmer. Even the next day seemed really easy in terms of workload, we walked the dogs, cleaned out some stables, shifted five wheelbarrows of horse poo then sat chatting with Nikki and her friend out on the porch, but it was fine by us. Unlike the farm we worked on as soon as we arrived in Canada, Nikki and Alan were a lot more laid back. We also sensed that they also just liked the company as much as the help sometimes. They also had a different view on workaways. Nikki said that you should enjoy it, it should be fun, trying things you've never done and are never likely to do again and it was a good attitude to have. You can sometimes feel subservient as workawayers, constantly trying to impress and be busy in order to earn your keep. With Alan and Nikki it actually felt as though you were the guests in their home. We were also really enjoying the time we spent with the dogs. Major was leader but soon reaching retirement, when Andrex would be taking over but he had such a presence for a dog, I felt really privileged when he allowed me to stroke him. Smiler was hilarious, he slept around the side of house in a big hole he had dug to keep cool. He was called Smiler for obvious reasons, when he approached you he bared all his teeth, not in a nasty way though. Some dogs do this and it is known as a submissive grin and is used to show that they are no threat, soliciting attention in a non-threatening manner. His coat was so thick and Helen spent ages each day brushing him and the other dogs.

One day Nikki and Alan had a long trip out to the supermarket, this is usually once a month. Helen and I cleaned the house, painted a fence, filled up water for the horses and started making a new clearing which would increase the size of a paddock. Alan and Nikki also left us the keys for the quadbike and told us to go for a ride and explore. That would have been great except we couldn't start it. When they returned though, Alan got it started and we went for a long ride. That evening Nikki mentioned that there is an open air drive-in cinema so we decided to check it out. It was 30 km away but thought it would be fine, however it was 30 km of gravel road. Halfway there, the car started making some horrendous screeching noises, so we turned round and headed back to the farm and stayed up drinking with Nikki and Alan. Nikki and Helen carried on until the early hours and both were feeling a little tender in the morning. Our time here had flown by and we were already on our penultimate day. We took a drive to look at some buffaloes and had another ride on the quad bike. In the afternoon, all the wood and branches we had cleared from the previous day, we fed it all through a wood chipper. It was a beautiful sunny day and we were just wearing Shorts and T Shirts, it was now October and we purchased hats and gloves on the way here! Saska and Shep then joined us for a walk before our last lovely evening meal with Alan and Nikki.

Before we left the next day, Alan looked at our car, the noise was made by stones that had got stuck between the brake disc and the wheel, so we had to take off both back wheels to clear them. Soon we were back on the road waving goodbye to Alan, Nikki and all of the dogs. We had an amazing time in their company. The work was so light in comparison to our other workways and the hospitality was on another level and that friendship is what made it so memorable. During our short stay, it really didn't feel like a workaway, and when there are 10 dogs, that is always an added bonus. The only regret from our stay there is that I didn't post any photos of the farm, our hosts or the dogs on Instagram. Instead I posted three photos of sunsets, as Saskatchewan is known as the land of the living sky. INSTAGRAM POST 116, INSTAGRAM POST 117 and INSTAGRAM POST 118. In the last one I also managed to get a flock of Canadian Geese on their way south for the winter.

That night we stayed in Kindersley, near the provincial border of Alberta that would put us within a four hour drive of Calgary not including our stop at Drumheller. Drumheller is famous for Hoodoos, Canyons, Badlands and dinosaur bones, and it was a nice afternoon admiring the scenery on the 50 km looped scenic drive. INSTAGRAM POST 121, INSTAGRAM POST 122 and INSTAGRAM POST 123. It was just before dark when we arrived at our Airbnb on the outskirts of Calgary. The house was enormous with eight bedrooms. It was busy and there were people all over the house. It reminded me of some sort of cult and the owner looked very similar to Elon Musk. We were not really in the mood for socialising so decided to grab an early night before our house sit started tomorrow. I still managed to really offend someone when I walked into the bathroom and she was sitting on the toilet. She had a go at me and said I should knock, I told her she should consider locking the door next time. There was a note in my journal about how we couldn't believe we had made it all the way across to Calgary. And yes, there was also a note about me walking in on a woman sitting on the toilet. When we started and would look at the map of Canada, Calgary just looked so far away, it never seemed we would get there but we had driven over 4,000 km since buying the car in Montréal. It was always Alberta and British Columbia that attracted me to Canada, these were the provinces I was excited about, the picture postcard scenes you have in your head when you think of Canada. So far Canada had totally exceeded our high expectations and we still had our favourite bits to come. As the guide book put it "Alberta does lakes and mountains like Rome does churches and cathedrals. Rome has never really appealed to us, but Lakes and Mountains, now you're talking.

The day of our house sit had arrived. Before heading over to Cochrane, we stocked up on some groceries from the supermarket. The weather was noticeably cooler now so we also bought some thermals and a hoody each. Just after lunch we pulled into the drive of our new house sit for the next two and a half weeks. We were met by Jeremy and Anne and their two gorgeous dogs, Addy and Lilly. They are Goldendoodles, INSTAGRAM POST 120. Some of you may have noticed the photo order is slightly out of sync as the Drumheller photos are appearing after the photo of Addy and Lilly. I apologize, I don't know what happened, I was probably traumatised after the lady and toilet incident. The same goes for INSTAGRAM POST 119, this is Glenbow Ranch Provincial Park, I'll tell you about it in a bit. Anyway, the house was great, the dogs were lovely and when we all went for a walk, we realised the area was pretty special too. We had lucked out on this one. Jeremy and Anne were not leaving until the day after tomorrow so it meant we would have another full day with them. That day was a handover day, explaining everything we needed to know. Jeremy gave us a tour of Cochrane and we took the dogs to the pooch parlour for a shower. They also showed us the places where they usually took the dogs for a walk. One of them was an off leash area which runs alongside the Bow River. Jeremy and Anne's house is also close to the river but about 2 miles further along from the off leash area. INSTAGRAM POST 124.

They set off at around 7am the next morning, we were up and about to help load the cases in the car and wave them off. Today it was snowing. It seemed like we missed autumn and went straight from summer into winter. We were wearing shorts in Saskatchewan this time last week. Borrowing some of their thicker coats we took Addy, Lilly and the next door neighbour's dog, Boomer out for a walk. We didn't just help ourselves to the neighbour's dog. We were told they regularly take him out on their walks as his owners are at work, so they have a key to their house. Boomer was a great little dog, well behaved as were Addy and Lilly, so walking them at the off leash park was easy. This was our routine in the early days, it was pretty cold so we would walk the dogs in the morning after breakfast, back to the warmth of the house for the rest of the day and then we would go out again before it got dark or after dinner we would walk them around the estate under the streetlights. At night we would snuggle up in front of the open fire they had in the basement and watch Netflix. Addy and Lilly warmed to us really quickly and followed us everywhere. It didn't take long before they were sleeping in our bedroom, Jeremy warned us it might happen but we liked it that they had accepted us so quickly. One day we took the dogs to Glenbow Ranch Provincial Park, just outside Cochrane. INSTAGRAM POST 119. We loved it here, there were lots of trails for walking the dogs and they seemed to like it as well, even though they had to be on their leads. To get back to Cochrane you drive back on the 1A road and on this day the skies were clear and we caught an amazing view of the Canadian Rockies. They are only about 30 km west of Cochrane but they stretch North to South as far as the eye can see. The total length is 1,450 km stretching North West all the way to top of British Columbia. So two days later we headed west, after walking the dogs in the morning, we then took them out for a scenic drive. It took us about 45 minutes to reach the Rockies and we drove down the highway on the eastern side along Kananaskis Country. Coming from a place in England that is very flat and rarely sees much snow, this place was breath-taking to us. INSTAGRAM POST 125, INSTAGRAM POST 126, INSTAGRAM POST 127, INSTAGRAM POST 128, INSTAGRAM POST 129 and INSTAGRAM POST 130. We let the dogs stretch their legs and we went for a walk around the side of Barrier Lake under Mt Baldy. It was so quiet, almost scarily so. We had seen signs saying that there had been some Grizzly bear sightings around here so that added to our nerves. A story Jeremy told us before he left also played on our minds. Jeremy is a retired vet and once he was called to examine the stomach contents of a grizzly that had been killed. He said he found parts of a human including some fingers. Unlike the cute Black Bears we saw back in Ontario, Grizzly bears can stand up to 3m tall and should never be approached. There are plenty of warnings of what to do if you spot a grizzly. Avoid eye contact, back off slowly if it is not approaching. If it charges stand your ground, you can't outrun it. Speak in a soft monotone voice and wave your hands to let the animal know you are human. Don't scream or yell (that would be tricky). If you have bear spray use it when the bear is within 25 feet. If you are attacked curl up into a ball or lie on your stomach. We didn't have any bear spray at that time but we would definitely be buying some. When walking it is advised to carry a bear bell, this warns them of your presence from a distance so they won't be startled. Instead of thankfully seeing a grizzly bear that day, we did encounter some deer and Rocky Mountain sheep.

A few days later we drove to Canmore, a little further into the Rockies. With the dogs, we walked the Grassi Lake Trail, INSTAGRAM POST 131 and INSTAGRAM POST 132, again the scenery and the walk were stunning. The walk was supposed to be "easy" but we found it quite tough. The altitude was probably having an effect. Cochrane, where we are staying is at 1,159m and Ben Nevis 1,345m. We were certainly feeing more sluggish than we normally would. Our time in Cochrane looking after the dogs was really enjoyable. Our days were spent walking them either along the River Bow, at Glenbow Provincial Park or just on the outskirts of the Rockies, only now we had bought some bear spray. One evening we decided to take Addy and Lilly out for a walk when it was dark. We were walking around the estate under the streetlights and then decided to cut across a field. Helen wasn't sure where we were heading and just as I turned around to say "follow me", I tripped and fell flat on my face. Helen was in stiches and the dogs were jumping on me as if it was some sort of game. Helen begged me to make a note of it in the journal for some reason. Anyway, I did and that's why I've told the story, I would have conveniently forgotten about it otherwise. Soon our two and half weeks looking after Addy and Lilly came to an end when Jeremy and Anne returned. We would miss them so much even though we had them for such a short time. Helen even shed a tear when she said goodbye to them. This was a new benchmark in house sits. We learnt that the ideal house sit comprised of three things. Firstly, the location, was there a lot to do in and around the area? Secondly, was the house itself nice? And thirdly, the pets you are looking after? Are they sociable, are they active?

With just over a week until we had our next house sit in Calgary this gave us the perfect opportunity to spend time at the world famous resort town of Banff. On arrival we were amazed how small the town is, there is only a population of 9,300 people. Banff is the service centre to the surrounding park, so it is full of hotels and restaurants to cater for the tourists. As Banff sits in the National Park, there is a charge to enter, you are then given a sticker to put on your windscreen. Unlike other accommodation in Canada, the ones in Banff do not come with a microwave or fridge. This was a problem in two ways, firstly for Helen's insulin and secondly for our food. We had managed to travel across Canada living on sandwiches/snacks for lunch and then something we could microwave for dinner. Here, it was not possible, I presume they wanted you to spend your money in the bars and restaurants. To save money, as the motels were a lot pricier in Banff than anywhere else we had visited in Canada, we ended up buying a cheap kettle and living on pot noodle type meals for our stay and still making sandwiches for our hikes. Reception also kindly stored the insulin in their fridge. On our first full day we headed straight to the tourist information centre to pick up a map of all the different walks we would do over the next few days. Our first walk was the Bow River Falls and Hoodoo trail, this was a great walk from the town centre and took us about three hours.

INSTAGRAM POST 133, INSTAGRAM POST 134, INSTAGRAM POST 135, INSTAGRAM POST 136, and INSTAGRAM POST 137. At the end, on the way back towards Banff there was a huge Elk just strolling along the main road. INSTAGRAM POST 138. The next day we drove north about 20 km to try the Boom Lake Walk, INSTAGRAM POST 139 and INSTAGRAM POST 140. There was quite a bit of snow on this walk, ankle deep in places, but so worth it for the views. The snow was so powdery it never made our clothes or boots wet, it just shook off, not like the snow in the UK. It snowed even more on the way back but we decided we wanted to spend more time in this area as there was so much to see and explore. That included a 16 km walk along Lake Minnewanka at Stewart Canyon. INSTAGRAM POST 141. About 50 km north of Banff is Lake Louise. It is a picture postcard turquoise lake that is surrounded by mountains and forests. Obviously it is a major tourist attraction and there is a rather ugly hotel sat at one end of the lake but you cannot take away the sheer beauty of the place. It snowed overnight and they seemed to have a lot more up here. We walked up to Fairview Point through the snow, sometimes knee deep to get a better view of Lake Louise. INSTAGRAM POST 142 and INSTAGRAM POST 143.

If you did an internet search for the most scenic drives in the world, I'm pretty sure that the Icefields Parkway would be one of them. It is Highway 93 linking Banff to Jasper 230 km north. All along the drive you can marvel at glaciers, waterfalls, lakes and just pure breathtaking scenery. There is a handy map available at the tourist information that lists all of the attractions by kilometre markers depending if you are driving North or South. After visiting Lake Louise, we decided to drive a short part of the parkway although the road was really bad. Only one side, unfortunately not ours, had been snow ploughed so it was pretty scary. We ended up having to turn around in the end. The following day, the weather had improved so we decided to give it another go, and this time the road was much better. We covered about half of the Parkway that day taking in a couple of hikes at Bow and Peyto Lakes. INSTAGRAM POST 144 , INSTAGRAM POST 145 and INSTAGRAM POST 146. At Bow point summit we reached the highest point on the Parkway, 2,135m. With still so much to do in Banff, the next day we hiked the Tunnel Mountain trail overlooking Banff, we were finished by 1pm so decided to walk some more of the Bow Falls Trail. INSTAGRAM POST 147. Later in the afternoon we drove up to Mt Norquay for more views over Banff and then headed over to Canmore for some groceries and a trip to the laundrette. In what was a nice change to the noodles we had lived on for the past week we decided to treat ourselves to a veggie burger. Also with the amount of snow around we decided to buy some snow spikes to put under our shoes, this gave us a better grip when hiking, especially for tomorrow when we were going to hike up Sulpher Mountain on our last full day in Banff. This is a great hike, you can take the easy route up via cable car, but this would have cost over $100 for the both of us. From the bottom the elevation gain is nearly 800m over 3.5 miles. What makes it trickier is that half way up you reach the snow and ice so the shoe spikes we purchased came in handy. The hike was pretty tough and we managed it in just over two hours. Sulpher Mountain is a big tourist attraction in Banff and rightly so as the views were amazing looking across the Rockies in every direction. INSTAGRAM POST 148 and INSTAGRAM POST 149. If you hike up the mountain, you are entitled to free ride down in the gondola, so we did. To celebrate our hiking success we went for a beer or two, or three. With the lack of food, altitude and the fact that I had hardly drank in Canada, I really couldn't handle my beer, and when we got back to the motel I realised how drunk I was. I ended up being rather ill and if I wasn't fed up with noodles before now, I was when I saw them for an unexpected second time that day!

As you can expect, the next day I was feeling pretty rough, but we had a lot to do. We needed to pack, check out, get petrol, and return all our empty bottles and cans (soft drinks and water, not beer!) to the recycling centre and then drive all along the Icefields Parkway to Jasper. Banff had been great and we would love to return in a different season as some of the trails were closed due to the weather. INSTAGRAM POST 150. Helen was a star and drove the whole way whilst I admired the view with my window down, just in case, but I was feeling ok again by mid-afternoon.

Jasper was to be the most northerly destination for us in Canada, really pretty but it seemed like a ghost town compared to Banff. It was almost like the season hadn't started here yet. That evening we just wanted a quiet night. What we didn't realise when we had booked into the cheapest motel in Jasper, it was above a bar. We also didn't register that it was Halloween and they were having a huge party which went on into the early hours. After a restless night we decided to drive to Maligne Lake. This is a must do scenic drive when in Jasper and again didn't disappoint as we saw lots of wildlife including elk, deer and mountain goats. We were faced with a roadblock on the way at Medicine Lake, INSTAGRAM POST 151. Maligne Canyon was also a stopping point on the drive, a steep narrow gorge shaped by the river with a numerous waterfalls. INSTAGRAM POST 152. This was to be our only full day in Jasper, it seems that there is a lot to do but it just seemed empty during our time here. Jasper is a place very much like Banff that I would love to come back to in the spring or summer to hike the many trails.

Our drive back to Banff would take in all the sights on the Icefields Parkway that we didn't stop at on our way up the first time. Highlights driving south included a lot of waterfalls, namely Athabasca Falls, INSTAGRAM POST 153 and Sunwapta Falls, INSTAGRAM POST 154. However the most impressive sight for us was the Athabasca Glacier. This glacier is one of six "toes" that runs from the huge Columbia Icefield. It is the most visited Glacier in North America due to the ease at which it can be reached. You literally pull off the Parkway into the car park, and then you have less than a mile to walk to it. It is 6 km long and 1 km wide. When we arrived, there were only a handful of people and by the time we reached the glacier we were on our own. Sadly the glacier is disappearing at quite a rate and there are stark reminders on the walk to it. Signposts indicate where the edge of glacier reached in the years prior to its retreat. Estimations are that the glacier is currently retreating at about five metres per year. The walk to the glacier was so windy, it seemed the wind funnelled all the way down through the glacier and was like an ice cold hair dryer, we really had to shield our faces up there but it was worth it. INSTAGRAM POST 155 and INSTAGRAM POST 156. On the video you can really get a sense of how windy it was from the sound. It was truly a special sight and was a great end to our time on the Icefield Parkway. There were sights along that 230 km road that we will never forget. It is these sights that appeal to us, pure natural wonders like mountains, lakes and glaciers. Give us these over a cathedral or museum any day of the week. It was dark by the time we arrived back in Banff, we parked our car in one of the heated covered carparks and checked into the motel. After such a great day we decided to treat ourselves to a Beaver Tail from the store on the main high street.

Our arrival at the new house sit was arranged for early evening so for our last day in Banff we hiked the Sundance trail and followed it with a veggie burger from A&W Burger. At 6pm we pulled into the long drive leading to our house sit. By coincidence it was very close to the Airbnb we stayed at a few weeks ago (the one where I walked in on someone on the loo). We were greeted by Jean. Jean was in her late 70's but has the energy of someone a lot younger, and she lives on her own with her nine year old Wheaton Terrier called Bloom. Jean is American and she was going south over the border to visit family for a few days. We enjoyed a really pleasant evening getting to know Jean and Bloom. Jean took us to the supermarket the next day and showed us the walk where she usually took Bloom, just a short one around the neighbourhood. Her house was stunning, hidden in amongst trees, it was huge, there was even a lift in the house and the downstairs was a really nice open plan layout. Jean left the next day so it was just us and Bloom. Bloom was absolutely lovely, she was very friendly and enjoyed her walks. The week went really quickly. During that time we would go for runs, Skype our parents and watch Netflix. One day Helen shouted me to come out to the garden, there was a huge porcupine snuffling around the undergrowth, INSTAGRAM POST 157. We had never seen one before so it was fascinating to see one so close up. During that week we took Bloom out to Glenbow where we used to take Addy and Lilly and another park in the city where she enjoyed meeting other dogs, INSTAGRAM POST 158. One afternoon we visited the Olympic park as it was really close to the house. INSTAGRAM POST 159. Calgary hosted the Winter Olympics in 1998 and for us Brits it was where Eddie the Eagle Edwards became a household name. It was also where the Jamaicans entered a team in the bobsleigh which then inspired the film Cool Runnings, and the actual bobsleigh is on display at the park. Whilst we were on this house sit Donald Trump won the US election, much to the displeasure of Jean when she returned from her holiday. We had a meal

61

waiting for her when she arrived home and chatted about her time away and ours here in Calgary. The next morning we all walked Bloom for the last time at the park we had been taking her to all week and I fed some birds out of my hand which was pretty special, INSTAGRAM POST 160.

It had been a short but enjoyable week in Calgary, but it was now time to leave Alberta behind and head into our final province of Canada, British Columbia. Again we headed in the direction of Banff to cross over the Rocky Mountains. We did actually stop in Banff on our way as we had some recycling to cash in, $8 for our cans and bottles, not to be sniffed at, as it then paid for our coffee and donuts at Tim Hortons. We spent the night in Golden and the next day drove through Glacier National Park, INSTAGRAM POST 161, and Mt Revelstoke National Park to Kamloops. Both parks had offered a glimpse of another beautiful province in Canada and it seemed to carry on where Alberta left off as we descended through the Western side of the Rockies. Another day of driving and we arrived at our destination, Yarrow, a small town just outside the city of Chilliwack. The reason for Yarrow was that we had another house sit, they were stacking up now, in part to our positive reviews from previous house sits. We even had another house sit to go to after this one. We were enjoying doing the house sits and they were appearing in our general direction. It was an opportunity for us to unpack our bags and feel homely, as well as looking after pets which we loved. In between the house sits, this was when we did our sightseeing. During the house sits we were quite happy keeping the pets company, going for runs, cooking some nice meals as a change to noodles and watching Netflix. This house sit was to last nearly four weeks so we would be here until early December. Peter and Amy were the hosts and they were trusting us to look after their house cats Gemma and Coco whilst they were going away on a bible mission to Fiji and some remote pacific islands. INSTAGRAM POST 162. Yarrow was one of those typical small towns we had driven through on the Trans Canadian Highway, even though it actually wasn't on the highway. Our house sit was right on the main road though so it was a relief to know that the cats were house cats and didn't go outside. The first night was pretty much like our other house sits. Our hosts cooked us a nice meal and we sat and chatted about where they were going, our travels so far and all the things we needed to know whilst they were away. This continued the next morning, but it felt strange for me not taking a dog out for a walk. The cats were very low maintenance, so we would have a lot of free time for ourselves. Helen and I did go for a walk in the afternoon and returned to see Peter and Amy leave around 5pm. One of our first jobs was to go to the supermarket for groceries, and we stocked up on fresh vegetables, something we had been missing. Our days were generally spent going for a walk and a run, or two to three walks a day just to keep ourselves occupied. I was amazed how much cats sleep and how easy they were to look after compared to dogs. Gemma and Coco were sociable when they were awake so we would play with them, it just wasn't very often that they were awake. Just outside of town we found a good running route and this lifted our spirits, also because we were both running well. It might have been due to our time spent at a higher altitude in and around Calgary at 1,200m that helped improve our fitness.

Yarrow is less than 10 km from the US border so one day we decided to drive along the road that ran parallel to it. I don't know what I expected to see when we drove there, maybe a fence or something but there was nothing. I did find a pillar indicating the border so I cheekily stood on the other side just to see if any sirens would start up. One thing that had been playing on our minds was whether or not we would be able to take our car over the border. Our time in Canada was coming to an end soon so it made sense that the only way we could really go now was south, into the US. But we had a car, we were British, would they let us? We phoned US security and they said it should be fine to take it into the US and then return to Canada afterwards to sell the car. That wasn't in our plans though. If we were going to the US, we might end up right down in the south. We wouldn't want to then have to return all the way back to Canada to sell the car. It was something we needed to think about. Another issue we faced was that our six month visa was due to expire on the 12th of Jan. Our current house sit finished on the 10th of December and our next one started on the 14th until the 28th. We still had a lot more of British Columbia to see but after our next house sit we were only left with two weeks. One day after a run my back was really hurting. I have always suffered with back problems since I was a kid. It meant no running for a while. Luckily I bought my back support with me and whilst Helen went out running I was housebound doing my back stretches.

It looked like our best option was to apply for a visa extension for Canada. That way it would allow us an extra six months and in that time you are allowed to leave Canada and visit the US before returning back to Canada. We didn't actually know what we were doing, but for starters it meant that we would be able to see more of British Columbia. Although there wasn't a lot in Yarrow, it did have a public library, so we spent a couple of days in there applying for our extensions. Over time my back started to feel better with stretching and not running, meanwhile Helen was getting faster on her runs. Unfortunately the weather was worse and it made even going for a run or a walk less enjoyable. It rained a lot, like England rain, grey and miserable for days, but heavy rain. Days like these were long so skyping friends and family helped as did watching hours and hours of Netflix. When it wasn't raining we made use of the time to get outside and hike. Cultus lake had some nice walks as were the hikes at Harrison Lake. One walk at Cultus Lake is called the The Teapot Hill Trail, so called as it follows a short trail up to the top of Teapot Hill. This walk was different though as there were dozens of teapots scattered and hidden throughout the hike. There had been so much rain though, one day we had to take our shoes and socks off to make it across a trail. Another day we spotted an ideal weather window to go hiking to Linderman Lake, INSTAGRAM POST 163. It took about 45 minutes to drive there and soon it started raining. We persisted, however when it started snowing heavily we decided that was enough and turned around to head back to the car. It had also been a while since we spent some money on keeping the car running, so $500 on new brake pads and windscreen wiper was an unwelcome subtraction from our funds.

In the last week we visited the hosts of our next house sit located in Abbotsford. Abbotsford is about 20 km west of Yarrow so it was no problem heading over to introduce ourselves. They were a really lovely family, Hannah, Sam and their two sons as well as Mick the dog who we would be looking after. Mick is an Australian shepherd mixed with a Ridgeback. He was really friendly with lots of energy so we knew we

64

would be spending lots of time walking him. Their house was lovely and there seemed lots of places to take Mick for a walk. This housesit also included chickens, which was a first for us.

On a rare clear day we headed out to walk up to the top of Mt Thom, it took us about an hour to reach the top and we were rewarded with great views of the Fraser Valley and Cultus Lake. INSTAGRAM POST 164 and INSTAGRAM POST 165. When we arrived back at the house, our parcels from home had arrived. My parents had sent me a better day pack that I had left at home with more padding on the back. They also included two pairs of thick socks and a birthday card as my birthday was approaching. Helen also received some socks and some more dextrose tablets.

Vancouver is about 70 km away from Yarrow and we had decided that the four days in between our two house sits would be an ideal opportunity to explore the city. The weather was worsening though and we were keeping a close eye on the forecast. The news was saying that Vancouver had not experienced snow for a thousand days, yet just before we were arriving, heavy snow was predicted for our region. Even Peter and Amy were concerned enough to send an email warning us of the impending snow and asked us to arrange for a plumber to winterise the bungalow. Helen went for a run and her water bottle froze. We drove over to Hope and walked the Nicola Valley trail. INSTAGRAM POST 166, INSTAGRAM POST 167 and INSTAGRAM POST 168. We had never felt the cold like we did on that walk. I was wearing a buff to cover my face but the condensation from my breath made the buff freeze solid stiff. The posts look like I have used a blue filter but that's exactly how it was, it was just absolutely freezing and we were wearing about six layers of clothing because our jackets were only lightweight. Despite that, it was a beautiful 6 km walk through the forests to the Othello Tunnels. The day before Peter and Amy returned was my Dad's birthday, so I Skyped home. We also enjoyed a last long walk along the Chilliwack River where Helen had spent a lot of time running and you can see why with the views. Running is great as you just switch off but when you are running in places when the scenery is like this it certainly helps. INSTAGRAM POST 169.

Peter and Amy were landing at 7am so we were up early to wash, dry and change the bed before they arrived. It was nice seeing them again, they were a lovely couple and it seemed that their bible mission had been a success. Considering we had only known them for a couple of days either side of their trip away we were amazed at their kindness when they invited us to join them on Xmas day. It wouldn't be possible as we were looking after Mick but it was a lovely offer and totally summed up the hospitality we had experienced from Canadians on our trip. Another house sit complete and friends made, we continued West past Abbotsford where we would be returning in four days to head to Vancouver. The 70 km drive was pretty scary. There had been a lot of snow overnight and it was falling heavily as we were driving. For some of the journey it was made easier by following a snow plough. Instead of staying in central Vancouver we stayed at an Airbnb just outside in a suburb called Delta. There is a 4 km spit at Delta so we drove out to that for our first glimpse of another ocean, the Pacific. The last one we saw was the Atlantic, over 5,500 km to the east. INSTAGRAM POST 170. Overnight it snowed even more, there was about 20cm of snow on the ground when we walked to the bus stop to head into Vancouver. Luckily it wasn't so bad in the city and there was hardly any snow, the temperature was also a bit warmer. My Fitbit recorded that we walked over 25,000 steps and nearly 20 km around Vancouver, we basically walked around the whole shoreline of Downtown taking in the magnificent 404 hectare Stanley Park. INSTAGRAM POST 171 and INSTAGRAM POST 172. The next day we crossed the Harbour to North Vancouver arriving at midday. Our Airbnb was only five minutes away from Capilano Canyon. There are a number of walks and attractions at the canyon and they are certainly not for those who suffer from vertigo. Before we attempted the famous suspension bridge we had a go at the Cliff Walk, a glass bottomed walkway that extends out into the canyon. INSTAGRAM POST 173. The suspension bridge was next, it is one of the longest (140m) and highest (70m) suspension bridges in the world, spanning the Capilano Canyon. INSTAGRAM POST 174 and INSTAGRAM POST 175. The final walk we gingerly attempted in the park was the Tree Top Trail. INSTAGRAM POST 176. The Park is a good place to spend a couple of hours but it was quite pricey, it cost $35 each. As we were nearing Xmas our tickets did allow us back in the evening when the park and bridge were decorated with fairy lights. If we were not a five minute walk from the park, I'm not sure we would have bothered, but it was the first time we really sensed that Xmas was only a fortnight away as we had not really thought much about it. In between our two visits to the Capilano Canyon we drove a bit further north and walked a part of Capilano lake and the Cleveland Dam, INSTAGRAM POST 177. Our mini city break in Vancouver was over, but it was nice, there were a lot of green spaces and there are plenty of outdoor activities within reach of the city if you want to escape the buzz. Before our drive back to Abbotsford, we were able to fit in one more walk at Lynn Canyon Park, INSTAGRAM POST 178 and INSTAGRAM POST 179. This park was free and less crowded with plenty of walks and suspension bridges.

Arriving in Abbotsford at 3pm, we only had a couple of hours with our hosts before they left, it was no issue though as we had already visited them the previous week and they had prepared a welcome pack. This is a good tool on the house sitting website which allows the hosts to note down anything they think the house sitters will need to know about the pets and the house. It was now the 14th of December and we were here for two weeks so this is where we would be spending Xmas. Hannah and Sam had asked if we wanted them to put up a Xmas tree, we declined and I think they were quite relieved. The first couple of days in a house sit we try and get our bearings of the local area. We scour google maps and the internet for places to go for long dog walks and running routes. Skyping parents usually happens in the first couple of days to give them a view of where we are staying and we also tend to do our large grocery shop. Abbotsford was still suffering from the bad weather, in our first week there was a covering of snow most days so it was impossible to go for a run anywhere but it didn't matter as Mick enjoyed his walks and we would take him out to various places two or three times a day. INSTAGRAM POST 180 and INSTAGRAM POST 181. Walking Mick anywhere around the neighbourhood was tricky as the ice was treacherous from when the snow has melted slightly in the day but then froze after the sun disappeared. Helen and I both ended up on the floor a number of times despite walking with our shoe spikes attached. The chickens were very low maintenance, we were concerned how they might cope with the unusually cold weather but they had a light and a lamp in their pen and seemed fine, even providing us with a few eggs. More surprising to us was the hummingbird that appeared at the house every day to feed. They do migrate (I looked it up) but this one must have thought it was still ok to hang around for now. INSTAGRAM POST 182. The 20th of December was my mum's birthday so we Skyped to wish her well. My Uncle Martin and niece Lucy were around at the time so it was good to catch up with them. Good news arrived just before Xmas, we had been accepted on another house sit, at a place called Summerland, about 300 km back east in the Okanagan Valley, an area we missed out on as we travelled from Banff down to Yarrow. It was starting on the 29th, the same day that Hannah and Sam would return. The new hosts had asked if we could be there at 11am. Hannah and Sam were returning early in the morning on that day so we worked out we should leave at 6am.

When Christmas Day arrived it just like any other day. There wasn't a Xmas tree or decorations to remind us it was Christmas, but it did when we went onto social media and all our friends and families were posting. The UK was already tucking into it's dinner when we woke up as they are five hours ahead of us. I looked out the window along the street, the neighbours would be up and exchanging presents. Cars were soon arriving at houses or leaving to visit relatives. We Skyped our families and that was quite sad, it must have been especially hard on Helen's mum who was really missing her. Throughout our travels we felt incredibly fortunate at what we were doing, but today it felt like we were the ones who were missing out. Xmas day was the day that we missed our families the most throughout our travels because it is the time when we are all usually together. Helen and I had already agreed that we wouldn't buy each other any presents either. We put Mick in the car and drove him to the dog park. There were a couple of people there who we had a chat with and Mick had a great time playing with their dogs.

Back at the house it was time for Xmas dinner, cheese sandwiches and a packet of crisps! Mick had another walk later in the afternoon and I made an effort at a Xmas dinner with veggie sausages, lots of veg, roast potatoes and Yorkshire puddings. Instead of sitting with our families playing board games or watching the Xmas film on TV, Helen and I watched re-runs of UFC fights. It would certainly go down as a Xmas unlike any other we have experienced.

It snowed heavily on Boxing Day luckily just after Helen had been out for a run and I'd walked Mick. Soon we would be moving on again so we started the usual routine of packing our rucksacks and cleaning the house. The 28th was my birthday and I shared it with Emma, my niece. We Skyped and wished each other Happy Birthday and we also Skyped our parents, thanking them for the cards they sent over in the post to Chilliwack. Since arriving in Canada, I was yet to have a haircut, it was starting to get quite long so I decided to go the hairdressers. Helen also hadn't had a haircut but she decided to just keep growing it and eventually have a pony tail. For the rest of my birthday we walked Mick, cleaned the house and packed our bags, as early tomorrow we were on the move again. Hannah and Sam returned home in the middle of the night and slept in the spare room and we crept out just before 6am.

The journey was a scary one to say the least. On Netflix there is a reality series called Highway through Hell. It is a Canadian reality based TV show that follows a heavy vehicle rescue and recovery company. They are based in Hope, not far from our house sit in Yarrow, and the program follows them out on the roads mainly in horrendous conditions rescuing lorries and keeping the roads open. Having watched it quite a lot we had heard the name of the infamous Coquihalla Highway. It always seemed to be the highway where vehicles were getting into trouble and is considered one of North America's most dangerous roads in the winter. The reason for this is due to elevation (1,200m) and the steepness on both sides at the summit. In winter, snowstorms are common and the road becomes very treacherous with poor visibility. As we headed out ourselves on the Coquihalla, it started to snow, I followed a snow plough for most of way gripping the steering wheel like never before, INSTAGRAM POST 183.

At 10.45 am we arrived at our house sit in Summerland. Kathy and Terry were worried we might not even make it as they had heard the Coquihalla was now closed due to the weather. They introduced us to their dogs Shannon and Goofy. Goofy is an 11 year old Pomeranian and Shannon is a big white mixed breed. Shannon is a really nervous dog, but lovely so we had to be extra careful not to scare him. They also had two cats, Luna and Nero. INSTAGRAM POST 185. The house was gorgeous, set on a hill overlooking Okanagan Lake, INSTAGRAM POST 184. After a very quick tour of the house and feeding requirements, Kathy and Terry were on their way and would return in six days on the 3rd of January. It was a very short hand over. More good news arrived today, our visa extension applications had been approved, and they just required an address to send the documents. We contacted Peter and Amy and asked if it was okay to have them posted to their address. They were fine with that so we arranged to pick them up on our way back through BC.

New Year's Eve was now upon us. Although it was bitterly cold, the sky was clear so we drove to Giants Head Mountain and walked with Goofy and Shannon to the top. INSTAGRAM POST 186 and INSTAGRAM POST 187. The views were amazing, this part of Canada is stunning but not visited by many tourists as they are usually heading to either Banff and Calgary or Vancouver, although it is very popular with Canadians. The 180 km Okanagan Valley is prime wine region and all along the terraced hills there are dozens of vineyards and wineries as in the summer, this area is one of the sunniest parts of Canada. On the house sitting website we had been looking at an assignment a bit further south down the valley towards Osoyoos in a place called Oliver. We sent a message notifying them of our interest. New Year's evening was a typical quiet affair watching Netflix accompanied by Goofy and Shannon, the cats kept themselves amused and we were in bed by 11.30pm. Who knows where we will be this time next year?

New Year's day we found a really nice walk along a creek in the morning and the river was barely visible through the snow and ice. INSTAGRAM POST 188 and INSTAGRAM POST 189 and then we walked part of the way up Giants Head Mountain again. Kathy and Terry returned on the afternoon of the 3rd and it was a bitterly cold day at -18 degrees, so Shannon and Goofy only had a short walk. As we only spent a very short time with Kathy and Terry before they left, we stayed until 6pm with a few beers (Helen was driving). There had been no news regarding our potential house sit so we were a bit in limbo. It would be a nice house sit as it was looking after two dogs and we really liked the Okanagan area. Penticton is a town further south in between Summerland and Osoyoos so we decided to spend a couple of days there. It just seemed to be getting colder and colder, and walking around the shore of Lake Okanagan it had frozen out to about 100 metres, INSTAGRAM POST 190 and INSTAGRAM POST 191. Our potential house sit then made contact, her name was Marjorie and she had invited us over to visit in a couple of days time. We extended our stay in Penticton as we still had plenty to explore. One place was Munson Mountain, this was on the other side of the lake, INSTAGRAM POST 192. As we were staying in a motel room, it made sense to be outside exploring even though it was really cold. We drove to the Naramata Creek trail where the waterfall was completely frozen, INSTAGRAM POST 193. Somehow we managed to make it around the top of the fall and we joined the Kettle Valley Trail. The trail, high on the valley side used to be a 650 km railroad system that stretched from Hope to Castlegar. Now decommissioned, it is a recreational trail, and best of all, it was flat which came as a welcome change to all of the hills we had been walking up and down. This turned out to be one of our favourite walks and we ended up walking 10 km to and from the little tunnel. INSTAGRAM POST 194, INSTAGRAM POST 196, INSTAGRAM POST 197. Again it was bitterly cold, so much so that our drinks froze. INSTAGRAM POST 195,

The next day Terry also contacted us saying I had left some things at the house so we headed back to Summerland to say hello and collect my belongings. On the way we stopped off for a walk to visit Hardy Falls, where again it was frozen, but you could see the water cascading through the ice. INSTAGRAM POST 198. Terry and Kathy asked us if we had ever been to see a game of ice hockey, which we hadn't and were delighted when they invited us to spend a typical Canadian Saturday night watching the Penticton Vees. It was a really enjoyable evening, we found it difficult to keep our eye on the puck as it is such a fast paced sport, but were told it is something your eyes get used to. INSTAGRAM POST 199.

On the Sunday we arrived at Marj's, she wasn't leaving until the Thursday but kindly let us stay as she was working during the day and we could keep the dogs company. Marj was lovely, she had a great bubbly personality and we instantly clicked with her. Her dogs were Winnie and Lucy, both mixed breeds, they were great but Lucy bless her was another dog who had anxiety issues. INSTAGRAM POST 200. The days leading up to Marj leaving we took the dogs out for walks and had dinner ready for when Marj returned from work. We found a great walk along a river but poor Lucy was scared of travelling in the car. Helen sat in the back to comfort her and our intention was to help her overcome her fear of cars whilst Marj was away. The house itself was right next to the main road, sat in the middle of a vineyard. At the top of the vineyard, there were fantastic views across the valley. INSTAGRAM POST 201 and INSTAGRAM POST 202.

On the day Marj left it coincided that we had now been travelling for six months and were having the time of our lives. The kindness and generosity of the Canadian people had made our travels so much easier and the country had exceeded our high expectations. Buying a car in Montréal was the best decision we made, it may have cost us a bit more to keep it running but without your own vehicle it is not possible to explore Canada properly. Helen and I had not spent more than a couple of hours apart in the past six months but our relationship seemed as strong as ever. House sitting had allowed us to go further with our budget as we were not spending as much money on accommodation yet we were still getting to experience so much of Canada. Whilst walking along the river, we stopped to chat to a local man who told us that he had lived here all his life and had only seen the river freeze over twice in 40 years. Today it was frozen! Another time when we were out, a guy stopped his car and said we were crazy walking out in this weather. I suppose when a Canadian tells you it is too cold to be outside you know you probably shouldn't be. Before she went away Marj left out a lot of clothes for us to borrow should we get cold. We were now both wearing them to keep warm. The weather channel was saying that the temperature was now -30 degrees. When it seemed too cold to go on a longer walk with the dogs we would take them for a quick walk in the vineyard that surrounded the house. At the back of the vineyard, the valley rose up to the mountainside. A number of times the dog's ears pricked up to the distant howls of coyotes. Marj had warned us about them, and had seen some herself but there was a fence at the back of vineyard so we didn't feel too concerned. They did wake us up though at night on a few occasions and it is a very eerie sound, the type of which we had only heard in films. Along the river we used to regularly walk, there was a tree that always used to have golden eagles perched in it. It became a bit of a game as to who could guess how many eagles would be in the tree today. The closest we ever managed to get to them was when we spotted one feeding on a carcass in a field, INSTAGRAM POST 203. The weather obviously affected the car, one day it wouldn't start, the battery was dead but we managed to get it going by borrowing some jump leads from the owner of the vineyard. Another trip to the garage was due, we consoled ourselves with a Tim Hortons muffin and coffee, a double double for me, whilst we waited for the verdict. $200 for a new battery.

For the first week we didn't do a great deal due to the weather. My brother's wife, Amie celebrated her 40th birthday that week so we Skyped to wish her a Happy Birthday. They also gave us some great news. They told us they were flying out to L.A for a week at Easter. Meeting up with my brother and his family at the beginning of April would be amazing, that was just over two and a half months away.

In the second week, the temperature started to rise at last and there was a bit of a thaw. This made walking the dogs easier and we both managed to start running again. INSTAGRAM POST 204. Most hosts are happy to be kept up to date with emails and photos of their pets, but with Marj we would have a video chat which was fun and gave her a chance to see Winnie and Lucy. The final week arrived and we were out running every day in addition to walking the dogs twice. Sometimes we would still go out on our own for a hike; these included the Golden Mile trail and McIntyre Bluff, INSTAGRAM POST 205. Our car also needed to be re-registered, Rebecca had forwarded on all the details. Basically we had to write a letter with all of the details and enclose a postal cheque which we found slightly bemusing in this day and age, in that you couldn't simply reapply and pay online. This therefore meant a trip to the post office. The day before Marj returned we started our usual routine of packing and tidying the house. This house sit was really enjoyable, we could say we had experienced a proper Canadian winter during our time in the Okanagan Valley and the pets we had looked after were great company. Helen in particular had really bonded with the shy Lucy who had come out of her shell and was far better at travelling in a vehicle than she was three weeks ago. The morning Marj returned we drove over to Mt Baldy on the other side of the valley, stopping for views over Osoyoos from the Crowsnest Highway on the way. INSTAGRAM POST 206 and INSTAGRAM POST 208. The road leading up to the ski resort was pretty dicey so we had to take it slow and steady. INSTAGRAM POST 207. At Mt Baldy, there was a small ski resort and today there was a fat bike demonstration where you could hire out some bikes. It was great fun riding around the ski slopes on our bikes with enormous thick tyres. INSTAGRAM POST 209 and INSTAGRAM POST 210. Marj returned and she was over the moon to see her beloved Winnie and Lucy. In the evening Marj kindly took Helen and I out for a drink and paid for an Indian takeaway and we all had a good catch up. As ever it was always sad to say goodbye to hosts and the pets we had grown fond of, but we had a three hour drive along the crow's-nest highway back to Chilliwack. The drive as expected was stunning and a lot less scary than the Coquilhalla highway. We stopped numerous times to admire the views including the famous spotted lake. INSTAGRAM PHOTO 211. The reason for the spots is the high concentration of minerals in the water. Before checking into our motel for the night we made a quick stop at Hannah and Sam's house to collect a parcel that hadn't arrived by the time we left. As both of them were at work we offered to take Mick out for a walk, so it was good to see him again before the short drive back to our motel in Chilliwack. Amy answered the door when we turned up at our old house sit. It was really nice to see her, unfortunately Peter was out today. I wasn't sure Coco and Gemma remembered us, but we did play with them for a bit. The reason we were here was to collect our paper work for our visa extension, this meant we were now eligible to stay in Canada for another six months. After a couple of hours catching up with Amy we drove onto another motel where we spent the afternoon planning what to do when we crossed over to Vancouver Island tomorrow.

The ferry terminal was at Tsawwassen (I don't have a clue either how you are supposed to pronounce it). Driving onto the ferry, we were saying good bye to mainland Canada, from Vancouver Island we would be taking another ferry into the US. The ferry departed at 10.15am and took about two hours to cross to Nanaimo on the north east of the Island. After stocking up on groceries we drove the 100 km across the whole island on Highway 4, the only road to Ucluelet, a small town with a population of 1,600. We had booked into a really nice motel and were surprised to find the owners were two British guys. We checked in and with our hosts providing us with directions we set out and walked the short 2.5 km lighthouse trail. Across the Pacific Ocean, there was nothing in between us and Eastern Russia. It was made even more special by viewing some seals. It felt different seeing the sea. For the last six months we had not seen it and now here it was crashing into the rugged coastline INSTAGRAM POST 212. The next day, waking up to beautiful sunshine again, we would be walking along the Great Pacific trail. Filling up on a great breakfast prepared by the motel we set off on our 17 km walk. The whole of the walk was beautiful and we also included the Half Moon Bay and Florence Bay hikes. It was a full day of hiking but we both really enjoyed it. INSTAGRAM POST 213.

What a difference a day makes. Yesterday we were wearing shorts and T shirts, but waking up this morning we were faced with 10cm of snow. It wasn't going to stop us though, we had planned another full day of hiking and that's what we were going to do, snow or no snow. We walked more trails in the Pacific Rim National Park and also stopped at Cox Bay Beach and Long Beach. Despite the snowy and cold conditions there were still surfers riding the waves. INSTAGRAM POST 214. The main tourist spot in this area of Vancouver Island is Tofino, a sleepy, surfers and walkers town, so we paid it a visit and indulged in coffee and cake in one the many quaint coffee shops. It was our last day on this side of the Island, we said our goodbyes to Ray and Stuart at the motel before having another drive back up the coast to Long Beach again where we went for walk, the weather had improved a lot since yesterday and most of the snow had melted on this side of the island. INSTAGRAM POST 215. Highway 4 took us north and up through the mountains again when it started to snow. This made us unable to visit Little Qualicum Falls. Nanaimo was now covered in snow and after checking into our motel we headed out in the car again in search of the Abyss Fault. I had stumbled across this when looking for things to do on Vancouver Island, it isn't a huge dramatic canyon, but it a very large crack in the ground, about 16 inches wide. I know I'm not selling it very well, look it up you'll see. I can't reference an Instagram post here as we couldn't find it due to the snow and even worse I ended up getting the car stuck in deep snow. I spent ages underneath the car digging out the snow with just my hands but there was too much. Then as luck would have it, a recovery vehicle drove past on his way no doubt to help someone else in a similar predicament. He stopped and with his shovel we were able to shift a lot more snow. Both of us pushed as Helen managed to reverse out of the deep snow back onto the road. We drove back to the motel very relieved, and the kind man didn't charge me either.

The rumours were true, British Columbians (and two English tourists) really didn't know how to handle the snow. The next day we drove to Sooke, bypassing the capital of Victoria as we would be returning here. The drive was horrendous, probably scarier than the Coquihalla highway. We witnessed two cars spin out on the drive to Sooke. Determined not to let the weather beat us we arrived at our Airbnb and headed out to view the Sooke Potholes, these are large holes carved into the rock from the last Ice age and in the summer I'm sure would be great for swimming in, but not today, as we were walking in sleet. Our evening consisted of keeping warm and dry, playing solitaire on the Ipad and watching the end of the Super Bowl.

Surprise surprise, the next morning we woke up to even more snow but we still decided to make the most of Vancouver Island and drove along the main road to Port Renfrew and circled back to Sooke where we saw some seals and dolphins. The drive back was even worse than yesterday. We met a car without winter tyres struggling to make it up a hill, 30 seconds later we saw it slide backwards and we passed it again but this time on our side of the road facing the wrong way, so were pretty relieved to make it back to the motel. Deciding to have a break from driving we just walked the Whiffin Spit at Sooke before driving to Victoria. When we left Marj she gave us a Tim Hortons gift card so we popped in for a coffee and was amazed that she had put $50 dollars credit on it, a really nice gesture. The weather had cleared up today so we walked along the Galloping Goose

Trail around Victoria. Our last evening in Canada consisted of having a clear out and getting rid of anything the US customs would find a reason not to let us into their country. We probably went overboard with the clear out as we had read some horror stories on the internet but we didn't want to leave anything to chance. Our final morning involved walking the other way on the Galloping Goose Trail where we saw two really cute racoons. I know they are considered pests but they look so cute! As we had come to expect, it started snowing again so we remained in the motel for the rest of the day.

Departure day and what should have been a relaxing morning turned out to be quite stressful. We received an email from Montréal saying they had not received the postal cheque we sent two weeks ago. This is why we should have been able to pay online. We visited two post offices to try and find out what happened to it but they couldn't track it as we didn't pay for a signed package. We were never offered to pay for a signed package in the first place. We were told that the postal cheque was travelling by road and the bad weather had probably caused the delay. An online payment would have taken a minute to complete.

The Ferry port was only a short drive from the motel sitting in James Bay, we were early, and sat there awaiting our fate. Eventually a serious looking official walked up and down the lines of cars, handing out paperwork to fill in. Our car was never checked. Asked to leave our vehicle, we were then told to queue up at a building and wait to be called by an immigration officer. We eventually arrived at the front of the queue. The officer asked us a few questions such as why we were visiting the US, how long we planned on staying, where we visiting and our reason for visiting. All pretty straightforward, we answered confidently and put on our best British accents in the hope that it would help our cause. Whether it did or not we don't know but the officer stamped our passports and we were now allowed in the US for three months. Today was the 9th of February, we could stay until the 9th of May and my brother and his family would arrive in LA on the 2nd of April. That was seven and a half weeks away which gave us plenty of time to explore what America had to offer us. The ferry journey across the Salish Sea would take an hour and a half before arriving in Port Angeles.

We were feeling a range of emotions on the crossing. Yes there was excitement that we were about to embark on a new chapter of our travels in America. There was also relief that we were allowed in with the car. I think we (me especially) had worked ourselves up a bit too much on that but whilst there is a tiny seed of doubt, you are always going to feel unsure. But probably the biggest emotion was sadness in that we were leaving Canada behind.

I took a photo looking back at Victoria as we were leaving the harbour. INSTAGRAM POST 216 and the post read as follows. "We had an unbelievable time in Canada, such an amazing country. Epic in both size and beauty, and the Canadians were so friendly all along our journey, we met some amazing people. Happy 150th Birthday Canada! Thanks for some awesome memories" And what memories they were, no one can take those last seven months away from us. If we hadn't been allowed into the US I think we would have stayed in Canada until our extension ran out, and we would have still looked upon it as an amazing adventure. Most Canadians would never travel all the way across the width of their country so we felt very privileged that we had the opportunity to do so. Out of the 13 provinces, we visited all but 3, the Yukon territory, Nunavut and Northwest Territories. These were all located in the north and the winter had already started to set in by the time we arrived in Alberta. We fell in love with Alberta and British Columbia and spoke already about returning in the future during summer and they are also places we could easily see ourselves living.

However, we were now about to set foot, well actually drive into country number two, The United States of America.

PART 2 – THE UNITED STATES

Following the line of other vehicles off the ramp we were met by another immigration officer. He asked us similar questions to those we faced on the other side of the Salish Sea. The process was quick and he welcomed us to Washington, and we were soon on our way to our motel. After checking in and emptying the car of our belongings into the room, we headed out for a pizza and started to work out where we would now be heading. We only had two choices as north was back to Canada, and west was the Pacific Ocean. That left east or south. Our intention was only ever to go south. Los Angeles was 1,200 miles south (the US isn't metric like Canada) and we had seven weeks to get there. That would be no problem based on the distances we had been driving in Canada. Heading east would have kept us in winter territory and actually, by now we were craving for some warmer, dryer weather. Since we crossed from Saskatchewan on the 4th of October, four months ago, we had pretty much experienced constant winter. And in the Okanagan Valley, it was a proper Canadian winter with temperatures as low as minus 30 degrees. We also faced the unprecedented snow in Vancouver and on Vancouver Island, the likes of which had not been seen for years. When entering the US though, all we had planned was where we were staying on our first night, nothing more. Because of the uncertainty as to whether we would be allowed to take the car across we had not applied for any house sits just in case we couldn't make it. We didn't want to let the homeowners down or potentially have a negative review on our profile. The Oregon coast is famous for it's rugged stunning scenery so our rough plan was to head south along the coast, apply for some house sits and see where it takes us. So we booked our next accommodation, Ilwaco, situated just on the Washington and Oregon border.

One thing we had to get used to quite quickly was using the imperial system instead of the metric system when driving. Our car's speedometer was in kilometres but now all the speed restriction signs were in miles per hour. We fiddled about and eventually changed the settings on our sat nat. Petrol was sold in gallons and not litres and when paying, instead of converting US dollars back to UK sterling, we were working it out in our head back to Canadian dollars. To head south from Port Angeles, the easiest route is to go clockwise around route 101 and the Olympic National

80

Park, with Mount Olympus the centrepiece in the middle of the park at 7,965ft (I don't know what that is in metres). The distance to Ilwaco was only 200 miles but it took us nearly five hours. There were so many different speed restrictions. On our drive we passed speed restriction signs for 25, 30, 35, 40, 45 and 50 mph. It seemed like we spent more time looking at our speedometer than we did looking at the road in front of us, fortunately we had cruise control which helped a lot. On the way we did call in at at one of the Olympic park entrances as we had read buying a National Park Pass was a good idea. In the US, like most of the National Parks in Canada, you are required to pay an entrance fee, whilst in America we planned on visiting a few so it made sense to buy an annual pass for $80.

Florence was the next day's destination, 200 miles further down the Oregon coast. We left Washington state via the impressive four mile long Astoria-Megler Bridge. Again the 200 miles took us around five hours to complete. It didn't help that Helen wasn't feeling well either as her sugar levels were all over the place so we just wanted to get to our motel. A few hours rest on arrival and she was feeling better so we headed out to the local sports bar. Over a couple of beers we decided to stay put in Florence for an extra day. The driving time was taking longer than we expected and by the time we had checked in, emptied our bags and had something to eat, we then needed to find somewhere to stay the next night and make sure we looked up places to see and visit on the way. It all just seemed a bit rushed and we wanted to have a better idea of what we were doing and also spend a decent amount of time researching and applying for house sits. Our motel was situated quite close to the beach so Helen took advantage and went for a run in the morning. I walked instead but we had the whole beach to ourselves and Helen loved the hard, flat wide beach as she hadn't been able to go for a run since we were house sitting for Marj in minus 15 degrees. In the afternoon we drove back north a little way to view parts of the Oregon coast that we couldn't stop at the previous day as Helen hadn't felt well. We stopped at a few towns along the way and walked along the beaches taking photos. Some of the spots we stopped at were used as locations for the 1985 Steven Spielberg film the Goonies as most of it was filmed in Oregon. INSTAGRAM POST 217. It was hard not to be impressed by the beauty of Oregon's coast, mile after mile of jagged cliffs, pine forests, sandy beaches, seaside towns and lighthouses made it a great scenic drive. INSTAGRAM POST 218, INSTAGRAM POST 219, INSTAGRAM POST 220, INSTAGRAM POST 221. The nights also seemed to be drawing out a bit, now it was 6pm by the time the sun went down and this allowed us to go for a walk on Florence beach when we returned. There was a house sit that appealed to us in San Francisco so we applied in the hope we might be accepted. Also it had been a while since I had spoken to my parents who had been away on holiday and had trouble with their Wi-Fi so it was good to catch up. My mum was going into hospital tomorrow and might require an operation depending on the results so I wished her well.

Back on the road again south we pulled in at Coos Bay, it was supposed to one of the nicer stops along the Oregon coast, the distance wasn't too far or time consuming for driving either. Coos Bay is famous for its sand dunes so we headed out for a walk which ended up further than we expected, over 5 miles in total. By now we were three quarters of the way down the Oregon coast, and our next coastal stop was Gold Beach. Over the past few days we had developed a familiar routine. Arrive at our motel at 2pm on the dot, when we can check in, then we empty the car, dump the whole lot in the room, and head out for a walk to stretch our legs and explore the new area. The routine was same in the mornings, breakfast, shower and then re pack, Helen then makes lunch for the day whilst I start loading the car again. There was a sigh of disappointment when we opened the curtains the next morning to see torrential rain. It was to be expected I suppose as overnight the wind was so strong we thought the motel door was going to blow open. Our day in Gold Beach was now going to be a "zero day". A zero day is a term which we took from the books we were reading about long distance trail walking. These included the Pacific Coast Trail and the Appalachian Trail which are considered two of the most famous in America. These trails are thousands of miles long and take the hikers months to complete. After camping out on the trails for days, eventually hikers will reach a town which is used as a stop to resupply and visit the laundrette. These days involve very little walking and are as such called zero days by the hikers. As a result of the weather we would be taking an enforced zero day in Gold Beach. We also visited the laundrette, INSTAGRAM POST 222.

We had now reached California, Crescent City to be precise in the very north of the state. It wasn't the Californian sunshine we were hoping for either as the torrential rain continued. Sitting in the warmth and dry of our motel we applied for two more house sits and then received an unexpected email. Before we started travelling we researched which bank had the best card to use abroad. Norwich and Peterborough was our choice and we were happy with it as it had served us well so far. The email informed us that Norwich and Peterborough was closing down and therefore so would our bank account. There was going to be a period of six months before we couldn't use it so we figured we would worry about it nearer the time, we hadn't a clue where we would be in six months anyway.

Looking at the weather forecast on TV, there was heavier rain further south so we opted for another day in Crescent City. Despite the weather we still visited Jedediah Smith Redwoods State Park to admire the enormous Sequoia or Redwood Trees. INSTAGRAM PHOTO 223. The size of the trees was just unbelievable, it was a really special place even though we ended up absolutely soaked. Our spirits were lifted though when we received a notification telling us we had been accepted for a house sit. It was in Salt Lake City, 850 miles due east from Crescent City but it didn't start for another three weeks, and my brother was arriving in six. Our plan now was to keep heading south through California and then east from L.A up to Las Vegas and north to Salt Lake City. Waking up to no rain, Helen went for a run before it arrived later, we also managed to fit in a nice coastal walk as well. Unbelievably we were accepted for two more house sits. One was in San Francisco in a week's time at the end of February and the other was further south in Ventura in early March. At last we were now starting to land some house sits, they were much needed. The constant rain was starting to get to us. On a house sit it doesn't matter, you are in a house, you can go to another room for a change of scenery. When you are just in a dingy motel room it can drag you down. When we did decide to venture out inevitably we would get drenched and then it was difficult to dry our shoes and clothes before we moved on the next day. The town of

Eureka was our low point, we really didn't like the place, couldn't wait to get out of it, the weather was miserable and there was no Wi-Fi in the hotel to book our onward accommodation. The weather really can have an impact on morale.

In order to be closer to San Francisco we drove 300 miles to Santa Rosa, this would allow us a couple of days of sight-seeing in the city before our house sit. It rained heavily the whole way but it was made better by taking the scenic drive through the Avenue of the Giants to see more amazing Redwood Trees. The rain just continued, we didn't think it could get much worse, and we decided against visiting Point Reyes National Seashore. In our motel room we were glued to the weather channel, all around us there were flood warnings and mud slides but luckily we managed to buy the last ponchos for sale in Walmart. The heavy rain resulted in a scary drive through the crowded San Francisco traffic to Concord just on the outskirts. Our house sit started in three days so we had time to explore the famous city. It would have to wait until tomorrow though as it was chucking it down and even our new ponchos couldn't persuade us to step foot outside. Nearby in San Jose there was a mandatory evacuation of 14,000 people at risk because of flooding, and rainfall records were being broken all over California. Northern California saw its wettest winter in over a century. Damage to roads was estimated at over $1bn. A large section of the Big Sur coastal road, one of the most famous scenic drives in the US which we had planned to drive along was closed due to a collapsed bridge and mudslides. It eventually took a year to clear the road from the landslide and fix the road.

Our first full day in San Francisco started with rain but we took the train to downtown and walked along the harbour front. Whilst on the train, we panicked when a guy all of a sudden started screaming that we were all going to die. It seemed he was living with a mental illness and sadly it was a sight we saw quite a lot of whilst we were in America. Pier 39, there are a lot of piers, is one of the most famous as it's a resting place for sea lions, so we sat watching and listening to them for a while. INSTAGRAM POST 224. The rain appeared again a few times during the day but we managed to walk all the way around to get a closer look at the Golden Gate Bridge and book ourselves on a tour of Alcatraz for the next day.

The tour was fantastic, really interesting and we'd recommend it as a must for anyone visiting San Francisco. The tour cost $35 each but was well worth it, starting with a 20 minute video and then an audio tour which involves walking around listening to commentary through headphones. INSTAGRAM POST 225, INSTAGRAM POST 226, INSTAGRAM POST 227, INSTAGRAM POST 228, INSTAGRAM POST 229 and INSTAGRAM POST 230. San Francisco was the first major city we visited in the US. The weather put a bit of a dampener on it, no pun intended, but we enjoyed our short city stop.

On the day of our house sit we were kicking our heels a bit as we had to check out of the motel at 11am, the house sit was only an hour away and they asked us to be there at 8pm. That was a lot of time to kill so we took the scenic route and drove up and around the Berkley and Oakland Hills and managed a couple of short walks. Did I mention that it wasn't raining today? We even pulled into a park and both of us had a nap. Dinner was at McDonalds and then we knocked on the door at 8pm. The house was owned by two Scottish guys, Adam and Simon. They had four cats, Zoe, Prince, Blanche and Giudecca. INSTAGRAM POST 231. This was only a short house sit, four days whilst Adam and Simon went away for a weekend of birthday celebrations. They left early in the morning and we fed the cats and cleared out litter trays. In the afternoon we took a drive to the top Mt Diablo which gave stunning views all around as far as your eyes could see. That evening we had our first proper cooked dinner, for the last three weeks we had to put up with meals we could nuke in a motel microwave. The next three days passed by quickly, we would go for a run in the morning before it was too hot, the rain was firmly behind us now, and just spend time with the cats. Also we took advantage of the washing machine, it is nice to be able to wash our clothes on a housesit. We Skyped our parents, my mum had an operation a couple of days ago so it was good to catch up and see how she was feeling, obviously groggy but on the mend thankfully. Adam and Simon were not due back till the evening but we had arranged to leave that day. Our motel for the night was at Monterey, via

Santa Cruz as we were going to see a potential future house sit, if we were accepted we would be returning in three weeks after the house sit in Salt Lake City. In effect our route was going to be a big loop, down the west coast, east and up, then west and back down again to L.A. Prior to the storm we had originally intended to drive the Big Sur just south of Monterey but as a result we had to take the less scenic inland highway 101 down to Morrow Bay. After checking in early afternoon we walked to Morrow Rock, an enormous volcanic plug that sits proudly in Morrow Bay, INSTAGRAM POST 234. It seemed we were now far enough south to enjoy the warmer weather and had escaped the storm that had permanently hung over us for the past few days, so we enjoyed a run around Morrow Rock the following morning. Our house sit in Ventura started that evening and we were asked to turn up at 8pm so that gave us plenty of time. Due to our diversion via the 101, we had heard there was a stretch of the coastal road north of us still open and we had read about a place called Piedras Blancas. On a stretch of beach about a mile wide, there is a huge colony of elephant seals, hundreds of them. INSTAGRAM POST 232 and INSTAGRAM POST 233. Joining all the other tourists, we spent a good hour observing these amazing creatures from the boardwalk just above the beach before setting off to the delightfully named Spooners Cove for a really enjoyable sunny cliff top walk. Our leisurely drive also took in the sights of Santa Maria and Santa Barbara before we pulled up in front of what would be home for the next few days. There we were greeted by Andrew and Lisa, a nice couple with a young child, they were going away for just three days. As is usual, we enjoyed a meal, good conversation and found out all we needed to know about the house and looking after their dogs whilst they were away. The dogs were called Inca and Sydney, INSTAGRAM POST 235. They were lovely dogs, Sydney was disabled on her two back feet so she can only walk for five minutes with protective rubber shoes on her paws. Inca didn't walk very well either so fifteen minutes was enough for her. Andrew and Lisa left in the morning, we did some grocery shopping and then we just spent our time with the dogs, except when we ventured out for a run. The remaining two days were the same. In that short space of time Helen really bonded with Inca and she would follow her around everywhere. Andrew and Lisa were returning at 5pm, but we left at 2pm, even though it was a really short house sit, it breaks up the constant travelling and is even better when you have the company of two great dogs like Inca and Sydney. Los Angeles was only an hour south of us but we wouldn't be spending any time here for now, so we skirted above it and took highway 15 to Las Vegas, taking five hours, no thanks to the notorious LA traffic. Today was the 5th of March, we had to be in Salt Lake City, 420 miles north on the 9th.

Las Vegas is very polarising, you either love it or loathe it, and we fell into the latter category. This was due to the fact that we were on a budget, so we stayed in a cheap Airbnb about 30 minutes walk from the Strip. When most people come to Vegas, they immerse themselves in it, money isn't an issue, but having a good time is. It would have felt wrong to completely ignore Vegas so we spent one full day there. The walk to the strip showed us a different side to what the tourists see staying in the big hotels. We were amazed at the amount of homeless people living under the bridges, a really sad sight. During our one day we walked the whole length of the strip on both sides, yes it is an impressive place but it just wasn't our thing, in the way we were travelling. INSTAGRAM POST 236. Instead we were really looking forward to the next couple of days visiting Zion and Bryce National Parks.

We left the hustle and bustle of Vegas well behind us as we departed early knowing we would already lose an hour crossing time zones into Utah. Hurricane is a small town close to Zion and it is used as a base for visitors. At 2pm we checked in, dumped our bags and headed straight to Zion National Park. Zion is another one of those places where it stops you in your tracks and you just have to admire it and take it all in. Niagara Falls did it, the Rockies did it, as did the giant sequoia trees on the east coast. Entering the park via the canyon, you are enclosed by the walls, up to 800 metres high. The canyon itself runs for 15 miles through the park. INSTAGRAM POST 237. Eager to enjoy as much of the park as we could we headed out on a couple of trails including one to Upper Emerald Falls, a very thin waterfall with snow and ice still visible at the bottom. INSTAGRAM POST 238. After hiking, we had enough time to drive as far as we could down into the canyon, making a mental note of where we pick up the trail start points for our return tomorrow. During April to October, the peak visitor period, vehicles are prohibited in the park, instead you use the free shuttle buses that allow you to hop on and off as you please. Tomorrow we would be returning to hike the famous Angels Landing Trail, a strenuous 5.4 mile hike, with 548 metres of elevation gain.

We were both starting to enjoy the US more now, we had a couple of house sits lined up and a plan to take us up until my brother's arrival. It's amazing how the difference in the weather can change your mood without waking up day after day to torrential rain.

Back at the motel we were really excited by the arrival of an email into our inbox. Thinking ahead to where our journey could go after the US, the obvious direction was south and that would be Mexico. Helen and I had a holiday once in Mexico a few years ago, we enjoyed an all-inclusive without ever leaving the confines of the hotel. To be honest we could have been anywhere in the world where the weather was warm. As much as Mexico was an option, it seemed like the easy option. This was a once in a lifetime trip so we were keen to look at alternatives. One of which was the Caribbean. In the US, we are not supposed to participate in workaways as it is seen as taking work away from citizens so it had been a while since we even looked at the website. But when I did, I spotted one which seemed interesting. It was in the Caribbean, on the twin island nation of St Kitts and Nevis. It sits in the north of the Caribbean between the islands of Montserrat and Anguilla. This workaway was asking for volunteers to help at their dog shelter on the smaller of the two islands, Nevis. I mentioned it to Helen as an option rather than going through Mexico and she was keen, so we applied. The email we received was an acceptance and the dates were Mid-April to Mid-May, about five weeks in total. My brother and his family were due to fly home early April so that gave us a week in the United States before we had to get rid of the car and be on a flight to the Caribbean. We were over the moon. It was early March and we now pretty much had a plan that took us up until Mid-May.

On top of the news of going to the Caribbean, we woke up excited about the prospect of a full day in Zion, and the notorious Angels Landing Trail. Some have called it one the scariest hikes in the US, but that doesn't start until you are near the top. The route is continually uphill, 548 metres of constant plodding in the heat with plenty of breaks for a drink and to admire the scenery below as you get higher and higher walking up the 21 switchbacks. INSTAGRAM POST 239. We eventually reached a point where everybody else seems to take a welcome rest, this is called Scouts Lookout. This is where you either say I'm done or you carry on the scary part up and along Angels Landing Spine. We took in the views and had something to eat. INSTAGRAM POST 240 and INSTAGRAM PHOTO 243. Even though we were in early spring, it coincided with Spring Break and the trail was too busy. Zion was the first busy park we had visited in the US and the selfie generation during Spring Break were out in their numbers. Helen wasn't bothered about heading up the spine, I decided to have a quick look but it didn't last long. I ventured across about 100 metres along a slope with a sheer drop and just a chain to hold to. Look it up on Google. People were coming from the other way and it just seemed way too crowded with some trying to pass instead of waiting for a clear opportunity. Surprisingly there have only been five recorded deaths on this trail. After safely making it back to Helen we headed up the opposite way to the spine to get a better look across, INSTAGRAM POST 244. It was a really hot day and even though we didn't make it all the way across Angels landing it was a great to experience one the most iconic trails in the US. The walk up was punishing on the calves but the walk down always takes it out on the quads. Nevertheless we were going to take full advantage of Zion so we pressed on and completed the Riverside Walk, INSTAGRAM POST 241, and the Canyon Overlook Trail, INSTAGRAM PHOT0 242.

Even with only a day and a half, Zion was a magical place, and a hikers dream as the scenery was just unbelievable. To be honest we would have preferred an extra day in Zion than the one in Vegas. We left in the afternoon as we needed to drive onto our next park.

Bryce canyon is about a two hour drive northeast of Zion and we stayed at a lodge just on the outskirts. Despite it being sunny, it still felt cold as we were at 9,000ft. Picking up a map at the park entrance, we quickly decided the easiest thing to do was to drive all the way to the end along the Rim Road Scenic drive, turn around then stop off at all the scenic look outs on the way back. We only had one day at Bryce and we still had a four hour drive ahead of us to reach Salt Lake City for our house sit. The views out across Bryce canyon are other worldly, thousands and thousands of hoodoos, shaped and formed by the elements over the years. Hoodoos can be found all over the world, we saw some in Drumheller and Banff when we were in Canada. Here at Bryce Canyon though you can see the largest concentration of anywhere in the world and what a sight it provides. INSTAGRAM POST 245, INSTAGRAM POST 246, INSTAGRAM POST 247, INSTAGRAM POST 248, INSTAGRAM POST 249. We seemed to be stopping every couple of minutes, such were the views. It is possible to walk around inside the canyon itself, (although it is not actually a canyon) unfortunately with all of the snow melt it was pretty muddy and quite difficult to actually get back up on the slippery slopes but well worth it to get a different perspective of the hoodoos. After a few hours of sightseeing we needed to get moving in order to reach Salt Lake City, most of it along highway 15.

It was a welcome sight when we pulled up at the house, it was a lovely place. Laurie our host welcomed us in and we were met by her two little gorgeous dogs, Maddie and Oreo. INSTAGRAM POST 250. Laurie showed us around the house and to our room which was located in the basement with its own bathroom, kitchen and living area. We couldn't be happier. It looked like there were plenty of things to do and places to walk in Salt Lake City, but also the house was fantastic as were the dogs. We had hit the bullseye of our wish list criteria. Laurie wasn't leaving until the day after next so there was no rush in getting to know the routine of the dogs and how everything in the house worked, so after a chat with Laurie we had an early night as we were shattered.

The following day was very relaxed as we took Maddie and Oreo out on our first walk around the estate, and after grocery shopping we just hung out with the dogs all afternoon. That evening, Laurie very kindly took us out to a restaurant and bought us dinner. We were joined by a friend of Laurie's and we all had a really enjoyable evening. It wasn't a late night though as Laurie was leaving at 5am for her holiday. Making sure we were up to see Laurie leave, we had a long relaxed morning of breakfast, walking the dogs and skyping both of our parents. I mapped out a 5 km run on the laptop, a great thing about the US is the straight roads so it seemed quite easy to find a route. Or so it would seem, Helen tried it but somehow ended up lost so I had to head out in the car to look for her. Salt Lake City seemed to have a lot of parks when looking on the map so we tried one out for the dogs in the afternoon. Because the dogs are small, they have little booster seats to sit on so they can look out of the windows, they looked so cute. It was nice to be back in a house sit for a while, enjoying just cosying up with a couple of little dogs for the evening in front of the TV. After just one day they were absolutely fine around us and especially Helen. Maddie was particularly fond of her. The days followed the routine of a little walk for the dogs in the morning followed by a run and a longer dog walk in the evening, then on the sofa watching TV at night. INSTAGRAM POST 251. One day we took the dogs to the grooming parlour so with a morning to ourselves it was time for some retail therapy as we needed some new clothes.

The weather was great and it didn't start to get dark now until about 8pm so we tended to take Maddie and Oreo out a bit later when it had cooled down a bit. One evening, it was a surprise for us to see a guy walking his baby in a pram with a gun holstered and clearly visible. It just looked so bizarre to us coming from a country where there are virtually no guns.

One afternoon we booked our flights to St Kitts. This is where Google flights came in handy by using the map option and working backwards. Typing in the start destination as St Kitts, you are then able to scroll around the map of the US and find where the cheapest destination is. Then assuming it works in reverse we soon found that the cheapest place to fly out from was Denver. This was a bit further away from LA than we hoped but any flights from there, San Francisco, San Diego or Vegas were so much more expensive. It didn't matter to us though, as we now had a route to Denver, Colorado that would take in the Grand Canyon, a place we missed on our journey up to Salt Lake City. Our loop of the United States was now turning into a loop the loop. One day we decided to take the car with the dogs over the mountain range to our east and visit Park City. Park City sits at 7,000ft. and is a large ski resort. Utah Olympic Park is just to the north and hosted the 2002 Winter Olympics. It was a really nice day out, the dogs seemed to really enjoy it and we didn't get back to the house until early evening. Our house sit in Salt Lake City flew by and soon Laurie was back walking through the front door to be greeted by her doting dogs. As Laurie returned home at 9pm, we were spending one last night at the house so the evening was spent enjoying listening to each other's stories. After loading up the car and saying our goodbyes it was time now to head west across to the coast as our house sit in Santa Cruz started tomorrow. That was 800 miles away so our plan was to do half today and half tomorrow. It was sad to say goodbye to Laurie and her dogs. Maddie and Oreo had been great company for a few days and we visited a city and an area of the US we would have never intentionally visited.

The long cross country drive was very flat as we drove out of Utah through the Nevada Great Basin, INSTAGRAM POST 252. In the motel that night we applied to a house sit in the Caribbean, it was in St Vincent and the Grenadines. Shortly afterwards we had a reply asking if we would be free in the morning for a Skype chat. That night we couldn't sleep as we were too excited.

The Skype chat went really well, except at the end, they said they had spoken to another couple and would make their decision tomorrow. We decided to follow up the chat with an email saying it was lovely talking to them and how much we would love the opportunity. They replied straight away and said they had already made up their minds and the house sit was ours!

We were ecstatic; this house sit was for two months. The location was actually a tiny island called Bequia, part of St Vincent and the Grenadines, further south than St Kitts and Nevis. I say tiny, it is the second largest island but still only 7 square miles, with a population of approximately 4,300 people. It commenced straight after our time at the dog shelter on Nevis, so now instead of five weeks in the Caribbean we were going to be there for three months up until the end of July. The six hour drive across to Santa Cruz was no issue, we were buzzing all the way there. We faced unexpected weather conditions going over the Stanislaus Forest Range, it was a complete white out with the side of the road stacked up with over two metres of snow. Another scary journey when we thought we had seen the last of any snow. INSTAGRAM POST 253

For our house sit in Santa Cruz, we were spending five days looking after a cat called Missy. INSTAGRAM POST 254. We quickly realised this was going to be a lot trickier than when it was first sold to us a few weeks ago. We knew Missy had a stomach condition, acid reflux. Our own dog had also suffered from it. What we had to do with our dog in the morning was to try and get some food into her as soon as possible to settle her stomach, otherwise there is a build-up of stomach acid and they will probably be sick, at which point it is even harder to get them to eat. Getting Missy to eat was not a problem for us but her owner wanted us to feed her seven times a day starting at 7am and finishing at midnight. We watched her follow Missy around the house with a spoon full of food but she just wasn't interested. We also had a list of herbal and alternative medicines to add to the food as well. Our bed was a single bed and the room had no curtains. The cooker was out of use as it was used as storage for all of the herbs and medicines, as was the dishwasher. The washing machine was locked behind a door so we couldn't even wash our clothes. It soon became apparent that there wasn't much in it for us, fortunately it was only going to be a short stay. As her owner had asked, we tried feeding Missy as often as possible but sometimes she just wasn't that interested but luckily she wasn't being sick. In the end we started to leave a variety of different foods out for her and as we expected she came to eat when she wanted, and never had a single problem with stomach acid the whole time we were there. Some days we would manage to get out of the house and walk to the beach at Santa Cruz and watch the surfers INSTAGRAM POST 255, INSTAGRAM POST 256, INSTAGRAM POST 257 and INSTAGRAM POST 258. Thankfully the end of house sit soon arrived, it was a long five days but Missy had been absolutely fine under our care. We explained to her owner our method of leaving food out for her and she said would try it. A couple of days later though she emailed us to say she had gone back to following Missy around the house with food. It was a strange house sit for us, but an example of the lengths people go through to do what they think is right for their pets. When our dog Macy was coming to the end of her life, we took it in turns to sleep downstairs with her and look after her through the night. We ended up doing this for six months. It just becomes normal practise when you care for your pet and will do anything for them so we had a lot of sympathy for Missy's owner.

Instead of following the coastal road south as we had a few weeks earlier, we drove inland as we were going to be spending a few days with family friends of Helen's. Peter and Claudia lived in a place called Mariposa, just a couple of hours drive to the west of Yosemite National Park. Peter was Helen's neighbour years ago, but he moved to America after initially travelling, and Helen's mum still looks in on his elderly mother who still lives alone at the ripe old age of 104. The plan was always to spend some time with Peter and Claudia and it was so convenient for Yosemite which we were excited about visiting. Their house was lovely and they had a great dog called Winston. We arrived at about 6.30pm and spent the evening chatting after a fabulous cooked dinner.

Up early the next day, we had a lovely breakfast and then prepared our packed lunches for a full day at Yosemite. Claudia boosted our supplies with a generous helping of the American hiker's staple, trail mix. The queues were already forming as we approached the park on Highway 41, a stunning scenic drive in itself. As you emerge from the tunnel to the park, nothing can prepare you for the view that is laid out in front of you. It was another one to go on the list of jaw dropping sights. Tunnel View as it is called allows the perfect panoramic picture of the Valley. On the left is El Capitan, the monumental granite rock that has attracted the world's best climbers for years. Half Dome is in the distance, and Bridal Veil Falls is on the right. INSTAGRAM POST 259. Today was a day for having a good look around, Yosemite is huge compared to Zion, six times larger but the resemblance was there. It covers an area of 3,000 square km, although most of the four million annual visitors, like us, restrict their exploration to the 18 square km valley.

After driving down into the Valley we came to Bridal Veil Falls, this was only a short walk towards the bottom of the Falls, we didn't get too close as we met a lot of people walking back who were absolutely drenched. INSTAGRAM POST 260. Next up we headed over to the other side of the Valley to admire the sheer size of El Capitan. INSTAGRAM POST 261. A few days previously we had watched a documentary on Netflix called Valley Uprising, a really insightful programme about the history of rock climbing in Yosemite Park, and especially El Capitan. The programme features a climber called Alex Honnold. Just two months after we visited Yosemite, Alex made history by becoming the first person ever to make a free solo ascent of the 914 metre El Capitan in a time of just under four hours. This amazing climb was made into a film called Free Solo and won multiple awards, including an Oscar and I can highly recommend it. We then spent some time driving through the valley admiring the scenery stopping multiple times to take photos. The final walk of the day was the Mirror Lake walk which gave great views of Half Dome. Our first day in the park had totally lived up to our expectations. With over 800 miles of varied hiking trails it is possible to spend months here in the park. Unfortunately we couldn't, we only had two more full days in which to appreciate it. On the drive back to Peter and Claudia's we decided tomorrow we would hike the Vernal and Nevada Falls trail. We were delighted to return to another fantastic meal listening to Peter tell us about his hike up Half Dome. Half Dome is at 8,842 ft. and a strenuous 14 mile round trip where advance permits are required. We would love to come back one day and try it. After dinner we had a good play in the yard with Winston before collapsing in bed exhausted. Day two and we couldn't wait to get back to the Valley. Luckily it was another clear day and great weather for hiking. Vernal Falls was an amazing hike as you just skirt the side of it before reaching the flat outcrop at the top for a welcome rest with other hikers. INSTAGRAM POST 262. After a bite to eat we pushed on upwards to the next target, Nevada Falls. INSTAGRAM POST 263. Reaching the summit provided amazing views back along the Valley. INSTAGRAM POST 264. The walk back down also allows you to look over Vernal Falls, spotting the tiny specks of hikers taking a breather as we did a couple of hours earlier. INSTAGRAM POST 265. The whole walk should have only been an easy 9 km and the trail takes you back down a different way to which you ascended. However there was a sign saying that this route was closed due to snow. We therefore took another route down before joining up with John Muir trail, this ended up taking a lot longer and resulted in a lot more climbing. John Muir was a Scottish American who helped establish many of America's National Parks. He famously invited

President Theodore Roosevelt on a camping trip to Yosemite in 1903. The trip persuaded Roosevelt to return Yosemite Valley to Federal Protection as part of the Yosemite National Park.

Tired, but filled with the joys of another epic hike under our belts, it was nearly 8pm before we pulled into the drive at Peter and Claudia's for a welcome beer and a hearty meal, as always accompanied by a good chat.

Our final day in Yosemite involved another waterfall, or two, Lower and Upper Yosemite Falls. This was going to be the toughest hike in Yosemite but we were looking forward to it. INSTAGRAM POST 266. Yosemite Falls is the highest waterfall in North America at 740 metres. We were blessed with another clear day. Stopping for a water break allowed us to appreciate the beauty of the Valley below, it can be so easy to fall into the trap of just walking with your head down or forward and not realise what is behind you, INSTAGRAM POST 267. It also enables you to see how far you still have to go though when you are heading for the top of the Upper Falls! INSTAGRAM POST 268. It took us three hours to reach the top of Upper Yosemite Falls, INSTAGRAM POST 269, tired, we simply found a quiet spot and just gazed around the valley, taking it all in. These were the days we had hoped for when we decided to go travelling nearly nine months ago and sitting at the top we realised what an adventure we still had ahead of us for the next five months. Next we were going to Death Valley and then onto to LA to spend a week with my brother and his family. From there we would drive to the Grand Canyon and on to Denver where we would catch a flight to the Caribbean for four months. Was this really happening to us? Life was pretty damn good at the moment and I honestly remember sitting there thinking this is a special moment. We are sitting at the top of an awesome walk in Yosemite with no worries and lots to look forward to. After a good hour we started our descent, back through the snow we had encountered near the top, INSTAGRAM POST 270. It took us two and a half hours to reach the valley floor below. My Fitbit recorded 350 flights of stairs climbed that day. it was the end of an amazing three days in Yosemite, we could have spent another week in the park, no problem. This was certainly another place that would be on our return to list.

On our final day with Peter, Claudia and Winston, we all went for a walk in Redwood Sequoia Forest and then enjoyed fish and chips for lunch at Bass Lake. Peter and Claudia had been fantastic to stay with and had treated us like family. We had spent most of our time in Yosemite, however the time we did have with them was special and they made us feel so welcome. We said our goodbyes early afternoon as we needed to drive down to Bakersfield, which would be a good base to head in to Death Valley the following morning.

That morning we were on the road at 7am as it would take another three hours to reach Death Valley. This was somewhere that we really didn't want anything to go wrong with the car. We pulled into the last service station we could find to fill up with overpriced petrol and check our water levels. INSTAGRAM POST 271. Death Valley National Park is larger than Yosemite, in fact it is the largest National Park outside Alaska at more than 13,000 square km. It holds the US records for hottest temperature (134 F / 57 C) and the lowest point (Badwater, 282ft below sea level). Our planned route was to drive to a central village in the park, Stovepipe Wells, stay the night and then continue the next day out the other side. On the way we stopped at Father Crowley Point, a high lookout point which gave great views of some of the park. Arriving at Stovepipe Wells, there was a hotel, a visitor centre, a campsite and a petrol station to stock up on groceries whilst also selling even more ridiculously priced petrol. By looking online we knew that the hotel was expensive and it was full. Tonight we would be sleeping in the car on the campsite. Having sorted that out with the campsite official we headed into the park so see some of the attractions. First up was Dante's View. This offers one of the best perspectives of the park, as you see all of the Valley Floor below and across to the mountains into the distance. INSTAGRAM POST 272. This viewpoint is famous as you can simultaneously see the highest (Mt Whitney, 14,505 ft.) and lowest (Badwater) points in the contiguous USA. Finally we visited Zabriskie Point. The scenery here was different with loads of golden brown undulating ridges. Our first day in Death Valley was really enjoyable, it's not like Yosemite or Zion where you park up, pull on your backpack and go hiking for six hours. It is more about driving to different places where there is a scenic viewpoint but it was a nice change and just another example of the amazing dramatic scenery there is to admire in the US. Knowing we were to spend the night sleeping in the car, we needed to find somewhere we could keep Helen's insulin chilled overnight and also freeze the ice packs. This proved to be no problem as the friendly receptionist at the hotel happened to be a diabetic herself. After buying some sandwiches from the service station we ate them on a picnic bench, used the communal facilities and picked a spot in the campsite to park our car for the night. It was hot in Death Valley, our car earlier in the day said the temperature was 37 degrees but the problem though was the wind, so windy in fact that you couldn't have the windows open as the car would fill up with dust. Helen slept across the back seat and I reclined the passenger seat. It was completely dark by 8pm so it looked like we were having an early night. The night sky though was just incredible, the stars were so bright and seemed huge. However it was an uncomfortable night, with coyotes howling, neither of us slept well and we were up at 6am so just decided to get on and explore the park. After picking up the insulin and ice packs from the hotel, our first attraction was the Mesquite Sand Dunes. Early morning is the best time to visit the Dunes as the sun is still low and it creates long curving shadows along the dunes, with a stunning backdrop of distant mountains, INSTAGRAM POST 273. Before visiting the main attraction of Badwater basin we also took in the Golden canyon walk and the Artist's scenic drive. Badwater itself was dry when we visited, so today we could walk out onto the crinkly basin, and you could just feel the heat rebounding up from the salt flats. INSTAGRAM POST 274 and INSTAGRAM POST 275. We spent some time taking in the scenery, it was like nothing else we had seen before. Soon it was time to head out the other side of the park, where we were fortunate enough to see the spring flowers, these on their own are a huge attraction for the park. It seemed strange that we were currently in the quiet isolation of Death Valley and yet tomorrow we would be in the hustle and bustle of city life in L.A. Tonight though we aimed for Barstow, about halfway to LA. Our motel for the night was on the famous Route 66.

Today was the day my brother Simon, his wife Amie and their two girls, Lucy and Emma arrived in LA for a week, obviously we were really excited as we hadn't seen them for nearly nine months. After crawling

98

through the LA traffic we arrived at our accommodation at around 4pm. It was great, a huge complex where we had all rented a two floor apartment on Airbnb, which was so much better than any Airbnb we had previously stayed in. The complex also had a swimming pool and there was a large gym. They were due to arrive around 9pm so we went to the supermarket and bought some pizzas, chips and garlic bread so they could eat when they arrived, and some beer. We saw them arrive at the complex in a taxi, and were waving and shouting from balcony but they couldn't see or hear us. Running down to the entrance, it was such a great feeling to see them in person and we all hugged. After helping carry the suitcases to the room we all had a look around the complex together before settling in for the night with some food and a really good catch up. They also bought some parcels from home that we had ordered to replenish our backpacks.

Our room was on the ground floor just next to the living room and it was a great sight to walk out the next morning to see the familiar faces of Emma and Lucy sat on the sofas. After discussing what the plan for the day was, it was decided we would visit the famous Hollywood Boulevard with the Chinese Theatre. It was also possible to see the famous Hollywood sign in the distance. INSTAGRAM POST 276. We took our time taking in the sights and reading all of the famous names on the Hollywood Walk of Fame, INSTAGRAM POST 277. At a junction ahead we could see a crowd gathering so we decided to take a closer look. It turned out they were filming a scene for the TV series NCIS Los Angeles and we didn't have to wait too long to see a car pull up, and LL Cool J step out to shoot his scene. Just a typical day in Hollywood! That evening, my brother and I attended a concert. He is constantly entering competitions and always seems to win. Knowing what dates he would be in L.A. he entered a competition to win two tickets to see Richard Ashcroft at the Wiltern Theatre. He won. We travelled there using the subway and enjoyed an amazing gig especially as I hadn't been to one in such a long time. INSTAGRAM POST 278, INSTAGRAM POST 279 and INSTAGRAM POST 280. Waking up the next day with my ears still ringing, today we were all visiting Universal Studios and it was brilliant, Helen and I were a little sceptical at first but after going on the first ride, the Harry Potter one, we couldn't wait to join the queues for all of the others. It was such a fun day spending it with Simon, Amie and the girls. Rides and attractions included the Simpsons, The Walking Dead, Minions, Animal Actors, Special Effects Show, Shrek, Transformers, Jurassic Park and also a tour of the studios. The adults enjoyed it as much if not more than the girls. That evening we didn't make it back to the apartment until nearly 9pm, a full but really enjoyable day.

With typical LA weather, the next day was a beach day, we all jumped on the Metro to Santa Monica Beach with its famous pier. INSTAGRAM POST 281. Lunch was sat on the sand then we walked all the way east to Venice Beach where we watched the bodybuilders at Muscle beach, some basketball and the skateboarders. INSTAGRAM POST 282. Instead of walking back on the beach we returned to Santa Monica Pier along the famous boardwalk, stopping to watch the impressive gymnasts. It was another long day but that was fine, we were spending it in the company of Simon, Amie and the girls and we were having a great time.

Another day, another activity, this time it was of the sporting variety. Baseball at Dodgers Stadium, home of the LA Dodgers. INSTAGRAM POST 283. I don't think any of us really fully understood the rules but we had a better grasp of it after nearly three hours. It was great entertainment cheering along with the crowds sitting out in the sun, high up in the stadium. As the way back to the apartment was all downhill, we decided to walk it and on the way back I promised the girls I would join them in the swimming pool. So the late afternoon was spent splashing around with the girls.

The following day, as we enjoyed it so much and the passes were still valid, we all returned to Universal Studios. INSTAGRAM POST 284 Even though we spent a full day there only two days ago we didn't get a chance to do everything so we ticked those off our list first, then returned for more goes on our favourite rides. Simon and I left at 4pm though as we were going to see a football match, I still can't bring myself to call it soccer. Helen, Amie and the girls stayed at the park for another few hours. Simon and I took the metro through South Central LA, passing through Compton, where I admit I was slightly nervous, but in the end had no reason to be. LA Galaxy won 2-0, we arrived well before kick-off to soak up the pre-game atmosphere. INSTAGRAM POST 285. For the penultimate day, we didn't actually spend it with them. They all went to visit various museums around the city and took in some retail therapy whilst Helen and I did some admin. We needed to print off our flight tickets so found a local library to do that. We also reorganised all our gear and sorted out what Simon could take home for us. The practise packing of our backpacks went well, for eight months all of our possessions had expanded and spilled out to fill the car but soon we would need to downsize and everything we wanted to keep had to fit within our backpacks.

Our final day together was obviously very sad, we all made the trip to the Griffith Park observatory and had a picnic at the top where there were better views of the Hollywood sign, INSTAGRAM POST 286. It was difficult to fully enjoy those final few hours together not knowing when we would see them again. Also we knew that we had at least a six hour drive ahead of us to be within easy reach of the Grand Canyon. The final goodbye came at 2pm, it was really sad for us waving goodbye as we pulled out of the apartment complex. The last few days had been absolutely everything we wanted. Even though we were on our own holiday, the last few days had felt like a holiday within a holiday which is a rare and special feeling. We loved spending time with the girls just talking about anything, they are great girls and brilliant company. Simon and Amie have done a fantastic job in raising them the way they have. We arrived at our motel just after 11pm.

There are two rims of the Grand Canyon, the quieter North Rim and the South Rim which we were visiting. To get from one side to the other by car, it would be a 200 mile journey. Grand Canyon Village is the main hub on the south rim. It was here where we parked our car and queued up for a shuttle bus. We chose to take the shuttle along the West of the canyon as we would be taking the easterly 64 route ourselves tomorrow as we head in the direction of Denver. Like most National Park shuttles, it is a jump on and jump off affair and we decided to jump off about 7 miles from Grand Canyon Village and walk all the way back along the rim. Most people have seen photos of the Grand Canyon so you have an idea of what to expect. The sheer size is the first thing that hits you visually then you try and focus on the details, but you are still trying to absorb the enormity of it all. It is just vast. You notice the tiny trails snaking down towards the Colorado River, the layers and layers of rock and the delicately balanced rocks which look as though they could fall at any second. For someone who is trying to do something slightly different with a book and take you on a journey with my Instagram Posts, I am under selling it if I say the photos don't give the Canyon the justice it deserves. Judge for yourselves. INSTAGRAM POST 287, INSTAGRAM POST 288, INSTAGRAM POST 289, INSTAGRAM POST 290, INSTAGRAM POST 291 and INSTAGRAM POST 292. We took a lot of photos that day walking along the South Rim trail and when we went through them that evening we both said the same thing, it just doesn't get across the scale. Choosing not to enter the Canyon due to limited time, I'm sure you would get a different perspective by being inside rather than viewing down. One of the most popular hikes is the Bright Angel Trail, an 8 mile descent down to the Colorado River, but it is advised to start this trail at dawn in order to make it back up to the rim in good time.

The following day we drove east on the Desert View drive, stopping regularly to take even more photos along the 26 mile route. On highway 163 we soon saw the signs for another area we had been looking forward to. Monument Valley. This was a landscape filled with red formations of rocks eroded by the elements. A lot of the formations have starred as the backdrop for many western films and the route is one of the most famous scenic drives in the US. INSTAGRAM POST 293, INSTAGRAM POST 294 and INSTAGRAM POST 295. It is possible to leave the highway for closer views but this 17 mile loop is unpaved and we didn't think the car would be up for it. It also looked like a place where you definitely didn't want your car to breakdown. Some days the driving can be a bit boring, most of the time though we have been able to admire the scenery everywhere we have been and today was certainly one of those days. It was quite a surreal drive, driving along the south rim of the Grand Canyon and then onto Monument Valley, we've definitely done worse.

Things were about to get even better. We had three days until our early morning flight to the Caribbean from Denver and we were a day's drive away. Looking through the guidebook on the Kindle, Helen came across a National park we very nearly missed but actually turned out to be up there as one of our favourites, Arches National Park. Staying just south in Bluff the previous night, it was only a 45 minute drive to the park in the morning, so we arrived early to beat the queues of traffic waiting to get in. The park is obviously as the name suggests, famous for Arches, lots of them, in fact the world's largest concentration of sandstone arches. Over 2,000 in total, ranging from 3ft to 300ft. As the park wasn't too large we could pretty much see all of the most popular arches in one day. Delicate Arch is probably the most famous; this is a 3.5 mile roundtrip on its own. INSTAGRAM POST 296. Other Arches we hiked to included the really impressive 300ft Landscape Arch, INSTAGRAM POST 297. Partition Arch, INSTAGRAM POST 298 and Double Arch INSTAGRAM POST 299. It was one our favourite days, the hikes were really good, not too taxing as it was a very hot day but it was just amazing to see all of these arches everywhere. We were really pleased we found it otherwise we would have driven straight past this little gem of a National Park. It was early evening before we pulled out of the gates to drive north to our accommodation in Grand Junction.

The route to Denver meant driving over the Colorado Rockies. At the bottom the temperature was so warm I remember I was driving without wearing a top as our air conditioning didn't work. As we climbed the digital temperature display kept dropping and dropping. We reached altitudes of 11,000 ft. and it felt really strange seeing people skiing down mountain slopes as I drove by shirtless when the temperature outside was just above zero. Soon we arrived warm, and dressed, at our motel, choosing one that ran an airport shuttle service. Our first job on arrival in Denver was to visit a friend of Marj's. She had forwarded on some paperwork for us to a friend who lived in Denver so we went round to collect it. The rest of the evening I spent looking for a way to sell our precious car. I had one day to sell it and I found a place that offered me $300 US. Including repairs, the total cost of the car was just under $2,000 CAD but it was priceless though for the memories we had made as a result of having our own transport. It had covered over 27,000 km in total. From Montréal to Vancouver Island and the big loop the loop in the States. It had endured -30 to nearly +40 degree temperatures. Most importantly it had taken us to places we would have never reached or seen without it. It was our constant travel companion for the last nine months and really performed when we needed it to. This now felt like a bigger chapter was finishing for us, as Helen and I were now continuing without our car onto a new part of our travels.

When we first started in the US, the weather really didn't make a good first impression and the culture shock of going from the more reserved Canada to the more in your face US took us a while to get used to. But it really grew on us. Yes all the cultural stereotypes are still there, some Americans were loud and enthusiastic compared to us more reserved Brits. It is busy, crowded and intimidating at times, but on the whole they were a very friendly nation. But what they do have is some of the most stunning National Parks we have ever visited. 58% of Americans do not own a passport, but actually when you realise the size of the country and what there is to do, you can't actually blame them for not needing to go abroad because it is all here for them. When foreigners visit the US, they usually stick to one destination, so to visit six states and see so much, we count ourselves incredibly lucky. The Lonely Planet had a list of 25 top experiences and destinations for the whole of the US. In our time here which was just three months, we managed to tick off seven of them.

That evening we packed everything into just our two backpacks and then went for a walk before having an early night as our shuttle left at 5am. Our flight left at 8am with a stopover in Dallas, then onto Miami. INSTAGRAM POST 300. The flight from Miami to St Kitts was nearly empty, there were only about 25 people on the flight. We landed in St Kitts at 8.30pm. A long days travelling, but another new and exciting part of our adventures lay ahead.

PART 3 - THE CARIBBEAN

A - ST KITTS AND NEVIS

Stepping out of the plane at the Robert Bradshaw Airport on Saint Kitts we immediately felt the humidity. It was hot considering it was 8.30pm and that was fine but we were not used to the humidity. As you would expect, the airport is quite small so it didn't take long to pass through immigration and baggage claim. The dog sanctuary was located on the smaller neighbouring island of Nevis, so for tonight we had booked into an Airbnb and our plan was to catch a ferry tomorrow. After a long day, we positioned the fans and collapsed into bed exhausted.

Saint Kitts and Nevis is part of the British Commonwealth and located in the Leeward Islands chain of the Lesser Antilles. It is the smallest sovereign state in the Western Hemisphere, both in area and population. The capital is Basseterre, this is on Saint Kitts and where we flew into. Nevis is the smaller island and lies about 2 miles southeast across a shallow channel called the Narrows. The population of Saint Kitts and Nevis is around 53,000, approximately three quarters of the population live on Saint Kitts, meaning Nevis has a population of just over 11,000. In terms of size, Saint Kitts is 168 square km shaped like an oval with a long neck and small peninsula at its south-eastern end. Nevis is cone shaped and only 10 km wide covering only 93 square km. Nevis Peak is in the centre of a chain of mountains and it is the highest point at 965 metres. Charlestown is the capital of Nevis.

Helen and I have been to the Caribbean before, my brother and Amie married in Jamaica. We have also been to the Dominican Republic and Cuba. On each occasion we mostly stayed inside the hotel complex and never experienced the true Caribbean. Except once, when we were in Jamaica, my brother and I got on well with the pool guards and they invited us to go with them to watch a local football match. It was amazing, we were the only tourists, everyone reversed their cars up to the pitch with music blaring out and drinking. We had such a good time and it felt like we were experiencing the true Caribbean, and that is what Helen and I would now hopefully be experiencing together.

We were woken up the next morning by someone banging on our door. I quickly got dressed and answered the door. It was the Airbnb host telling us today was Easter Sunday and there was only one ferry today but it was leaving in 30 minutes, so a taxi was on its way. Still half asleep and trying to process everything, I told Helen and we rushed around trying to get ready. We hardly know what day it is when we are travelling let alone the date, so we had no idea it was Easter Weekend. Catching the ferry just in time we also managed to phone our hosts and let them know we would be earlier. The journey took about 45 mins and as Nevis drew closer the clouds were covering the top of Mt Nevis but the cone shape of the island was clearly visible, INSTAGRAM POST 301. The ferry pulled into Charlestown and we were met and welcomed to the island by our host Paul, he drove us about 15 mins to the dog shelter, which is actually in the grounds of their house. We parked at the gates and were immediately met by a dozen very excited dogs. The walk through the gardens and up to the house is about 100 metres on quite a slope and then there was an external staircase up to a large outside decking area on the first floor. The ground floor was never used, it consisted of a library and a studio. At the top of the stairs we were met by Karen who ran the dog shelter. Dropping our bags on the decking we sat down for some breakfast and had a long chat with Karen and Paul whilst meeting the dogs and learning all of their names. Karen and Paul had moved to Nevis a few years ago, having previously spent a lot of time in the Caribbean. Paul was a yacht captain by trade, and spent time running private yacht charters for the rich and famous. Karen came from a chef background, also on yachts and that was how they met. They decided to settle on Nevis and as dog lovers they were appalled by the conditions of the dogs on the island. We soon found out that there are no domestic vets on Nevis, only a livestock vet so it meant a ferry ride back over to Saint Kitts if a dog or a cat needs treatment or medication. Immediately we noticed the passion in the way they talked about the plight of the islands dogs, the lack of vets, educating the locals on animal welfare and the troubles they have faced with the current government. They were clearly frustrated with the situation and rightly so but great credit to them, they had managed to rescue and re home around 650 dogs in their time on Nevis. There was another workawayer staying at the shelter but she wasn't there at the time, her name was Tara, she came from Maine where she was a seasonal crab fisherwoman. During our chat we discovered the dogs that had met us at the gate and were sitting with us outside were referred to as the "House Pack". Most of these were Karen and Paul's pets, ones they had chosen to keep for themselves after rescuing them. The number they had as pets had steadily climbed to ten over the years. The house pack consisted of Guinness, Sam, Charlie, Minx, Rascal, Kenya, Genie, Canelle, Pino and Roxy. The other dogs currently in the house pack were mainly puppies; Charlot, Buttons, Spyder and Oscar. There was also Kono who belonged to a neighbour but she stayed here when they returned to the US. It was then time to meet the shelter dogs. They were in various pens in the back garden or at the side of the house. To the side in the bottom pen there was Rickie, in the middle there was Ruby, next to her were best friends Nita and Twiggy. At the top of the garden in one pen was Snoopy with Turtle next door. Then in another double concrete pen were mum and daughter Tigger and Baloo. Then next door were a group described as feral. In total there were six dogs in here but we never saw them, as they were so scared of humans, they all hid, huddled up together in their enclosure. Bluebell was the mum and she had five puppies, four girls and a boy. The back garden section was known as Momma's pack. Momma had been here a while and she was great with the younger dogs. In here were Shelley, brother and sister Louis and Ella, Jingle, and other siblings Kane and Rexie. These we would soon be affectionately calling the "crazy gang" for obvious reasons. In total there were 36 dogs at the shelter including the house pack. After being shown where we would be sleeping we took some of the dogs out for a walk. The route is simple, out the gate turn left, this then steadily climbs until you reach a another smaller road and turn left, still climbing. Reaching the highest point of the road, turn left again and downhill, then reaching the bottom another couple of left turns and we were back on the same road as the shelter where we would start the uphill section again. It was basically a rectangle measuring just over a mile that ran along a quiet road with a fair bit of elevation, my Fitbit recorded 26 flights of stairs for one lap including the walk back up the garden path. One thing for sure was that we would be getting plenty of exercise whilst we were here.

However on our second day, there was to be no walking at all. A torrential tropical storm had hit the island and the rain was like nothing we had seen before. The house was a bit leaky in parts to say the least and all morning we did nothing apart from soaking up water from inside the house. Water was coming in through the skylights and running down the walls. We lost count of all the buckets of water we mopped up. After lunch Paul gave us a tour of the island, there is basically a road that runs around the bottom of the mountains circling the whole island. On our third day Tara took us to the police station to register for a temporary driving licence for the island. They were very insistent that we always wore our seatbelts and obeyed the speed limit. When I asked the police officer what that speed limit was, she didn't know. Tara then took us to Pinney's beach where there are few bars and we sampled Carib for the first time, the lager of St Kitts and Nevis. Tara was leaving at the end of the week so was basically having this week off as a holiday before returning to the US. Back at the shelter we were still trying to get used to feeding 36 dogs, knowing who has what, remembering where they have their bowl and in what order to feed them. That first week we were starting to get into a routine of feeding the dogs in the morning, walking them until lunchtime and then either going to the beach in the afternoon, INSTAGRAM POST 302 or staying and hanging around with dogs. After only a short while Helen was already making good progress with the feral dogs. Helen and I had stopped referring to them as the feral dogs, it was a word we didn't really like. Helen used to spend a lot of her spare time sat in the enclosure just reading her Kindle so Bluebell and her puppies would just get used to her and not see her as a threat and it seemed to be working. One thing Helen and I were determined to do was make sure every dog that could, would get a walk every day. Workaways are supposed to work for about four hours, five days a week, but we knew what we had signed up for. Working at a dog shelter is a 24 hour operation and we knew we would be working longer than 4 hours and not having weekends off. That was not an issue to us, in four weeks time we would be house sitting in Bequia where we could laze around as much as we liked, so we wanted to help the dogs and Karen and Paul as much as we could during our time here.

The dogs are not usually walked on a Sunday but we didn't mind taking them all out. We were already up to feed them and we would only be sitting around anyway so we still walked them. By the fourth day Helen and I were walking 21 dogs between us, the ones who didn't were either too young, too old, not well, or not able to be walked (Bluebelll and her puppies). The house pack would be first and we would have two or sometimes three each so walking all the house pack took two laps. Then we would move onto the outside shelter dogs and work our way through them. It was important to know which dogs got on well with each other and which ones didn't. Also the house pack had to be locked up on the decking so they wouldn't be in the garden when we walked the shelter dogs, apart from Pino who seemed to get on well with everyone. They would all be fed again in the evening at about 5.30pm and then we would collect and wash the bowls.

Just after our first week a decision was made to release two of Bluebell's puppies back to where they had been picked up, Bluebell was in season and couldn't be kept with her boy, and one of the female puppies was also chosen, so that he wouldn't be on his own. This was devastating news for Helen who had been working so hard with them. We had to accept the decision, hard as it was. That afternoon we decided we needed to get away from the shelter so Tara took us to a beach. Whilst there we heard what sounded like a flurry of loud bangs but thought nothing of it. The next day we were told that those bangs were gunshots and someone was killed in a drive-by shooting about a mile away from where we were on the beach. Supposedly it was retaliation against a murder the previous week. This should not put people off coming to Saint Kitts and Nevis, this was exceptionally rare and the locals know how much they rely on tourism and the effects it would have on their livelihoods if tourists stopped coming to the island.

We then discovered that our time in the Caribbean was to be extended even further. After our house sit in Bequia, we were then travelling further south to Grenada for another three month house sit. This would now take us up until October. Helen was also talking about the possibility of returning back to Nevis to help out again afterwards. I didn't have an issue with it. It felt so rewarding helping out at the shelter, especially when you see some of the dogs being adopted, like little Oscar, INSTAGRAM POST 303. That meant we could be in the Caribbean until possibly December.

On May Day, there was no dog walking, instead we took part in the Booby Island Regatta. Booby Island is a small rocky island between St Kitts and Nevis and there is a small regatta every year. Paul took Helen and me, along with his friend Tony in his boat as one of the entrants. We didn't win but we had a great time, INSTAGRAM POST 304. There is also a later photo, INSTAGRAM POST 309, one of the photographers took of me in charge of the boat. The days flew by with feeding, watering, walking, picking up poo and swapping dogs around for front garden time, it was hard work in the intense humidity and heat but it was great. Helen was really in her element, her work ethic amazed me. There were times I was shattered and just wanted to have an afternoon nap and Helen would be in the back garden playing with dogs or going round doing jobs. I couldn't have been more impressed with how she was doing, she was such a natural around dogs and was really enjoying herself. In the third week Karen went to the US for a conference and we also started taking some of the puppies to the beach in the afternoon. Little Charlot was a character and loved it, as did Ella and Louis. Buttons was far more timid. She was about six weeks old when an expat found her on the side of the road after being hit by a car. Her pelvis was broken and she had a badly injured leg. She is fine now but has a limp and her back leg can't lift like the others so tends to drag on the floor. Obviously she is scared of a lot of things so we really made an effort to increase her confidence.

Most of our walks tended to include other animals, there is a lot of livestock on Nevis but none of the animals are fenced in, they are just left to roam. When driving, there were always sheep or cows on the road that you would have to swerve to avoid. This was another reason for the mistreatment of dogs, the farmers would blame them for attacking livestock and so they would attack them with machetes or leave poison out for them to eat. By now we were used to seeing some distressing sights but it still wasn't very nice to witness. Seeing monkeys started off as a novelty but they are everywhere on Nevis, estimations are that there are about 7,500 on the island and as the shelter was at a higher elevation, we would see a lot of them. The dogs hated them, it sent them crazy if they saw a monkey running around on the roof of the house. There was a papaya tree just outside one of the windows and they would always try and steal them.

111

INSTAGRAM POST 305. The house pack caught and killed one in the front garden once so myself and Paul had to bury it away from the house.

Driving around the island you would see all sorts of dogs in terrible conditions. One dog Helen and I tried to rescue was suffering from terrible mange, it was almost bald, it hung around the food vendors living off scraps, unfortunately we were never able to get anywhere near it before we had to leave. INSTAGRAM POST 306.

One day a puppy was bought in with a badly injured back leg, it had been attacked either by other dogs or possibly a monkey. Because of her injury she would be part of the house pack, we called her Gigi and she slept in our room. INSTAGRAM POST 307. That's the thing with working at a shelter, it's not always cuddling little puppies, you have to deal with the sad times and the distressing sights. It is a real rollercoaster of emotions and you know you can't save them all but you do your best to save and help those that you can. It really was a case of appreciate the good times because you don't know when something bad would turn up on the doorstep. INSTAGRAM POST 308 is one of our favourite photos, it was taken one afternoon in the front garden with some of the dogs running towards me and it captured little Charlot in mid-flight. That week we were uplifted by the news that Shelly and Louis were going to be adopted. But as is the case, two leave and more arrive, two more puppies, Amber INSTAGRAM POST 310 and Sassy INSTAGRAM POST 311. Gorgeous little Amber was found on a deserted beach, obviously abandoned, she was delivered to the shelter and Paul and Karen spent ages removing ticks from her tiny body. Sassy arrived a day later, found lying next to a busy main road. Unfortunately the story of Amber didn't end well. She sadly died a few days later. One afternoon Helen and I took a break from the shelter to go across the narrows and visit Saint Kitts. INSTAGRAM POST 312 and INSTAGRAM POST 313. It felt weird, we had done all of our jobs, all the dogs had been walked but we felt guilty leaving the shelter as there is always something to be done. But downtime away from the shelter was a necessity sometimes. With the pressure of all that needed doing, tempers would often boil over. With both Karen and Paul spending years working and living with strangers on the small enclosed environment of a boat, arguments and disagreements were over and forgotten about almost immediately as you couldn't escape any other way. For me and Helen it was difficult to be over something so quickly. If there was a fiery moment it felt really strange to us that everything seemed to be normal again five minutes later when we would still be running it through in our heads, but by then Karen and Paul had already moved on.

In our final week we were supposed to hand over and show the ropes to two German workawayers, however they cancelled at the last minute. That meant there was no wind down for us in the final week but that wasn't what annoyed us. It meant Karen and Paul would be alone so we knew not all dogs would able to make it out for a daily walk. Our five weeks at the shelter were over so quickly, we said our goodbyes to the dogs and on the 24th of May we took the ferry again across to Saint Kitts. It was an unbelievable experience, one that we felt we made a difference. We were both keen on returning after our two upcoming house sits and both Karen and Paul were happy for us to return. Agreeing to keep in touch we headed south to St Vincent and the Grenadines, via stopovers in Antigua, Dominica and Barbados.

B - St Vincent and the Grenadines.

We arrived late afternoon in St Vincent and the Grenadines and had an Airbnb booked for two nights in Argyle near the airport. There wasn't a great deal to do so we would go for a walk on the beach, INSTAGRAM POST 314 and the hosts let us borrow their car to go to the supermarket. They also gave us a lift to the ferry terminal in the capital Kingstown to board the Admiral Express for the 45 minute, 15 km crossing. Approaching Port Elizabeth, the main town on Bequia, the island looked like a typical Caribbean island. The water was so clear, there were lots of yachts bobbing in the shallows just off shore and the island was very hilly and green. We sensed that this would be a true Caribbean experience on this tiny island with a population of about 5,000. Our hosts were waiting for us, Peter and Elizabeth, a couple in their 70's. Elizabeth was Canadian and Peter was originally from England but moved to Canada when he was 14. They had both been coming to Bequia on holiday for years before deciding to move permanently to this tiny paradise. The drive to their house was only five minutes, after all, the island is only 18 square km in size. It sat at the top of a very steep hill in an area where a lot of ex pats lived, near an area called Spring Estate on the Eastern side of the S shaped island. The house was on the side of the hill with three different levels with a huge sloping garden. The bottom level was essentially a shed, the next level was where we would be sleeping, there was a gorgeous bedroom with en-suite, a living room and a small office. All of this had a long walk around balcony. On the top floor was the open plan kitchen and diner with Peter and Elizabeth's room. Again there was a large wraparound balcony. It was a gorgeous house, there were no windows in the kitchen section, just wooden slats but the views were simply stunning from the balcony, INSTAGRAM POST 315. Peter and Elizabeth were a lovely couple and within 30 minutes of arriving I'd already had a rum and a beer. They were due to leave in two days time so it would be fun to spend a bit of time with them. Our responsibility whilst here was to look after their beloved three dogs, Molly, Maggie and Sandy, all rescued island dogs. They were great and very friendly. There was no gardening or cleaning to be done as a gardener and a housekeeper came to the house once a week. One thing they failed to mention though was that the house was rented, and that the landlord would be coming around to do some renovations and painting whilst they were away. One of our first requirements was to head back to Port Elizabeth with Peter to sort out a visa extension and a driving licence. Afterwards he took us to a bar for another beer.

Our final day with Peter and Elizabeth was very relaxing, we walked the dogs, went for a walk ourselves in the afternoon and met the neighbours, Colin and Claire who were originally from the UK. They were a really nice couple and were heading back themselves so we would have some fellow house sitters as neighbours soon. Going for groceries really gave us a perspective what island life was like and how small this island was. The main supermarket was no bigger than what you get on a high street in England, like a small corner shop. Some things are a lot more expensive as there is the extra travel and import costs added on top. The best thing is to eat as the locals eat and I realised I was going to have to scratch cook for pretty much our duration here. Things like frozen pizzas that you take for granted back home are so expensive here. Cheese was more expensive so too was peanut butter. Beer was cheap, and there was actually a brewery on the island and we were sometimes able to buy Coke Zero for Helen, but occasionally it would be past its sell by date. Grains, pulses, rice and pasta were all bagged up in little plastic bags but you would have to take out all the bugs once it was emptied into a pan and it was hit and miss if there was any bread on the day you visited. Peter and Elizabeth told us, if you see what you want; buy more as you will never know when it will be available again. There was another store on the island called Doris' and it catered for the yachts that would come and go. Price wasn't an issue if you owned or chartered or a yacht and especially if you had been at sea for weeks and craved something. As a result prices here were very expensive but it was amazing the things you could buy in here. One week we accepted defeat and paid £15 for a jar of Nutella. Peter and Elizabeth left at lunchtime on the day of their departure, we took the dogs for a couple of walks, not too far as Sandy was a little overweight. We found a short, but as with everywhere on the island, steep walk that was ideal with plenty of shade. The dogs didn't usually get walks, the property was not fenced and the dogs were free to roam as they liked. On our first night alone with the dogs, they woke us up at 5am barking. The reason, there was a herd of cows walking across the garden! That evening we were shattered and in bed by 9pm, it was going to be a case of early mornings and early nights whilst we were here. Also that night as we were watching TV, a mouse ran across the room. The second morning was the same, woken up really early by barking, but there were no cows in sight. I went for a run but even though I had been up since 5am I left it late and it was hot, very hot. It was a 5 km run but I was slow. The heat, humidity and hills took their toll. The worst part was the walk back up the really steep hill to the house, I had to stop three times.

Bequia has no running water on the island, all the water is rain water. So for a shower, you turn it on for about 15 seconds, get wet, turn it off, lather, turn it on again and rinse off. That's it, showers took no more than a minute. Again, just something you take for granted back home. The water was safe to drink but Peter and Elizabeth purchased their drinking water from St Vincent so it would be delivered on the ferry, they always ordered about five enormous bottles which then sat on top of a dispenser. We decided to do the same although I ended up drinking the tap water, and in the afternoon we headed down to Port Elizabeth to collect our water. There was no system, once the cars had pulled off the ramp, everyone just heads on to the boat to fetch whatever they think is theirs.

Later on we visited the famous Princess Margaret beach, named such because the Queen's sister came here visiting from the neighbouring island of Mustique. It is a stunning beach, clear water, golden sand, yachts moored out in the bay and also within walking distance from Port Elizabeth. INSTAGRAM POST 316. You will notice there are now multiple photos, it was at this time when Instagram allowed you to include up to ten pictures per post. Some of the beaches on Bequia, Princess Margaret included, had an abundance of Manchineel trees. This is one of the most toxic trees in the world, it has a milky white sap which contains numerous toxins and causes blistering, the sap is present in every part of the tree: the bark, the leaves and the fruit. Standing beneath the tree during rain could cause blistering of the skin from mere contact with a falling rain drop. The sap has also been known to damage paint on cars.

Wednesday was the day the gardener and housekeeper came. Mark the gardener was a really nice guy, he started at 6am. Again, it seemed everyone started early to beat the heat of the day and we were his second house. He didn't own a lawn mower due to the steep gradient of the garden, so he used a strimmer or weed whacker as they were known in the Caribbean. One thing we will remember from our time in the Caribbean is the familiar sound of a weed whacker. It seemed everyone owned one and because of the sun and the rain, the grass would grow quickly so you would probably hear the sound of someone using a weed whacker almost every day. I drove to Port Elizabeth to pick up the housekeeper, as arranged under the almond tree on the beachfront. Leaving them to it, we headed to the beach again returning at lunchtime to drive her back to town. As with other house sits, we were already starting to find a routine, an early start and walk with the dogs, followed by a run, maybe the beach and normally spending the afternoon back at house with the dogs. Then another walk later on when it was cooler with some Netflix after dinner and bed by 9.30pm!

June 1st was now officially the start of the rainy season, the reason why a lot of ex pats return home for a while, to avoid the weather and potential hurricanes. On June 2nd, there was a big rainstorm. When it is sunny in the Caribbean, it is glorious; when it rains it is important to find something to occupy your mind. One expat I met explained to me to that it is so easy to sit around and do nothing but drink all day, so he had given up alcohol completely. Peter, Elizabeth, Colin and Claire all did a lot for the island, helping out at the school through fundraising and donations and but also helping the islands stray dogs, it was a way of giving back and occupied their time. In the first week the landlord had called round twice unannounced, so it looked like this trend was going to continue during our stay. In the evening we had a meal round at Colin and Claire's. Their house was amazing, we also met the couple who would be house sitting for them, they were currently house sitting about a mile away for someone else and seemed to have the monopoly on the island by house sitting for various ex-pats totalling around six months of the year. It was funny as all of sudden Sandy, our dog appeared, he had walked over from our house on his own and fell asleep under the dining table. As the days went by the dogs were a lot easier to walk and were really warming to us. Sandy was losing a bit of weight and could go a bit further on the walks. They now also slept in our room so they couldn't be running around outside barking, helped by the humming of the fan which kept the mosquitos away. Helen was getting ravaged by them, especially upstairs in the kitchen where there was no draught.

We would Skype home usually once a week, there was a lot of downtime, so we decided to sign up for a VPN to be able to access shows back home, especially with the Tour de France coming up. One Sunday at Princess Margaret beach the jeep wouldn't start. On Sundays, everyone goes to the beach and there is music blaring out everywhere. Not having a clue what to do, I approached a group of guys and within 30 seconds the bonnet was open and they were tinkering inside. Within two minutes the car was running again. Something to do with sea air affecting the battery, everything rusts on Bequia as a result of the sea air. Our runs were also now getting easier as we were adjusting to the heat and humidity. It would nearly be a year since we left home and Helen's insulin supplies were running low, so one day we went to see the Island doctor, it seemed it might be tricky to purchase some whilst here, so we spent some time looking on the internet and Grenada, where we were heading next looked to be our best bet.

One day we were walking the dogs and heard an animal in distress, upon closer inspection, a goat had obviously chewed through its rope and wandered off but the rope had managed to get wrapped around a tree. Now the poor thing was in a right mess with its foot all tied up and strangling itself so it could hardly breathe. After a few minutes we managed to free it so that was our good deed for the day. Other creatures we would often come across were huge land crabs with an enormous claws and tortoises. INSTAGRAM POST 317. They would often walk across the garden or we would see them when we were running. Another day, Helen picked up her baseball cap to see a mouse staring back at her from where it had been hiding.

One day we decided to drive around the island and see the places we hadn't been to yet, that didn't take very long! By now we were used to island life. Helen remarked once that when she went for a run, at a quiet secluded part of the island just before the road ended she met three men walking towards her all holding machetes. A few months ago she would have been terrified of an encounter like this but not now. Machetes are everywhere in the Caribbean, it is the tool of choice for gardening and opening up coconuts. Helen simply replied to their "Good morning" and carried on running past.

One morning I woke up in absolute agony, it was my kidneys. I think I was dehydrated, I ran the previous day and spent all day lying in the sun and probably hadn't drank enough water. The pain was horrendous, Helen had to walk the dogs and it looked like I might need a doctor. I decided to drink a lot of water and see how I felt. I drank a lot that morning, not too much as I know the dangers of drinking too much too soon, but it was still after lunchtime until I needed to urinate.

The cricket season had also just started again on Bequia so every Sunday I would head down to the cricket pitch on the island to watch a couple games of Twenty20. INSTAGRAM POST 318. It was great sitting watching some sport, the crowd really got into it and you could also hear singing coming from the nearby church.

Hurricane Brett was heading towards us, one of the first of the season because the name began with a B and they are named alphabetically. There was a lot of wind and rain but it actually missed us by some distance but it made you realise the power of a hurricane.

Our letting agent emailed us with some sad news, we had a family renting our house back in the UK and the mother had died suddenly from a heart attack. It was a shock, we had never actually met them but felt terrible for the family.

The ex pats on the island who helped out with the stray dogs had arranged a vet to come over to the island to spay and neuter as many dogs as possible, both the strays and the pets. Our job was to help with the strays and there was one in particular that needed help. It was always around Port Elizabeth and was in a sorry state. The mange was so bad it was completely bald and sore from scratching. There was also an issue with its bottom jaw. Helen managed to leash him with the lure of some dog food and he was put in a cage and taken off to the school were the vet was set

119

up. The problem was that there was nowhere to keep a stray dog overnight. All the others were released again after they had recovered from their operations but this one, now called Tarzan was found to have a lump on his leg that needed removing. He was therefore kept in a garage belonging to an ex pat, not ideal when he had just had an operation but better than nothing whilst he recovered. Over the next couple of days, Helen and I regularly checked on him, kept him company and even took him out on a couple of walks, but it was obvious he just wanted to be back at the beachfront. When we visited him first thing one morning he wasn't looking very well. Jen, the owner of the garage where he was being held, contacted someone who ran the volunteers group, and they contacted the vets on St Vincent. They agreed that we should send him over on the next ferry. I loaded him into a crate and Helen helped me lift it into the back of Jen's old jeep and then she headed back to the house. When I say old, Jen told me her jeep was over 40 years old. I would be going with Jen in the jeep to help load Tarzan onto the ferry. As we set off, Jen said that the jeep can be a bit temperamental sometimes. The route to Port Elizabeth was flat to start with then you have to climb a hill then descend down the other side into the town. On the way there I was leaning over the back with my hand in the cage stroking Tarzan to keep him calm. The next thing I know I am waking up on the floor in the road.

It appeared that the brakes had failed as we were coming down the hill into town. As we were gaining momentum and getting faster, Jen tried to steer down a side road but this old jeep did not have power steering. We basically ploughed into a small wall and luckily a tree on the other side stopped us going over a drop. The force of the impact was on my front side and as a result I was thrown forward and the door flew open and that's how I ended up on the floor. I wasn't wearing a seat belt as I don't think there was one to wear and I was turned round in my seat looking after Tarzan. I was helped to my feet by some people who saw the accident and I went to check on Jen. She was obviously shaken from the ordeal and had hurt her wrist on the steering wheel but was otherwise ok. I then needed to check on Tarzan, he was fine. Someone was looking after Jen so a passer-by let me load Tarzan into their car to take him down to the port. It was here when it finally hit me what had happened. I had a big lump on the back of my head, my shoulder, hand and ribs were sore and I had a cut on my leg. I realised it could have been a lot worse. Jen did the right thing as we were gaining speed and there would have been a lot of people at the end of that road. She didn't say anything, whether that was because it happened so quickly or I might have reacted and tried to grab the wheel, I don't know. Meanwhile Helen was oblivious to any of this but word got back to her. As there is only one road back to the house, Colin and Claire passed the car on their way back and saw Jen who explained what happened. They then called in on Helen to tell her and she came down in the jeep to find me. We never told our parents about it as I knew my Mum and Dad would be worried, hence there wasn't a photo on Instagram. A couple of days later I popped into the garage to look at the jeep and the guy assured me the jeep would be up and running again once the parts had been shipped over.

I didn't do much for a couple of days after as I was sore but soon got back into running again and my times were getting better. I was also getting up at 3am to watch the British Islands Rugby team play their matches from the tour of New Zealand. The landlord was making more regular visits much to our annoyance and one day he had a go at me for leaving the hard white plastic sun loungers out in the sun. That's what they are for isn't it, the clue is in the name? On another stressful afternoon the house keys fell through a hole in my backpack when we were walking the dogs, so we had to retrace our steps and luckily found them on the beach.

There were always coconuts lying on the beach so I tried my first attempt at husking one. It took me a lot longer than it should have but it was worth it. INSTAGRAM POST 319. From then on we quite often came back after a walk with the odd coconut or mango. Princess Margaret Beach was still our favourite beach but we also used to spend a lot of time at Lower Bay Beach, a bit further on. INSTAGRAM POST 320, INSTAGRAM POST 321 and INSTAGRAM POST 322. It was another typical stunning beach and a great place to just relax.

The next morning I waited for Helen to return from her run before I set off. On finishing, when I reached the estate entrance there was a puppy, it had obviously been dumped. I was told this happens sometimes, when a local doesn't want to keep a dog they drive out to the estate where the ex-pats live and dump them as they know they will try and do something about it. I didn't know what to do. I decided to leave it there and headed back up the hill. We would then phone the group who look after rescue dogs on the island and they could hopefully help us out. When I reached the house and told Helen, we heard the dogs barking; we turned round and saw the puppy just standing there. It had followed my scent all the way up the hill. Molly, Maggie and Sandy barked to start off with but then couldn't be bothered. The puppy was already lying down and had decided it was staying here. It was really skinny, had lots of fleas and hair loss because of mange. No one could help us. Someone in the group of helpers accused me of picking up stray puppies, and the vets were not interested. We emailed Peter and Elizabeth and fortunately they said it could stay until it something was sorted out and he was better. We spoke to the couple who were looking after Colin and Claire's house. Luckily Claire emailed us straight away and said she had a dog pen in her garage and some medication to treat the mange and fleas. The next day we tried the VSPCA in the hope they could help us. It was a real concern, our duty was to look after Peter and Elizabeth's three dogs but then this poor puppy had made itself at home here as well. Frustratingly the help group were not assisting in any way. In all our "guest" stayed with us for eight days and we never left the house. We separated him from the other dogs in his own pen and thankfully he was getting stronger every day. Eventually and much to our relief, the VSPCA, through a Facebook appeal had managed to find a sponsor and someone who was going to cover any medical bills. A local couple would be fostering "Titch" as we had named him until a home could be found, he was renamed Lucky. Today was also July 12th, exactly a year since we left the UK. Never in our wildest dreams a year ago did we think we would be on a tiny island in the Caribbean, trying desperately to find a home for a puppy that turned up on our house sit.

After a week of not leaving the house, we ventured out again and hiked to the northern tip of the island, Bequia Point, INSTAGRAM POST 323, INSTAGRAM POST 324 and INSTAGRAM POST 325, returning with some mangos. We also ate the fruit from the garden. There were some delicious refreshing miniature apples we regularly ate, and a pomegranate tree. The gardener told me about a fruit called soursop that also grew in the garden. INSTAGRAM POST 326. It looked revolting but tasted really nice, especially in smoothies.

After a lot of research we decided that the best way for Helen to get her insulin was to go home for a week whilst we were house sitting in Grenada. Her mum was missing her and insulin in Grenada was really expensive. It would be a chance for Helen to see her parents, have a check-up at the doctors, opticians and also change some clothes for us both. The cost of insulin in the Caribbean for a year was about the same price as the return flight home.

The final couple of weeks were not that enjoyable, the landlord was at the house nearly every day, all day decorating or gardening. As a result we spent more time walking the dogs or just going out on our own. Sandy was now able to go on longer walks, both the gardener and the maid mentioned how he had lost some weight and was looking a lot healthier. They used to get really excited when they knew they were going for a walk. They would all excitably yap when we appeared with the leads and Sandy would run off straight away and we would have to put the lead on him when we caught him up. They loved walking down the hill and across the field to beach at the bottom of the road, INSTAGRAM POST 327, always looking down the holes in search of the land crabs. They were really sweet dogs, a lot of work to begin with but such great fun and they really enjoyed the company and would lay with us in the evenings when we were watching TV. INSTAGRAM POST 328.

On one of the decorating days, Helen and I drove into Port Elizabeth and walked to Fort Hamilton, situated at the northern end of Admiralty Bay. The fort was built by the British in the 1700's and even though little of the fortification remains, there are still some cannons and there is a great view back across the bay to Port Elizabeth. INSTAGRAM POST 329.

Our upcoming house sit in Grenada was to last six weeks but we also applied and were accepted for a workaway position on a chocolate plantation for a couple of weeks afterwards. Grenada is famous for its chocolate and it seemed interesting to experience making some ourselves.

With those dates confirmed we also booked our one way flights back to the dog sanctuary on Nevis, not knowing how long we would be there for.

The end of July was here, Peter and Elizabeth returned and we picked them up from the ferry. Peter had really missed Bequia saying he wouldn't want to leave the island for more than a couple of weeks in the future, this really was his home now and you could tell he had missed it. We let them unpack and unwind in the afternoon so Helen and I headed up to Mount Pleasant, one of the only places we hadn't seen on the island in our time here. INSTAGRAM POST 330. In the evening we all went out for a meal, and we had a really nice catch up. They asked what we would be doing next year and if we would want to house sit again. We enjoyed our time on Bequia, it was a once in a lifetime experience of staying and sampling life on a proper tiny Caribbean island. There were certainly a few stressful times but it was something we would never ever forget. The islanders were really friendly and it's amazing how you get to know people so quickly on a small island such as the other spectators at the cricket matches or the guy where we used to buy our fruit and vegetables from. And it goes without saying we loved spending time with Molly, Maggie and Sandy.

On the day of departure we packed our bags and weighed them, I took the opportunity to weigh myself and was amazed to see I was down to nearly 70kgs, I was about 82kg when we left the UK. Peter drove us to the small airport on Bequia on the far south of the Island. The plane was tiny, INSTAGRAM POST 331, we were the only passengers on the flight and we were sat right behind the pilot. INSTAGRAM POST 332. It was due to stop over at Canouan but there was no one to pick up so we carried on to Carriacou where we were joined by some fellow passengers. INSTAGRAM POST 333. The flight was amazing, such a different experience flying in a small plane looking down on the Southern Grenadines, Mayreau and the Tobago Cays. We initially applied for a position on Mayreau looking after some dogs. Mayreau is the smallest inhabited island of the Grenadines at only 4 square km in size with a population of just less than 300 people! However, we found out that our accommodation had no electricity, therefore it would have been risky for Helen's insulin, so we had to decline. One regret we do have is not visiting the Tobago Cays, they look stunning but at the time the only way to get there was on a chartered yacht which seemed too expensive, in hindsight we both know we should have gone.

Our flight landed in Grenada at 11am, we were going to be on this, another Caribbean island for the next eight weeks.

C - GRENADA

With no international flight coinciding with our arrival we breezed through immigration and baggage reclaim, as Alan and Jennie picked us up from the Maurice Bishop International Airport. They are originally from the UK and moved here a few years ago. Their house is on the south of the island and the journey back took about 45 minutes. Today was Saturday, Alan and Jennie didn't leave until Wednesday so we had five days in their company. By house sitting standards, this is a very long time for a handover. Normally it is a day or two maximum and the one in Summerland, Canada was 30 minutes. Alan was a meticulous planner, wanting to ensure we would know how to look after his house and pets but he also said he would feel responsible if something happened to us whilst at his house. The house was amazing, it was huge, the largest all in one living and dining room we had seen. Their bedroom and a guest room were off to the right. To the left was a really nice kitchen and our bedroom and bathroom. There were also some stairs which led up to a viewing area. Outside was an enormous pool, it must have been 15m long with a big garden and stunning views out to sea. We were here to look after their pet dog called Rufus. He was a huge Doberman, easily 50kg, and a really sweet boy. After chatting and unpacking we joined them on a walk to the very end of the peninsula. Everything seemed very ordered and structured. The afternoon walk was at 5pm, always to the same place, stopping and sitting at the same rock on the way back for a few minutes. Morning walk was 7am, down to the beach and back in order to avoid any other dogs. And so it continued, in our room we tried to remember it all and the order list was huge. Each to their own though, people are habitual and like routines. During the day we went to the capital, St George's to sort out my driving license and we were also shown where the supermarkets are located. Yes plural, with American influence, comes western sized supermarkets and food, the type of which we had not seen for a long time.

Grenada seemed so busy compared to Bequia. It has a population of 112,000 covering an area of 348 square km. Unlike St Kitts and Nevis, Grenada is not part of the Commonwealth and was granted independence in 1974. There is a heavy American influence in Grenada and many American students study at St George's medical university. Such students were the reason given by the US administration to justify an American invasion of the island in 1983. It was to rescue them from the danger of a coup but the invasion was heavily criticised internationally. The coup was strongly linked to Cuba and the Soviet Union so President Reagan justified the overthrow of a communist constitution by rescuing the 1,000 medical students on the island. The International Airport is named after Maurice Bishop, the then leader of Grenada who was killed in the coup.

During the remaining time with Alan and Jennie we lazed around and were shown more procedures on how to use the mower and the weed wacker in order to look after the garden as well as to monitor the pool. Fortunately they had pool cleaners who came to do the complicated work. Alan also showed us what to do in case of a hurricane, now we were in the middle of the season. The last major one to strike Grenada was in 2004, Hurricane Ivan. It caused severe damage to the island, which is still evident as you drive through St George's and 39 people were killed. Alan showed us how to use a generator should the electricity fail and the large drums to fill with potable water. Even though five days initially seemed a bit much, this training was invaluable if something ever did happen so we really appreciated the efforts Alan went to. He explained the best rooms to shelter in, the ones with no windows or if things got really bad, the area underneath the swimming pool with the pumps. It really hit home how we were potentially at risk and Alan showed us the National Hurricane Centre website where we could track hurricanes forming in Africa and heading across the Atlantic. We checked this website daily from then on.

Wednesday came and we drove Alan and Jennie to the airport, our first day on our own and it rained all day and night. Still there was a huge pool, and a great house to occupy us. On our second day we did our big shop at the supermarket and filled up the car with petrol. On our dog walks we were always joined by four other dogs that lived further along the peninsula. Their owner was in the UK at the time and a gardener would come and feed them. Pippa, Missie were the names of two of them but we didn't know the names of the others so Helen named them Lilly and Princess. INSTAGRAM POST 334. They seemed really friendly but were a little apprehensive to start with. It was good to have them tag along as Rufus

127

would run around on the beach with them and get more exercise. Rufus was a good dog, he seemed fine with his owners absence so we sensed that he would be fun to look after and already we noticed that he had a cheeky side to him. INSTAGRAM POST 335.

Soon Helen's departure day arrived, not helped by the fact she had a bad hypo in the night. I drove her to the airport at 2pm for her flight just after 5pm. I was walking Rufus when I saw her plane pass by above me. I was a nervous wreck without Helen. Mentally she was far stronger than me, I realised how much I relied on her. In the past year that we had been away, the longest we had been apart was when my brother was here and we went to the gig and the football match. Here and now I was on my own and it just felt unbelievably lonely. I wasn't just counting down the days, I was counting down the hours until she would be back. I'm a worrier, always have been and always will be. I worry if I'm not worrying about something. I just can't help it. I started imagining nightmare scenarios where for some strange reason Helen would not be allowed back into Grenada and I would be here on this house sit on my own for another few weeks. I was also concerned about hurricanes. Leading up to Helen leaving we had been monitoring activity over Africa and it all seemed fine. Whilst Helen was away, I just tried to keep myself occupied mentally and physically. I would swim 100 lengths of the pool and then do various exercises and stretches. I couldn't go for a run as the road was far too uneven and covered in loose rocks. I would spend time cleaning the house and playing with Rufus. I also built him a treat toy, essentially plastic bottles with a piece of wood going through them, filled with treats. In order to get the treats he had to push the bottles upside down so they tip out. The football season had started back home and Alan had a digital radio that played through speakers out onto the patio so I would listen to games on 5 Live Sport. I managed to Skype Helen most days. Her time back home was busy. Doctors, opticians, hairdressers, catching up with family, both hers and mine. Helen spent time in her parents' attic looking for clothes to bring back but at the same time her mum was spoiling her with her cooking. Thankfully the day of her return arrived and I picked her up from the airport. Her flight landed at 3pm but there were other international arrivals so she didn't walk out until nearly two hours later. The relief was immense to see her again, normality with the two of us back together. It felt like Xmas with all the stuff she had returned with. Normal house sitting service resumed quite quickly with walking and gardening. Alan and Jennie took pride in their garden so we were determined to do a good job looking after it, probably too good a job. Over the weeks we spent hours weeding, cutting and strimming it. The rest of the time we didn't do a lot, apart from lay out in the sun and make use of the pool.

One day we drove north to visit the chocolate plantation where we were going to be volunteering. It was not as we hoped. It was a bit run down and the ex-pat guy who ran it reminded me of John Lydon from the Sex Pistols. He showed us where we would be staying and it was basically a tiny wooden shed and you used the waterfall to wash yourself and your clothes. They were not even producing chocolate at the time we would be there either. I didn't need to check with Helen on the drive home that we wouldn't be returning, so the next day we emailed and said thanks but no thanks. That put us in a dilemma, we had already booked our return flight back to St Kitts and to change our flights would cost us over £400. The choice was to pay the £400 or find some cheap accommodation on Grenada for a couple of weeks and catch our original flight.

Helen's birthday arrived on the 24th of August so we decided to take a trip to the famous Grand Anse Beach. It was a nice beach but there weren't many places to buy any food or drink so we drove around to Morne Rouge Beach and had a beer and an ice cream, INSTAGRAM POST 336. Back at the house we Skyped both sets of parents. Today saw the first major Hurricane of the season, Harvey, it didn't hit the Caribbean but caused lots of damage in the US with 106 deaths.

Grand Etang is a national park located in the middle of the island so we went for a look. It was a nice drive but as it was high up in the mountains, the weather can be unpredictable and it started raining as we set off for a walk. There was a group of people trying to spot monkeys in the forest, after seeing so many on Nevis it seemed strange, as seeing monkeys had been a daily occurrence for us.

Sometimes when walking Rufus we would bump into an ex pat called Nigel who lived further along at the start of the peninsula. He was a really nice guy and we would spend ages talking to him. It turned out he had an empty apartment under his house and he invited us to have a look to see if it was fine for us to stay in until we returned to Nevis. After viewing it, we liked it so it then just depended on how much he would charge us. A couple of days later Nigel came round to the house for a drink and offered us his apartment at a really good price, it was a deal, we would be staying just up the road for a couple of weeks.

The Hurricane Centre website had issued a warning for the Caribbean as Irma was heading west. We monitored it closely for a few days and it was clearly heading north of us but towards St Kitts and Nevis. Luckily Nevis was spared as Irma passed within 100 km, it was still strong enough though to blow nearly 100 tiles off the shelter roof. We were glued to the internet as we watched the Category 5 monster devastate Barbuda and St Martin. The next day it ripped through the Virgin Islands and into Puerto Rico. Irma was the first category 5 hurricane to strike the Leeward Islands on record with wind speeds of 170mph. In all Irma caused 134 deaths and $77bn worth of damage across the Caribbean. At the same time, another Hurricane Jose was forming in the Atlantic and on its way but thankfully that fizzled out.

On one of our morning walks we noticed Missy, one of the four dogs wasn't very well. She hadn't appeared in the usual place that we met them, and when she finally caught us up she seemed sluggish and uncoordinated. We contacted Missy's owner in the UK and she was grateful that we would take her to the vets. After some injections and tablets Missy returned to her normal self over the next few days.

After six weeks our house sit had come to an end. I fetched Alan and Jennie from the airport and Helen walked Rufus. I cooked in the evening and then we packed our bags as we were moving to Nigel's in the morning. We had already been to the supermarket to stock up as we would be without a vehicle now.

We said our goodbyes but we knew we would see Alan and Jennie again as we were only staying up the road. It felt strange when we moved into the apartment, we had no responsibilities, no routine we had to stick to. We would miss the pool though and the views though from their amazing house INSTAGRAM POST 337. It seemed like we didn't do a lot whilst we were there compared to Bequia but that wasn't a bad thing, the location was the main reason. Our two weeks in the apartment were fun, we would get up when we wanted and then go down and see the four dogs twice a day, taking them food. Sometimes we would catch a bus into St George's. The buses were small minibuses that you just flagged down from the side of the road. On one occasion I counted 19 of us crammed into a tiny minibus. The apartment overlooked a football pitch so I would wander down to watch whenever there was a game on.

At the beach one day I was swimming and came out trying to persuade Helen to come in. She declined as she was wearing her glasses and wouldn't be able to see very well without them. I carried on asking her and she eventually came in up to her waist still wearing her glasses. Then we were hit by a rogue wave, we didn't see it as we were facing the beach. It engulfed us and washed away Helen's glasses. We were devastated, and I felt terrible as I had been the one who kept asking her to come into the sea. We would need to buy a new pair when we returned to St Kitts.

Losing Helen's glasses put things into perspective when we heard another Category 5 hurricane was heading to the Caribbean. Maria turned out to be even more devastating than Irma, which battered the north only two weeks previously. It clattered Dominica, the US Virgin Islands and Puerto Rico. It was the deadliest Atlantic Hurricane since 2004. Damages totalled upwards of $91bn, but even worse was that it caused the death of 3,059 people. Nevis had been lucky, Irma and Maria had just passed either side of the island and Maria again had caused lost roof tiles and a couple of broken windows at the shelter. I always remember watching stories of hurricanes on the news back home but here when we were so close to two major hurricanes ripping through the Caribbean in the space of a fortnight it felt very real, and we were fortunate to be down south at the time. Before applying for the house sit in Grenada we were looking at others available on those islands that were hit. It made us thankful that Alan spent the time to prepare us in case one did strike Grenada.

Alan asked for help in the garden one day so I spent one morning around there helping him drill some drainage holes in his raised vegetable patch. They also invited us around one evening for pizza and cocktails and we had a really pleasant evening. Another time they were due to go out for an evening but Rufus wasn't very well so they asked if we could go round and look after him, which of course we did as it was always good to see Rufus. He didn't look his normal self but seemed pleased to see us. Alan and Jennie had obviously not settled into the Caribbean as much as Nigel, or Peter and Elizabeth on Bequia who had immersed themselves in to island life. Whether it was due to the isolated location of the house I don't know. Alan told us expats leave the Caribbean to return home for three main reasons. Number one is money, and obviously lack off. The second is health, expats have grown old here and need more help and the reality is the healthcare is better back home. The other reason is grandchildren, ex pats that moved here 20 or 30 years ago, their children now have children and they want to spend more time with the grandkids. I agreed with him. Having only spent nearly six months in the Caribbean, Helen and I both said we wouldn't be sure we would ever want to live here. Real life in the Caribbean is completely different to a holiday and if it is better weather you want, you might as well live in an ex pat complex in Spain. Unless, like Peter and Elizabeth you accept that things take longer with island life and embrace it, rather than let it frustrate you.

In our final week I was suffering from a painful earache that must have come from swimming in the sea. Our last night on Grenada Nigel took us to a tiny little rum shack owned by a friend. It was a great evening chatting with the locals in a tiny little wooden bar no bigger than a garden shed. I even ended up playing a few games of dominoes with the locals. INSTAGRAM POST 338. Strangely it felt like we experienced more of the real Grenada on that night than we had done in the previous few weeks. Overall Grenada was a lovely island, the locals were probably the friendliest we had experienced in the Caribbean. Just walking on the beach or along the road there was always a smiling face and a hello. That's not to say there wasn't on Nevis or Bequia but it was a lot more noticeable on Grenada. It also seemed so much greener, along all the roads there were mango and banana trees, it seemed like fruit was growing everywhere here. INSTAGRAM POST 339. The final morning we walked to say goodbye to Missy and the others for the last time. Even though we weren't responsible for them, we had grown really attached to them. INSTAGRAM POST 340. Nigel kindly drove us to the airport and we would soon begin our second stint on Nevis, via Antigua and Barbados. INSTAGRAM POST 341.

D - ST KITTS AND NEVIS (AGAIN)

Arriving back at Robert Bradshaw Airport, everything looked recognizable, it was nearly four and a half months since we left St Kitts and Nevis. When we first arrived in Mid-April, there was that sense of slight nervousness you always get when you walk outside an airport in a foreign country for the first time. Everyone wants you to jump in their taxi or help you with your bags and it can feel a bit overwhelming. Familiarity eradicates that fear, it was 9pm, we were drained from flying all day and stopovers, and we just wanted to get to our accommodation for the night so we jumped into the first taxi we could find and headed to the sea front at Basseterre. Our motel was in the now familiar main town centre as we wanted to spend the morning looking for new glasses for Helen and I would try and find a doctor to get medication for my ear infection. Fortunately the motel had a bar and a great balcony that looked out onto the main drag, our bags were quickly dumped in the room and we headed straight to the bar for some Caribs. Three bottles each went down no problem as we talked about being back at the dog shelter. How many are there now? Which dogs would still be there? Have they changed? What would the new dogs be like? How are Bluebell and her three girls?

My ear was feeling slightly better in the morning so I convinced myself I didn't need to pay for a doctor's appointment. We found an opticians, the glasses wouldn't be ready for another three weeks, not ideal but we had to accept it. Also by now our bank account with Norwich and Peterborough had closed down and so we were now using our Credit Cards when withdrawing cash. This meant withdrawal charges that we previously avoided with our other card. From now on we drew out more cash, but far less often to minimise the charges. Incidentally, the currency we used across the Caribbean is the ECD, the Eastern Caribbean Dollar and the rate is approximately 3 ECD to 1 Pound Stirling. Karen picked us up in the van just after lunch and we drove down to the southern tip of the island to catch the car ferry over to Nevis. It was good to see Karen again and she told us all about what had happened over the last few months. The island dodged two bullets when Irma and Maria passed by. Karen said all the beaches were ruined though as the tidal surges had shifted all the sand. The exclusive Four Seasons hotel on the island was busy rebuilding the beach for its high paying guests. It seemed Karen was not impressed with the volunteers who had helped in our absence, they seemed to be on Nevis for a holiday rather than helping the dogs. Straight away we knew that meant no one would have put time in to sit and socialise with Bluebell and her girls, they would have regressed. A holiday was the last thing on our minds, for the last four and a half months it seemed we had been on holiday. We were looking forward to getting back to working. When we arrived at the shelter we were met by Paul and the house pack. It was good to see all the dogs. It was a mixture of feelings seeing Buttons and Charlot again, obviously we were really happy to see them both, they had grown up but had not yet been rehomed. They were no longer small puppies and that is the prime time when the dogs get adopted, hopefully they hadn't missed their chance. After dumping our bags in the newly refurbished downstairs studio, we headed around the shelter to see who was still here. Unfortunately there were a lot of the same faces as last time, Ricky, Turtle, Ruby, Momma, Snoopy, Twiggy, Tigga and Balloo were all still here. However Tigga and Balloo were leaving the shelter tomorrow to be rehomed, so that was good news. Bluebell and her girls were obviously still here but it was amazing to see that they recognised us, Helen especially. It was great to see Bluebell wagging her tail when she saw Helen.

Our first full day at the sanctuary we were straight back into the familiar routine. Still determined to take every dog out for a walk that could be walked. Starting a 8am, Helen and I walked seven laps on our first full day and the results from my Fitbit said it all. INSTAGRAM POST 342. Tigga, Balloo and two other dogs left the sanctuary for good today, it would be great if four could be adopted like that every day. Having the studio was far better than having the room upstairs, we felt we had more privacy as we had our own toilet and sink and a small living room with a couple of sofas lined up against the back wall. The next evening we joined Paul and Karen for some food and drinks at Turtle Time, a popular bar at Pinneys Beach. Later we were also joined by Judy, their friend who had previously helped out at the shelter. It was great to see Judy again, she was so down to earth. There was never a discussion with Karen and Paul on how long we would be helping out at the shelter, we knew there was another volunteer arriving early December staying until the end of January, and then another couple arriving the day after. Four volunteers would probably be too many so we would be happy to stay until then. It was now early October so that would mean about three and half months here. In total that meant we would have been in the Caribbean for nine months, quite a bit more than the five weeks we had originally planned. Having more privacy in the studio meant there was less need to leave the shelter as well. Karen was right about the beaches. Oualie Beach was our favourite beach when we were here last time, now it was a mess. The storm had washed up the sand and the beach seemed to be about ten metres further out than it used to be. The problem was there was a part in the middle that was higher so when the tide came in, the water was not able to flow back with the outgoing tide. This created a lagoon which smelt bad. It was also busy with JCB's shifting sand to try and level it all out, therefore we wouldn't be visiting this beach for a while. Even though we still walked all the dogs on Sundays, we liked to go a bar in the afternoon after spending a couple of hours on another beach we found that was still in a decent condition. It was called Lovers Beach and was only just a bit north of Oualie Beach but around the corner so it was probably saved from the hurricane by being more sheltered.

We were pleased to start walking Buttons outside the gates. Buttons was the dog hit by a car as a puppy with a damaged hip and back leg which drags on the floor slightly when she walks. She has been at the shelter since a few weeks old but it was important to get her out of the gates, build up her confidence and build the muscles in her back legs. Her back paw would be covered with a rubber sock which would protect it from scraping. The house pack would all get walked first thing in the morning before breakfast and Helen would then take Buttons for a short walk whilst I started prepping breakfast. Already some of the dogs had started to join us in the studio in the evenings. The house pack slept where they liked around the house, but some of them had started to wander downstairs with us. Pino was a house pack dog who liked to keep himself distant from the rest, he spent all his time in the front garden and rarely ventured into the house. However he did like the sofa in our studio. He was joined by Charlot and Buttons. Buttons would sleep on a cushion next to Helen's side of the bed and Charlot would sleep on the sofa at the other end to Pinot. When Kono's owners were away and she stayed at the shelter, she would also stay in the studio. The studio dogs became known as the "Studio Crew". Little Shorty, the newest and youngest member of housepack would also stay over sometimes.

Aside from walking, feeding and picking up dog poo, maintaining the shelter also kept us busy. Some of the dogs were escape artists, particularly Julio who was an amazing climber so fences were heightened and re built. During our time at the shelter I used so many cable ties to keep the fences and shades maintained, it felt as though the whole shelter was held together with cable ties. Some days we would also have no electricity. It wasn't too much of a problem except it meant the pump for the water wouldn't work. Therefore in order to keep the dog bowls full, we filled up lots of empty bottles just in case as some days the electricity would not come back on until late in the evening. The water for the dogs was especially important as the heat and humidity on the island had really increased. Most of our walk was in the sun and by the end of five laps my top was soaked in sweat and I was burning 5,000 calories a day. It was a case of walk one lap, drink a pint of water, then onto the next lap and keep repeating to stay hydrated. Even at 8 o clock in the morning the temperature was around 30 degrees, but the dogs were more used to it than us humans. So we could finish slightly earlier, Paul started helping out with a couple of walks each morning, which was great as it gave us extra time to work Bluebell and her girls. Each day we were making progress with them. Previously they only had a small area outside of their pen, but we had started to let them into the larger section which they enjoyed and then we progressed into letting them have a run in the large front garden. Making sure all the house pack were locked upstairs, it was an amazing sight when we first opened the gate and let them out in the front garden for the first time. They just ran and ran, it would have been the first time in nearly a year that they really would have been able to run freely. They would follow us when we ran around in the garden and they really enjoyed being around us now. Bluebell and Star, the bravest of the puppies, were both now wearing collars and we were able to put a lead on Bluebell, so started practising walking her up and down the garden, INSTAGRAM POST 343. The progress was amazing and we truly started to believe we could help these dogs. The problem however was that they were fine with us but they were still petrified of anyone else.

As we knew we were going to be here for a couple of months, we decided to go to the charity shop and buy some clothes as we would end up ruining our own. Between both of us, we bought six tops and three pairs of trousers which were cut into shorts for just over £5. My earache had returned and I couldn't put it off any longer so I decided to go to the doctors who prescribed me with some eardrops and antibiotics. Helen's glasses were well overdue but Karen brought them back coinciding with a trip to the vets over on St Kitts.

On the same day we had a new puppy arrive at the shelter, a lady who owns a restaurant on Nevis amazingly had found him abandoned in a bin. He was therefore named Dusty. Only about five weeks old and covered in ring worm so he had a few bald patches but otherwise he was in good health and a real little character. Helen was in love. INSTAGRAM POST 344. Dusty was the first of a few puppies who arrived in a short space of time. Obviously the puppies don't need walking but they are a handful. The pens constantly need cleaning out and obviously they need a lot of attention to try and socialise them early on. And who doesn't enjoy a puppy party? Buttons turned out to be amazing with puppies, she had such patience with them and let them get away with things the other dogs probably wouldn't. We think she liked playing with the puppies as due to her injuries she couldn't play properly with the other dogs.

As keen triathlon fans we couldn't turn down the chance to watch the Nevis triathlon. It had only been going for a couple of years and wasn't a big event but it made a nice change to our routine. Through Instagram we arranged to meet up with one of the competitors, a fellow Brit, his name was Nick Butter, and he was here with Nevis Naturally on a travel writing / PR capacity and taking part in the triathlon. Nick was preparing for his own adventure starting in January where he was hoping to break eight world records. An ultra-runner, Nick was planning to run a marathon in every country of the world in just 550 days, whilst raising money for prostate cancer. At the time of writing, Nick has successfully completed his epic challenge and wrote a book about his adventures, INSTAGRAM

POST 345. It was also a surprise to see a TV personality from the UK taking part. Jason Bradbury, a presenter on the Gadget show, and keen triathlete, was also here as part of the Nevis Naturally team. INSTAGRAM POST 346.

For a few days it was touch and go as to whether one of new puppies at the shelter would survive so it was a huge relief when it seemed she started to strengthen and it became clear she was going to pull through. Her story is very sad but it highlights the lack of knowledge from the locals when it comes to looking after dogs. Her mother was killed by poison just ten days after giving birth to a litter of puppies. All but one of the puppies died and the remaining one, this one, then became covered in ticks. Unsure how to treat ticks, which is a simple treatment of Frontline, the owner thought the best way to kill the ticks would be by dunking the poor puppy in a bucket of paraffin. Obviously she ingested it and became extremely poorly and it was lucky an expat smelt her and she realized what had happened. She then brought her to the shelter immediately but was in a very poor condition. Karen managed to wash out all of the paraffin but she smelt of it for days. A few times it looked like she wouldn't survive, but the little fighter did, we named her Lilly and she was a fantastic little puppy that was doted on by everybody. INSTAGRAM POST 347.

On the 14th November, just over one month since we returned to the shelter we walked Bluebell on a lead, outside the shelter gate just a short way up the road and back. It was such an amazing feeling, we were so proud of her. Ricky was a dog who when on a walk, he wasn't interested in any other dogs so we chose him to accompany her and he was great. Two days later Bluebell completed her first full lap, she would now be added to the walking list. It meant an extra lap for us but that didn't matter, she was walking on a lead and loving it. We would not have believed it was possible five weeks ago and yet here she was, unbelievable. One down, three puppies still to go, this was just the start, but it was a huge milestone.

As is usual at a dog shelter, there are highs like Bluebell walking on a lead, but there are also lows. Charlie, the lovely house pack dog who had skin cancer was put to sleep the day after Bluebell first walked outside. It was still important for us to occasionally have some time away from the shelter and with electricity problems becoming more of a regular occurrence Helen and I would enjoy some downtime on the beach. INSTAGRAM POST 348.

On our laps we regularly met people who lived on the route and we became friendly with a couple who lived further up the hill. Vernon and his partner were a lovely couple employed by the government to monitor the monkeys on the island. They are green vervet monkeys, originally brought to the island as pets in the 17th and 18th century. Some escaped and the rest is history. It was rumoured that there were more monkeys on Nevis than humans but Vernon told us the population of monkeys is around 7,500 compared to 11,000 humans. On our dog walks it was common to see monkeys most days, sometimes the troop would contain 20 or 30 monkeys and it is amazing how blasé you become about seeing them, especially when you see the Four Seasons guests drive by on a paid monkey sightseeing trip. Vernon invited Helen and I to join him one Sunday to visit the feeding stations scattered around the island. We collected all the unused fruit from the island's hotels and distributed it at various feeding tables around Nevis.

Towards the end of November Paul returned to Europe for three weeks so Helen and I were now busier than ever. We were back up to five laps each as well as looking after the puppies. Dusty and Lilly were now best friends and it was lovely to see them playing with each other. INSTAGRAM POST 349. The lady who found Dusty was the owner of a restaurant on the island called Bananas. As a thank you for looking after him she invited Helen and I for a free meal at the restaurant, a rare night out for us getting dressed up instead of watching Netflix with the Studio Crew. INSTAGRAM POST 350. Dusty was also getting along really well with Charlot. Dusty and Lilly would spend most afternoons in our studio after all the dogs were walked and they formed a great bond with Charlot and Buttons. INSTAGRAM POST 351. It was moments like these that made the busy days seem better.

The new workawayer was due on the 4th of December so we had a busy two weeks, and Karen also told us we could stay as long as we liked which eased the pressure slightly regarding Bluebell and the girls.

Vanessa arrived and she was instantly a huge help. She was German and spoke perfect English, she was fantastic with the dogs and immediately dived into the work at the shelter. With Vanessa here, we were now walking three laps each which gave us extra time again with Bluebell and her girls. They all warmed to Vanessa which was great to see. It was with a heavy heart that we said goodbye to Dusty as he was flying to the US to his new forever home. It was always sad to see a dog leave but that is what you hope for, to know that they are going away to a better life as someone's pet. On the 10th of December nearly a month after Bluebell, Star took her first walk outside the shelter on a lead, two days later she also managed a full lap. She did so well, as on her lap there were lots of distractions from cars, people and other stray dogs but she coped really well with all of it. Two down, two to go.

At this time of year back home, the popular TV show I'm a Celebrity, Get me Out of Here! was back on the screens and we noticed how much my charity clothes made me look like a contestant. INSTAGRAM POST 352.

Again a high is followed by a low, after waving goodbye to Dusty, Charlot was leaving on the same day as Star's full lap. INSTAGRAM POST 353. He was heading to Chicago for a better life. Charlot was the happiest dog we have ever known, he was the house pack clown and we loved him. Karen took him to the airport where he would meet his flight sponsor who would sign him in as their own before handing over to the new owners upon landing in Chicago. But it didn't happen, flight rules are that if the temperature is too low at the destination airport the dog cannot travel. It was December, Chicago is cold, Charlot was not going anywhere and that was probably his chance gone as winter would be around for a while in Chicago. We were genuinely sad to see Karen walk back through the gates with him, although he looked over the moon. He spent the night on the sofa back in the company of his studio crew.

Flight sponsors or volunteers are wonderful people. It is expensive for a shelter to pay travel costs for both a dog, and a person to accompany it to its destination. Sponsors step in to accompany the dog on the shelter's behalf. Their flight home is already paid for, so the sheler only has to pay the cost of animal transport. The sponsor has very little to do as someone from the shelter deals with all the paperwork and checking in. At the other end, the dog's new owner is waiting and you can feel proud knowing you have played a part in giving it a chance of a better life. If you wish to help out, contact shelters at your holiday destination and ask if they are looking for flight volunteers, it is that simple.

The shelter took in two more puppies and Vanessa took them both under her wing and doted on them for the rest of her stay. Rose and Violet were quite a handful and kept Vanessa very busy. As it was leading up to Xmas the shelter was also used for boarding kennels to house dogs whilst their owners went away for the holidays. The number had increased to over 40 and the shelter now seemed overcrowded but this provided an extra bit of income. On the downside, too many dogs can lead to tension. We had noticed the dogs were on edge more, and if one dog seems unstable it can have a knock on effect on all the others. The house pack never really got on with the shelter dogs and would occasionally rush the fences barking and growling through the pens. This was now happening more and more.

There was a bar just a five minute walk away that had been closed since we arrived but it had recently reopened, so Helen and I paid it a visit. It was called Gabriellas and Gabriella herself was originally from Leeds back home in England, but she had moved back to Nevis to be with her family and open the bar. She was really nice and we would use the bar quite often for a quiet beer in the evening after all the dogs had been fed, it was so convenient to have it just down the street. On the 16th of December Paul returned, he bought back some parcels of things we ordered. Helen needed a new insulin pen after one of dogs chewed hers, luckily we carried a spare. I ordered some new headphones as they also had been chewed by the dogs.

A couple of days later the house pack charged the fences again, I went to break it up and one of the house pack dogs bit me on the leg.

It was election time in Nevis. The shelter had no luck with the current government. There is no vet on the island for domestic animals, only livestock. Karen and Paul have been campaigning for years to have one as part of their larger project for new premises. Every time the government had rejected their proposal to build a proper dog shelter for the island and have an onsite vet. This had gone on for years, rejection after rejection. The government in the past refused to let World Vets on the island to carry out a free spay and neuter service which would help reduce the number of strays. If the current government stayed in power, Karen and Paul would face the same obstacles again for another term. Mark Brantley was the leader of the CCM Party and he was the person who Karen and Paul did not want to win as they had previously had plenty of run ins with him, and he was opposed to any of their ideas of a purpose built shelter on the island.

The results were in the next day and unfortunately as expected, Mark Brantley won and the future of the shelter looked bleak. Paul and Karen were resigned to giving up on the island they had called their home for years. Who could blame them? They would never achieve their dream with this government. We felt sorry for them, they had done so much for dogs on the island and rehomed nearly 700 dogs over the years. They had a plan to solve the issue on the island but no one would listen. Bridges were too badly burnt and they would never be rebuilt. The shelter would be no more, it was official, so the plan was to clear the shelter and rehome all of the current dogs. Karen and Paul would move back to Europe but obviously whilst the plan was to re-home the dogs, they would still take in any if they had to. This placed extra pressure on Helen and me to get Bluebell and her girls ready for adoption. They needed time we didn't have. It was nearly Xmas but it didn't feel like it, last year we were experiencing a white Xmas in British Columbia, now we were in shorts and t-shirts in 30 degree heat. Decorations were put up in Charlestown but they didn't help with our Xmas spirits. INSTAGRAM POST 354. Although on Xmas Eve, another milestone was reached, Coby, the second of Bluebell's pups managed a full lap outside the shelter. In just over two and a half months, we had manged to walk three feral dogs outside on a lead. Saffy, the remaining youngster was going to be difficult, she was far more timid and flighty than the other two, but we would keep persevering, we had to if the shelter was closing and the four dogs needed to be transported off the island. Xmas morning was a day off, sort of, we made sure Bluebell, Star and Coby all walked a full lap, we had to keep momentum up on these three. They were way behind the other shelter dogs in terms of confidence and dealing with other fears which they would have to face in the future, but we needed to help them prepare as best we could. After walking the dogs we then Skyped our families. Karen then cooked an amazing Xmas dinner. INSTAGRAM POST 355. Afterwards Paul and I headed down to Pinneys beach for a swim and a few beers. In the evening we all sat and watched a film together.

Boxing Day was horrible, after a normal morning of walking, Helen and I headed upstairs to get a bite to eat. Paul and Karen were sat watching TV and Vanessa was in her room with the two puppies. Stood in the kitchen, Helen and I heard some horrendous squealing. Something was happening outside in one of the pens and it didn't sound good. In a flash me and Helen were outside and heading for Mommas area. Bursting through the gate I could see she was being attacked by two other dogs. One of them was clamped on Momma's head and I had to use all my strength to prise the jaws open. Momma was in a real mess, there was blood everywhere from bites all over her body but the injury to the top of her head was worse. The top of her head was like a flap with a huge deep bite. We will never forget those cries. Immediately I segregated the two dogs that attacked Momma and Helen ran in to grab some towels and fetch Karen and Paul. I just sat with Momma, trying to comfort her and reassure her. I was just in shock but I felt so sorry for Momma, she was a real favourite of ours, such a friendly dog. Karen and Paul took over, in no time at all Paul had Momma in the van and heading down to the beach to take a speedboat across to the vets on St Kitts. We just hoped she would be ok. The atmosphere at the shelter had certainly been changing in the past couple of weeks as new dogs were arriving and unsettling the balance all around the different pens.

Just when we thought things couldn't get worse, the next day I had to intervene again on another dog on dog attack. A really cute little puppy we had named Billy was having garden time on his own in the side garden. Again I was upstairs in the house when I heard that now familiar horrible squeal. Without thinking again I was in the garden as soon as I could and found another dog with virtually the whole of Billy's head in his mouth. This dog had climbed an 8ft fence to escape and attack Billy. Karen arrived on the scene shortly after me. Again I managed to prise open the jaws to free Billy's head. In doing so I pierced my thumb on a tooth such was the strength of his jaws clamping down. Amazingly Billy was ok. There was a hole where the tooth had pierced his head, we managed to patch it up and fortunately there was no need for a trip across to the vets on St Kitts. Helen, myself and Vanessa were constantly on edge now, not knowing when the next attack might happen. We would be double checking the locks on the gates every time we went through them. We just wanted people to come back from holiday and take their dogs back to reduce the numbers. At the same time we needed to get more dogs adopted. My birthday was two days later, I Skyped my parents and my niece Emma who also had her birthday today. In the afternoon Helen and I headed out for a bite to eat and a few beers at Pinney's beach. It was nice to escape the madness of the shelter, even if it was just for a couple of hours. INSTAGRAM POST 356.

The days up to New Year were busy as normal. We had no plans for New Year's Eve anyway but the night before we had a new puppy arrival in our room to watch over and she had us up at 1am, 4am and 6am so when New Year's Eve did arrive we were sound asleep by the time the clock struck midnight.

Another new puppy arrived on New Year's Day, three weeks old, found on the side of the road, all of its siblings were next to it but sadly dead. INSTAGRAM POST 357. Unfortunately this little puppy didn't make it and died the next day. Even writing this I am thinking how many sad sights we witnessed in our time at the shelter. We spoke to Karen and Paul about it, you can only do what you can. You don't become immune to the pain and suffering either, you have to deal with it at the time and it's only on reflection afterwards that you really think about it. The island also was becoming worse for poisonings. The farmers blame stray dogs for killing and attacking livestock so leave out poisoned food. This also affects pets though, we had people bring their pets to the shelter that had been poisoned, Karen would try and induce vomiting as soon as possible but some of them died at the gates, as it was too late. There were cases of poisoned meat thrown into people's gardens in order to poison dogs that bark. We had to be extra careful when walking the dogs that they didn't pick up and eat anything during their walks. When things are bad, it was dogs like Lilly that made it all worthwhile, she was developing into an adorable little puppy and Karen found a little T shirt for her to wear. INSTAGRAM POST 358. This was one of the success stories, for a whole week we thought were going to lose her but she pulled though. That's why you celebrate the successes. In addition Momma was now back at the shelter, she was now part of the house pack during her recovery.

Our three-month visa was soon coming to an end so we would have to apply for an extension. There was a slight concern they would say no, what would happen to Bluebell and her girls? Vanessa had not been able to walk them yet. At the government offices, we filled out the paperwork and were told to return in a couple of days to get our passport stamped, we did and thankfully it was approved. On the way back I took a photo of a road sign. INSTAGRAM POST 359. For my birthday Karen and Paul bought me a t-shirt with this sign printed on the front. One day I found a dead tarantula outside the studio, they are called donkey spiders on Nevis. It was missing a leg but still covered most of my hand when I held it. INSTAGRAM POST 360.

January was probably our lowest month. Tensions were high, not only with the dogs but also the humans. Karen and Paul were obviously stressed about the closure of the shelter and their future away from the island. We had plenty of rows with Karen that month about nothing in particular. We all just had a shorter fuse. On our scale Helen and I were probabaly on a 2. That meant we should just leave, but we couldn't. We were committed to helping the dogs, especially Bluebell and her girls who basically had no chance without us. Things were so bad we stopped skyping our parents as often as normal because it would be obvious that we were not happy. A week into the New Year, Helen and I had nipped out to the shops in the afternoon and came back to carnage again. Guinness, one of the house pack had been bitten on the neck and blood was pouring out, he was almost choking on his own blood. I carried him down to the van so Karen could take him across to the vets on St Kitts. Supposedly it was a monkey that had attacked Guinness. I found the monkey, it was dead and I disposed of it. There was no blood in or around its mouth or anywhere else on its body. The house pack tends to spend time in and around the same places. Three of them, Pino, Kenya and Charlot liked to hang around in the front garden, as they were the ones who liked to run around a lot and were the fastest. Others lazed around upstairs. I believe what happened is that one of Charlot, Pino or Kenya caught and killed the monkey by breaking its neck. It probably came into the garden to steal some fruit but was too slow. Then the other house pack would have come charging down and that's when I think it would have turned nasty between them all. One of the other dogs had a limp from a bite and was acting very sheepishly which is why I think it was a dog not a monkey. Yet again we were on edge, the house pack seemed unsettled.

Whilst the other shelter dogs could easily be transferred to other shelters in the US, this wasn't going to be the case for Bluebell and her girls. Karen said they wouldn't cope with the situation like the other dogs and would need to go to a sanctuary rather than a shelter. As the month drew on Helen and I spent our afternoons and evenings emailing as many sanctuaries as we could. Direct flights to the US from Nevis only went to Florida, Charlotte and New York, so those were the areas we focused on. In the midst of all the madness at the shelter, it seemed a bit surreal when we saw a Rock and Roll legend on our walk. He was walking in the opposite direction when he passed us. I said to Helen that he looked like Roger Daltrey, the lead singer of The Who. The next day we met him again and I noticed he had a necklace with a guitar on the end. We saw him four days in a row and ended up having a chat with him. He was really nice and was interested in what we were doing at the shelter.

To add to our misery the unbelievable then happened, the house pack turned on Momma and she was attacked for the second time in two weeks. Vanessa, Helen and myself were in the kitchen with Karen who was talking. We were listening but then Helen and I just turned and looked at each other. The sound was familiar; Helen and I were instantly charging down the stairs into the garden. I was at the scene first. Momma was on the floor surrounded by about five of the house pack. I shouted at the top of my voice and chased the dogs away, Momma ran to Helen for protection.

Karen arrived with Vanessa. Autopilot kicked in again, segregate the dogs, towels for Momma, drive the van up to the house and get her across to the vets as soon as possible. It was just too much to take in that Momma had been attacked twice in two weeks. Two days later she was released from the vets and never returned to the shelter again, she was fostered by a couple of ex pats who did a great job doting on her. She eventually flew to the US where thankfully she is now in her forever home.

We were having no success in finding a suitable place to take on Bluebell. The situation was becoming desperate and the alternative was that Bluebell, Star, Coby and Saffy could be moved to an enclosure on a farmer's land on St Kitts, if the shelter would fund the cost of fencing. The quote for the fencing was $2,000, so completely out of reach. The alternative did not bear thinking about.

Vanessa was leaving, and with a real happy ending as she was flying to the US with the two puppies she became so attached to, Rose and Violet. They were going to their forever home and Vanessa was delivering them. We were really sad to see Vanessa go, her work ethic was amazing, she had helped out so much in her time on the shelter. She wasn't here for a holiday, she was here to work and she certainly did that. In her free time she hardly left the shelter, she would rather stay with the dogs instead. Since her departure we have stayed in touch and will continue to do so. Her time at the shelter had been nothing like she expected and it had been difficult for her (and for us) to deal with some of the things we had witnessed, it was entirely to her credit and strength of character that she had stayed and continued to work tirelessly every single day.

The day Vanessa left I had a big row with Karen over nothing, and then again the next day. We were all stressed. My journal that day, 23rd Jan read "Possibly at my lowest point now, I have no appetite and giving up on any hope for Bluebell. not cried for years but I could now. Hate seeing Helen so upset, it's killing me. But so proud of her, she is so much stronger than she thinks she is, couldn't love her any more at the moment." That evening we were joined by two new volunteers Rich and Laura.

Rich and Laura were from the England, they were really nice, and full of enthusiasm. They had experience of helping out charities and were really keen to help out on that side of things. The reality though was that they would be walking dogs and picking up poo like us. With the impending closure of the sanctuary Rich and Laura did help in ways to get the dogs off the island, sourcing of crates and sending info to possible partner shelters. On their second day I gave them a tour of the island and we stopped at Pinney's beach for a beer at Sunshine Bar.

The first week Rich and Laura were at the shelter, we showed them the ropes and spent time explaining the situation regarding Bluebell. Karen had mentioned that she could not afford to feed four volunteers so it looked like our time here was coming to an end. We wouldn't be able to help Bluebell and her girls get off the island. We were devastated after all the hard work we had put in and the progress they had made. They were comfortable around Rich and Laura so hopefully they could carry on working with them. The day came when we told Karen we would be leaving soon once we had booked our flights. The next day, the 4th of February, Paul took me, Rich and Laura out on his boat. It was a welcome distraction but all I could think about was Bluebell and her girls.

5th of February, my journal entry read the following. "Amazing! A sanctuary has agreed to take on Bluebell and her girls. It's called Mutley's Miracles in Florida. It sounds ideal and the owner sounds really nice. Looking at about six weeks which is the middle of March. Told Karen and Paul and they are fine with us to stay."

It was a miracle, they had a chance and we would be able to see it through. There was a lot of work still to do but we had a place for them, that was the most important thing. The relief was immense, we really thought we had resigned to passing the baton onto Rich and Laura. Mutley's Miracles did seem perfect, they specialised in nervous and difficult dogs and had a large amount of land for dogs to run around in. Katherine the owner seemed lovely when we chatted to her on the phone, she had years of experience dealing with dogs as nervous as these. Our prayers had been well and truly answered.

149

There was now a need to renew our Visa extension a second time, again we were slightly nervous that it might not be accepted but luckily there were no issues. That Friday night, Helen and I took Laura and Rich to Gabriellas where we enjoyed a few beers after a pretty stressful week. Life was never dull here. The next day we were just about to start feeding the dogs at 5pm when a call came in about a stranded pod of pilot whales on a beach not far from us. Helen stayed behind to carry on with feeding and the rest of us jumped in the van to go and help. When we arrived there were a lot of people helping out. A group of veterinary students from St Kitts had come over for a party but dropped everything to help out. We joined a line stretching from the sea to a stranded whale, passing containers of water, whilst others tried to secure a harness and load it onto a flatbed truck. We were doing this for about an hour before it was driven to the port where it would be released. Sadly most of the stranded whales died but a couple were saved.

The shelter was now on a mission to clear the shelter. It was also agreed that Helen and I would fly Bluebell and the girls to Miami ourselves. We actually had no real travel plans after Nevis anyway. Things were improving still with Bluebell and the girls, we were slowly trying to get them used to crates by placing their food bowls inside. This progressed so that we were able to close the door with Bluebell inside. These were small steps but absolutely necessary to build their confidence. They have never had any vaccinations and to travel to the US they needed them. That meant being put in a crate, driven to the beach, a boat over to St Kitts, drive to the vets, injections from a stranger and then the return journey back to the shelter. This would need to happen twice as they would need two sets of injections. All of this would be a harrowing experience for them. Helen and I took Bluebell and Star to the beach one day to get them used to being in a car, we also walked on a different route just to get them out of their comfort zone. Crate training was also practised outside in the garden, not in their pen, as this is where they would be loaded into the van. For every scenario we thought about out how we could prepare them for it.

Towards the end of February was Laura's birthday, it was a fun evening at the shelter with lots of nice food and I overindulged on Carib and Rum. I was sick the following morning and dog walking in the heat was difficult.

The view from the shelter looks out towards the sea, and there is a large hill in the distance called Saddle Hill. Every day we woke up to the view of this hill but had never visited it. So one Sunday afternoon Helen and I decided to pay it a visit and walk to the top. It was a really enjoyable walk and gave a different perspective of the island to the one we were so used to. INSTAGRAM POST 361.

The shelter was now in full fundraising mode, we were asked to appeal to friends and family for donations, some of whom very kindly did. INSTAGRAM POST 362. Helen and I just carried on as normal, we had a rough date to work to and there was also the small matter of how we were going to get them from Miami airport to Malabar up the coast about three hours away. Hiring a van would be extra cost the shelter didn't have, and neither of us fancied pulling out the airport in a big van at night after a long stressful day. I therefore started to look into volunteer animal transport groups in the US to see if they may be able to help on the second part of the journey.

Seven dogs went out in one day. Karen took them all to Miami with some help from flight sponsors. Three little puppies in addition to Royale, Joey, Julio and Lilly, they were all leaving. As sad as we were to see Lilly go, we were really happy for her. After everything she went through it was so special watching her grow up. INSTAGRAM POST 363. After walking the dogs in the morning we always played with the puppies and Lilly, she quickly bonded with Buttons and as such became part of Studio Crew. In the afternoons she loved to come in and fall asleep underneath the bed and wait around for titbits from our lunch. She made these really cute little noises and she was definitely a favourite at the shelter. It makes it all worthwhile when you know that she is now part of someone's family in the US.

When Paul sold his boat, the fact the shelter would be no more seemed very real, they were making their own plans for the future and they would be heading back to Europe in a week for a scouting mission, leaving the four of us alone to run the shelter. A date was booked for Bluebell and the girls to receive their first round of medication. In the week leading up to it, we intensified the crate training. It was still a bit hit and miss at the moment, especially with Saffy who we still hadn't been able to walk on a lead yet. The day before, the weather turned and created large swells between St Kitts and Nevis. Although Paul had sold his boat, it hadn't actually changed hands. With his experience, he knew he needed to move the boat, which he did. Others weren't so wise and a couple of boats sank as a result. It was another three days before ferries resumed between the islands and the big day arrived for Bluebell and the girls to take their first trip off Nevis.

That day we were up 5.45am to let them have a run around in the front garden and go to the toilet, before we tried to coax them into the crates. It worked, all four were in. Rich was kindly up early to help, so with the dogs in the crates, he came down to help load them into the van. Then Paul drove us down to catch the ferry, me up front with him and Helen sat in the back with the girls. We had arranged to catch the 7am ferry as it is the only one that runs pretty much on time as it is the first one of the day. We arrived at the vets at 8am. The vet was really helpful, instead of unloading the dogs she agreed to administer the injections through the side of the crates. Helen climbed into each crate one at a time so the dogs would be up against the side and the vet could make the injections. After filling in the paperwork, meaning now the dogs officially belonged to us, we were done in half an hour and heading to catch the next ferry back. Everything went so smoothly, all the patience and practise had paid off, it was a major step in getting these dogs off the island permanently. Back at the shelter, Rich and Laura were waiting for us to see how it all went, they were delighted with the news. They kindly took on the entire dog walking that morning whilst we were away. That afternoon Helen and I walked down to Gabriellas to celebrate with a couple of Caribs.

The next day Karen and Paul flew back to Europe for two weeks leaving the four of us to run the shelter on our own. Whilst the duties at the shelter carried on as normal, life was a lot more relaxed and less stressful with just the four of us. With just four weeks until Bluebell and the girls would be flying out, we ramped up the training. There was the little matter of a return to the vets to contend with first. Then Rich and Laura had an idea. There was a retired vet who lived just up the road from shelter. One morning when I was walking the dogs I stopped to chat with him and asked if he could help us out. If the vets on St Kitts agreed to it, would he administer the injections for us? That way we wouldn't have to put the dogs through the stress of another trip across the islands. He kindly agreed, as did the vets when we phoned them. Two days later Helen and I made the trip across to collect the vaccinations. Another two days later we were all set to do this at the shelter. The time was arranged for him to come at 11am, that way all the dogs would have been walked and the girls would have had a good 30 minute run around in the front garden. That allowed us enough time to coax them into the crates ready for his arrival. All planned to run smoothly, except he walked through the gates 30 minutes early whilst they were still in the garden. This spooked them all massively as expected. I asked him to wait upstairs out of sight whilst we tried to get them in the crates. It was tricky but Bluebell, Star and Coby all went in. Unsurprisingly, Saffy was spooked the most and went running back to her pen. The injections were quickly given to the three in the crates but the issue was going to be with Saffy. She was terrified, and hiding at the back of her pen. The easiest option was just for me to go in and pick her up and hold her whilst the injection was given to her. It certainly wasn't the way we had planned the morning to go, but it was over. The girls were now officially allowed to fly to the US.

On the Sunday Laura, Helen and I were up early to support Rich who was taking part in the cross channel swim from Nevis to St Kitts. Laura jumped on the boat to meet Rich on the other side and Helen and I returned to look after the shelter for the day.

One day we received a call from an American holiday maker called Erin regarding a puppy she had found. Erin had been out walking and the puppy had appeared from nowhere and started following her. She had fallen in love with it and asked us to look after it whilst she looked into the possibility of adopting her and taking it back to the US. Rich and Laura became good friends with Erin during her stay and Erin was obviously very passionate about animals and wanted to help in getting the remaining dogs off the island through her contacts in the US. She would also help out as a flight sponsor for some dogs on her return flight.

Rich was stopped by the police the next day in the van and as he had not applied for a license, he was fined 150 ECD which is about £50. The problem was that I had never applied either when we returned and the van was very recognisable. I wasn't going to take the risk of being caught, especially as now our second visa extensions had also run out. It was too close to flying the girls out, we weren't going to jeopardise any chance of getting them out. Paul and Karen arrived back the next day and the evacuation plan continued, we were planning on leaving in about ten days. Our hopes were lifted in that there was a man with a private plane on a neighbouring island who was planning on flying to the US and there was a chance Helen, myself and the girls could join him. That would have meant not having to travel across and check in on St Kitts, but instead fly from the smaller Nevis airport. In landing we could also avoid the busy Miami airport and use a quieter private airport nearer to Mutley's Miracles in Malabar. Unfortunately that didn't work out and we were going to have to do it the hard way. This added to the pressure in that we still hadn't sorted ground transport out from Miami to Malabar and it looked increasingly likely that we would have to hire a van ourselves. It was now the 4th of April, almost a year since we arrived in the Caribbean. That day we booked our flights to Miami, and a volunteer animal transport charity came to our rescue. Wings on Wheels had managed to find a driver who would meet us at Miami airport and transfer all of us in his van up to Mutley's Miracles. This was amazing news. A few weeks ago we never even knew charities such as this existed but they do a wonderful job of transporting animals across the country. The organisation is amazing as some of trips require dozens of people driving different legs to hand the animal over to the next driver in a relay to deliver it to its destination.

We would be leaving in two days. We had spent six months at the shelter, far longer than we imagined, but we made a commitment to help Bluebell and her girls and stuck to it. It might seem crazy to people looking from the outside but this was something we wanted to do. Time in the Caribbean to others should be seen as relaxing, but ours was far from it. We knuckled down to work for our six months on Nevis and probably really only had a couple of days where we didn't do anything. The work was hard physically, but emotionally it was far harder than we ever imagined. It really wears you down seeing some horrible sights of mistreatment, especially as you are surrounded by the shelter 24 hours a day. It is all encompassing, there is no let up. We don't know how Karen and Paul managed it for so long especially with the uphill struggle against the government in opposing any of their plans.

On our day of departure, the dogs were walked as usual, all our packing was done the previous night. The girls were put in their crates at 11.30am and loaded onto the van. We said goodbye to all of the remaining dogs especially Charlot and Buttons then thanked and said goodbye to Paul. Rich was coming with us to help with the loading and unloading. We hugged and said goodbye to Laura, we were all emotional, we had only spent six weeks together but had been through so much in that short space of time. They were going to be spending a couple more weeks here, they too had committed themselves to helping out as long as possible with the view of continuing onto the US and flight sponsoring as many dogs as possible.

With Karen driving, we pulled out of the shelter gates for the last time. Instead of taking the car ferry we had decided to take the quicker option by crossing via the speedboat. Here we said goodbye to Karen, as Rich, Helen and I made the crossing with the dogs. On St Kitts we were met by our pre-arranged taxi van that then drove us to the airport. The process of checking dogs in at the airport is not easy, especially with dogs as nervous as these. Karen had explained the process in detail to us many times beforehand. After all the paperwork at the desk, we are then required to take the dogs out of the crates so the crate can go through an x-ray machine. The x-ray machine is in a room behind the check-in desk. Once the crate goes through the machine, the dog can be placed back inside and the crate closed, making it extra secure with cable ties. With any confident socialised dog, this still may seem slightly daunting but this was going to worse for these girls. This was the point where Helen and I were most nervous, we had talked about this moment so many times. With Rich we had come up with a plan to try and make things run smoothly. Helen opens the crate door I pull the dog out the crate on one of two leads attached just in case, with Helen holding the other. Picking her up, Helen then places a towel around the dog, in case she starts kicking and scratches us in the process. Not once did we think the girls would bite, in these situations they tend to just shut down though fear rather than fight or flight. Once I have the dog in my arms, Helen makes sure the leads are out of the way so I don't trip over them and Rich immediately picks up the crate and takes it through to the x-ray machine. I follow behind carrying the dog. Once we are in the room, Rich feeds the crate in to the machine, we walk round to the other side until it comes out and I place the dog back in then and then secure with cable ties. Job done, easy. The order was to be Bluebell, Star, Coby and then Saffy. Most confident first. Bluebell, Star and Coby went through fine. Then came Saffy, this was the one we were always concerned about, the most frightened of them all. She didn't want to come out of her cage so I had to pull her out. As she was the last one, Helen would carry the crate and Rich and I would shuffle behind with Saffy held in between us both. Saffy did not struggle at all, she shut down as expected and didn't move a muscle. They were through. All four were now being transferred onto the tarmac to be loaded up onto the plane. The airport staff then told us we needed to go through to the gate immediately. With barely anytime to say goodbye to Rich we hugged him and thanked him for his help before being ushered along by the staff. The whole airport process went just as we planned and it was so much easier having his help. It wasn't long before we were taking off and leaving the Caribbean behind. Almost a year ago we arrived in the Caribbean. Never in our wildest dreams did we think we would be here for this long, let alone have four dogs registered to us under our names and flying back north to the US. Whenever we used to finish a house sit or a workaway Helen and I would always say to each other "another chapter done" Although this was another big moment in our travels, it wasn't completely over as we still had to deliver the girls. There was no reflection time whilst we were in the air, we were concerned about other things, hoping the dogs were ok in the hold, what would we have to face at Miami airport and would Wings on Wheels be waiting for us?

Looking back now, ours wasn't a typical Caribbean experience, I suppose you could say Bequia was as we lived on a stunning little island for nearly three months. In Grenada we were probably too isolated to truly appreciate it and Nevis was mostly all work. The first time on Nevis was more relaxed and we enjoyed Nevis as a Caribbean island, on our return it was completely different. We learnt the difficulties Karen and Paul faced over the years and how it had forced them to abandon their plans for the island. It is a real shame the shelter had to close as the island really needs the help. The people on the island are not dog people, most see them as guard dogs and nothing else. They are scared of them and therefore they are fed scraps and not looked after. There is obviously a cost that comes with looking after a dog so it seems easier to some to simply abandon a dog that has fleas, ticks or ringworm. A dedicated shelter and vets on the island would have helped enormously but sadly it was not to be, and education for the younger generation of looking after and treating dogs was going to be part of Karen and Paul's plans. This is not isolated to the Caribbean, it happens all over the world, it was here though where we experienced it first-hand working for a non-profit charity. After all of that though, Helen and I look back at our time in the Caribbean with great fondness, and even though there were some major low points there were some awesome memories that will stay with us forever. I was also pretty useful with a machete by the time we left.

A few hours after taking off from St Kitts the wheels were touching down in the busy airport of Miami. We were back on US soil.

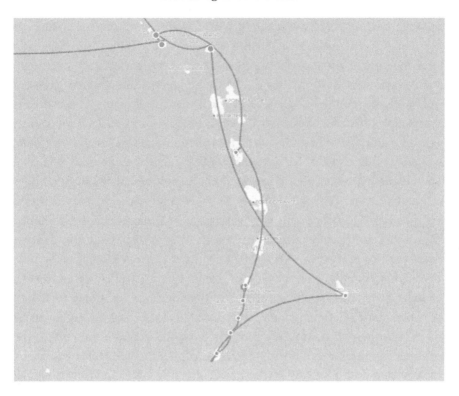

PART 4 - USA (AGAIN)

Our flight landed at 7.15pm. Miami airport is busy due to its location, it is the largest US gateway for Latin America and the Caribbean and also America's third busiest airport for International passengers. That meant queues. It seemed to take ages to go through security and immigration. All the time we were wondering what was happening to the girls. When we eventually made it through to baggage collection we asked at a desk where we would be able to pick them up. They pointed in a general direction so we started walking. Then we noticed the crates, they were just lined up in the middle of the crowded baggage collection hall, not even up against the wall, just sat in the middle with hundreds of people walking past with some occasionally peering inside. Who knows how long they were sat there or what was going through their minds? We rushed over and immediately tried to reassure them. Helen stayed with them, whilst I collected our backpacks. I then found an employee who returned with a large trolley so we loaded them up. He then led us through all of the checks with the dogs, fortunately they didn't need to come out of the crates but it still took a long time before we eventually walked out into the arrivals hall. Almost immediately a guy introduced himself to us as Jim from Wings on Wheels. It was such a relief to see him. He told us to wait out front whilst he went and fetched the van. The van wasn't large enough to fit all four crates in, so the girls would have to double up for the trip to Malabar. I sat up front with Jim and Helen sat in the back with girls, the crate doors open so she could stroke them. They seemed remarkably calm which was a relief. Malabar was 175 miles north up the Florida coast, the journey would take us three hours, eventually pulling up to the gates of Mutley's Miracles at 11pm. We were met by Katherine the owner. She was an elderly lady in a motorised wheelchair and she directed us to their new pen. It was a large octagon close to the main house. Jim drove the van as close as he could and kept the lights on so we could see what we were doing. We let the girls out and stayed with them for a few minutes to get used to their new home. It was getting late now, and Jim needed to get going. It was a huge help from Wings on Wheels to sort out ground transport and we were deeply thankful to Jim. Katherine showed us to our room and we crashed out on our separate single beds after a very long and stressful day. But the girls were here, they had made the trip and were now on US soil at their new sanctuary.

We were up early for our first morning at the sanctuary. Katherine had an assistant called Debbie, but she wasn't here as she was on her vacation. A young guy called Aaron was walking around filling up feeding bowls and moving dogs around. We checked in on the girls. They seemed fine, especially after we gave them some breakfast. It seemed as though dogs were everywhere. Aaron was moving dogs that spend the night in cages in the garage or the house to their outside pens for the day. I tried counting and think there were at least 50 dogs altogether. After some breakfast Helen and I explored the property, it was large, there were also about a dozen horses with stables on the property. The first thing that struck us is that there weren't many people here compared to the amount of animals. Like all shelters, money is scarce and they rely heavily on volunteers. In the afternoons, volunteers or school children who need to volunteer some time to help as part of their curriculum came to help. They walked the dogs that were moved outside in the morning and put them back in their cages for the evening. We had our first catch up with Katherine, she was lovely and obviously had a lot of experience with dogs. She made her first assessment of the girls and explained they can be helped but it would take time. She mentioned how it would be great if we could stay for a while and help with transitioning the girls to become familiar with other people, as for starters she didn't want them spooked. That was fine by us but it became clear that Katherine wanted us to stay longer than we had planned, about six months longer. We expected two to three weeks and then let the experts take over. But we couldn't stay here for six months. Our visa only lasted for three months anyway. Katherine showed us a dog that used to be scared of people and said it took them two years to grow her confidence. It was clear that Katherine knew her stuff, but her health wasn't great and she spent a lot of time in bed as a result. That just left Debbie with about 50 dogs. Helen and I were starting to become a little concerned that the shelter simply didn't have the human resources to help the girls, we certainly didn't think it would take two years. Even as early as that first day, our hearts were saying this place was great for the girls, but our heads were saying it wasn't. It was an amazing gesture by Katherine to say they would take the girls in, but that's what charities do, they take dogs on even when they are full themselves and don't have the resources. A lot of the dogs at Mutley's Miracles were dogs that were given up by owners and have issues, some were on their way to be put down but they were taken in. When time was convenient and there were no dogs running around, we would take the girls out for a walk, even Saffy. She wasn't on a lead but because the grounds were fully enclosed she was able to walk and run alongside us. INSTAGRAM POST 364. This photo was their first time at the lake, and they loved it. The crazy thing was that we were stressing and thinking this was probably not the place for them after all, but they were loving it. The reason why though was because we were walking them, if we were not there, they would not be walked and spend all their time in the octagon.

The next day we spoke to Rich and Laura and discussed our concerns and they said they would have a chat with Erin, the holidaymaker from Nevis who asked us to look after the puppy. Debbie also arrived back at the shelter, she was really nice and we spent a bit of time together on that day, walking other dogs and fixing pens and shelters.

It turned out Erin really wanted to help us out and was doing all she could to see if she could find anywhere else for the girls. Speaking by Skype, she could understand our predicament in leaving the girls here. In those first two or three days, we managed to fit some time in with Katherine looking at the girls. They seemed to be doing well, but again, our hopes could not be lifted too much as it was us who was developing them under Katherine's guidance. They would have a lot less frequent training and development in our absence. Towards the back of the shelter there was an enclosed field, much larger than a football pitch and all securely fenced. When possible we would take the girls into this field and let them all run freely. Moving the dogs around in the morning started around 8am so Helen and I started getting up just before 7am to allow them to have an hours run around in the field before the house and shelter started to stir.

Karen also made contact. Over the last few weeks, there was interest from a shelter in Wichita, Kansas for both Buttons and Charlot. The place had a great rehabilitation centre that would be ideal for Buttons with her hip and leg. Charlot was liked for just being Charlot. When we knew the girls were heading to Florida we told Karen, if you recieve confirmation and can get Buttons and Charlot to Miami, we would drive them ourselves to Wichita. Wichita is in the middle of the US. There are no direct flights going anywhere near, so it would have meant additional internal flights. That's when we offered to take them on a road trip ourselves should it become a certainty there was a place for them. When Karen confirmed there was a place for them, we were so happy they would be leaving the island and we would be dropping them off ourselves. Charlot and Buttons would be flying into Miami in two weeks time.

Meanwhile back on the shelter, when not helping out with the other dogs we were spending all of our time with the girls. Not long ago on Nevis we had noticed a change in Star, she was becoming more dominant over her two sisters, Coby and Saffy. Here at Malabar it seemed to be increasing. Bluebell, the mother didn't intervene. Katherine explained that Bluebell was basically done looking after her girls and Star was stepping up to be the dominant female. One day Debbie asked if we wanted to take Bluebell and Star along to an obedience class in town. They were fine travelling in the van, but it was a real struggle to get them inside the building. Once in there, they were fine with all the other dogs and owners, they were not taking part in the class, they were just there to introduce them to new surroundings. They loved the huge mirrors and looking at themselves and they both ended up falling asleep. Karen messaged and said she had booked us all in at a hotel next to Miami airport.

There was another phone call with Erin, she told us she was good friends with both the CEO and the Head Vet at Richmond SPCA and she had been talking to them about the possibility of taking in the girls. Helen and I were really unsure on what we should do. Rich, Laura and Erin would be heading there themselves in a week as this was where Erin was taking her Nevis rescue pup to be checked out. However this was a city centre dog shelter. Would this be ok for them? Would they be better to remain here for a long period of rehabilitation or do they just need to go to a big shelter in the hope that they are adopted as soon as possible. Officially we still owned the girls and they were our responsibility. We were leaning towards

Richmond and that night decided if they were accepted that is where they would go.

The next day, Erin confirmed that Richmond SPCA had agreed to take the girls. It was mixed emotions, after leaving Nevis we had hoped that everything would be ok for them but it hadn't quite turned out like that. Their journey was still not complete and we had to make sure it would end positively for them. Erin had arranged for us to have a Skype conversation with the head vet, Dr Ivey. She was lovely and immediately put us at ease about Richmond. She explained what would happen when they arrive, how they would be kept separate from all of the other dogs with only a small team of specialist workers looking after them. They would have all their jabs upon arrival, tests for Heartworm and be spayed. Richmond had a very impressive adoption rate as well which was encouraging and obviously all persons and homes are vetted prior to adopting a dog. When we told Katherine the news that we would be moving the girls to Richmond, she was pleased for us, there was never going to be any resentment. We would always be forever grateful to Katherine for accepting them in the first place, that allowed us to get them off Nevis. But the reality was Mutley's was under resourced and just didn't have as many potential adoption opportunities. But the people who own these shelters, like Katherine, do not like to turn any dogs away, so they will still say yes in taking them in. And for that we were extremely grateful.

Charlot and Buttons were arriving on the 24th, meaning we needed to hire a vehicle to drive the girls up to Richmond, and get back down to Miami, so we had about a week left at Mutley's miracles. The distance from Mutley's to Richmond, in Virginia SPCA was 790 miles, roughly the same as driving from London to Edinburgh and back. We would have to do it all in one go, passing through the states of Georgia, South Carolina and North Carolina, which meant we would leave early evening and arrive first thing in the morning. In all it would take about 12 hours of driving. The plan would be for us to spend the night in Richmond and then drive the 12 hours, 790 miles back to Mutley's. An overnight stay at Mutley's then another drive south back down to meet Karen with Charlot and Buttons in Miami. There was then the small matter of a 1,600 mile road trip halfway

163

across the country to deliver them to their foster home. There would be a lot of driving over the next couple of weeks. Rich and Laura had made it to New York after flying from in Nevis with seven dogs, including three puppies. They were heading down to Richmond SPCA with Erin to take a couple of dogs there to receive all of their medical treatment. Along with Erin's rescued puppy, now called Olivia they had another dog called Pepper. Pepper was a lovely dog who hadn't been at the shelter that long, he had a machete injury to his back left thigh.

Five days before our date to leave with the dogs, as usual we were out early with them in the field at 7am, when there was a fight between Bluebell's girls. It seemed that Coby and Saffy had enough of Star and her dominance and attacked her. Luckily we were close by and they weren't at the other end of the field at the time. I jumped in and picked Star up. She had sustained some bite wounds on her back left leg and Coby had a bite mark under her chin and near her eye. Bluebell wasn't involved and didn't step in at all. That was the end of the session, we put Bluebell, Coby and Saffy back in the octagon and Star came back to our room. A spare crate was set up in the corner of the room whilst we checked over her wounds again, they were ok and she wouldn't need to go to the vets. For us, it was sad to witness, we had seen them go through so much together but the reality was Star would not be left alone in the same run as her sisters again, but these things happen. If they had stayed at the sanctuary instead of going to Richmond, by now Star would have ended up in the crates in the garage with the other dogs. In the days leading up to the departure we carried on helping around the sanctuary, Aaron and I spent one morning putting up a fence and we also cleared away fallen branches and dead wood.

Another day, Debbie and I took Bluebell and one of her dogs to the beach. She did really well, not only in the van, but also on the crowded beach, probably a relief to be away from her daughters for the day. Mutley's Miracles is only about 30 miles from Cape Canaveral, so we were delighted when Katherine told us there was going to be a rocket launch. Katherine has seen lots over the years but she came out and showed us exactly whereabouts over the trees we would see it appear. INSTAGRAM POST 365.

The day before departure we booked our hire car, it was a people carrier and all the back seats could fold down so we would be able to fit the crates inside. On the actual day we decided to set off at 8.15pm. Prior to that we made sure the girls all had a good run around, separately now from Star, and then fed them. An hour or so later we let them have another session in the field to make sure they went to the toilet as they would be spending the next 12 hours in their crates. Loading the girls into the crates and then the car was no issue so we said a quick goodbye to Katherine and Debbie as we would be back in two days. Helen and I obviously took turns to drive all the way to Richmond, the girls were fine, it helped driving at night as they settled down and went to sleep. 790 miles later we drove into the parking lot at Richmond SPCA, it was a huge building, and it was surprising to see so many staff around considering it was a Sunday. The girls were brought inside in their crates and we filled out some paperwork, this was to officially hand the girls over to the SPCA. The lady we met who was in charge of looking after the girls was Jackie, she was the Behaviour Director. We immediately warmed to her and she put us at ease. The girls were then transferred to their own room in which there were six large pens. For now they were split into pairs, Coby and Saffy, and Bluebell and Star. It wasn't long before they all were all given two rounds of injections and then some food. The room was ideal for them, only certain employees of the SPCA would be allowed in the room so as not to spook the dogs and a sign was put on the door outside saying so. The staff designated to look after the girls were really sweet and gentle with them. In total we were probably there for about an hour, it was still early on a Sunday morning. Our accommodation for the night was supposed to be a Couchsurf but we cancelled it and ended up booking into a motel near the shelter. It was still too early to check in, so we went and had a McDonalds breakfast. Over breakfast we were again agonising if we had made the right choice for them, they all looked nervous, was it all too much too soon for them? Would they have been better to stay at Mutley's Miracles. It was too late anyway now, we had signed the papers and handed them over. The girls were now part of the SPCA and we had to trust that they were now in expert hands and they could carry on where we left off and hopefully find them all a forever home. This feeling stayed with us all day, after checking in at the motel and getting a bit of sleep we went for a walk with the same thoughts running through our minds.

The next morning we were back at the SPCA. This time we were met by Dr Ivey, the main vet we had chatted to via Skype, who then took us to see the girls. They seemed to be ok, nervous obviously as expected but it was good to see them again, and we sensed the feeling was mutual. We also met Robin Starr who was the CEO of the shelter. Robin and Dr Ivey gave us a tour of the facility. They took us down to the pre surgery area where Olivia and Pepper were waiting to be spayed and neutered. On the top floor of the shelter, there was a huge exercise area. There was no doubt that the SPCA was an amazing facility and very professional. It was agreed that we could return after transporting Charlot and Buttons and help out for a few days with the girls. Before leaving, Dr Ivey and Robin took us down to see the girls again, they reassured us that we had done the right thing and they could help the dogs gain confidence and find them all homes. It would take us ten days to collect Charlot and Buttons, drive them across the country and return to Richmond. It was exactly what we needed to hear before we set off for the 790 mile return journey to Mutley's Miracles. The journey took a little longer as there was a lot of rain driving back and we arrived 13 hours later at 10pm and went straight to bed.

The next morning we were up helping Debbie with the chores of feeding, moving the dogs around and cleaning out the crates. Karen would be landing early afternoon so we had to leave at lunchtime to drive back down to Miami. We had a really nice chat with Katherine and Debbie, they were genuinely happy the girls were taken in at SPCA and agreed they would do well with specialist dedicated trainers helping them. In the time we had spent at Mutley's, Katherine had shared so much of her knowledge and experience with us, we learnt so much from her. It felt strange to leave them and they will never understand how much they actually helped us. All those nights in Nevis when Helen and I were emailing shelters to see if they would take in the girls only to face reply after reply of declines. Katherine gave the girls the lifeline to get off the island, and even though

166

her shelter was not "the one", she provided us with the all-important stepping stone into the US. As a thank you we gave them a donation for all of their help.

Sadly less than a year after we left Mutley's Miracles, Katherine passed away in March 2019. The shelter would be closing and they were desperately appealing for help in transferring the dogs into other shelters or for adoption. Debbie was mourning the loss of her friend of more than 20 years whilst at the same time trying to find suitable new places for the remaining animals.

The drive down to Miami was awful with torrential rain and thunderstorms. After checking in at the hotel, we drove the short distance to the airport, parked up and waited in arrivals for Karen and the dogs. After the last couple of weeks it was great to see Charlot and Buttons, we had missed them so much. Back at the hotel, we dropped Karen off at her room and took the dogs back to our room for the night. It was good to think that we were going to deliver Charlot and Buttons to their foster home, and even better that they would be in it together to keep each other company. The next morning we had an early start, Karen and I drove to a shipping company who would be sending the crates back to Nevis. Back at the hotel we all had a big breakfast before loading up the car ready to set off on our road trip Wichita. Karen took our photo before we set off. INSTAGRAM POST 366. I'm wearing the "Monkey Xing" t-shirt Karen gave me for my birthday. The fourth photo showed our route, we would be leaving Florida and driving through the states of Georgia, Alabama, Mississippi, Arkansas, Missouri before reaching Wichita in Kansas, about 1,650 miles in total. After saying our final goodbyes to Karen we were on the road for 11.30am and heading north to Ocala, still in Florida. Buttons and Charlot were great travellers. Charlot used to be sick in the car when we took him to the beach on Nevis but it seemed he had grown out of his travel sickness. There was lots of room now in the car, for both of them to lie on the floor and enough for whoever wasn't driving to also lie down in the back and have a nap. Every so often we would stop for a toilet break or find a park where they could stretch their legs. Charlot was keen to explore everywhere but Buttons was always ready to go back to the safety of the car.

Day two of the road trip and Oxford in Alabama was our destination, about 450 miles away. Spending time with Buttons and Charlot took our minds off the girls and how they were getting on at Richmond. America has plenty of dog exercise areas so there no shortage of places to take them as a break from the driving. INSTAGRAM POST 367.

Another 300 miles on day three and we had already reached Memphis. INSTAGRAM POST 368. It would not have been right to be in Memphis without making a trip to Graceland, home of Elvis Presley. We had read that if you arrived early then there was no admission fee to pay and you could walk around the gardens and still be able to visit Elvis' grave. INSTAGRAM POST 369. Unfortunately dogs were not allowed on the property so we had to take it in turns to stand outside with Charlot and Buttons, but all of the walls were adorned with messages and tributes from fans so there was plenty to read. I'll be the first to admit we are not massive Elvis Presley fans but it was an enjoyable morning having a look around, and it was obvious how much Elvis was adored as the place was busy with fans from all over the world coming to pay their respects. Leaving Memphis, our next destination was 350 miles away in Joplin, however we weren't driving on the highways now so the speed restrictions on the road were reduced. All the time on Nevis, Charlot and Buttons were part of the house pack right from when they were puppies so they never socialised with any other dogs. Now here in the US we realised how important socialisation and experiencing things at early age is so crucial for dogs. Charlot is a lovely, friendly sociable boy but in a dog park when in the presence of other bigger dogs he was nervous, he didn't know how to react. It made us think how we could have done more whilst on Nevis to help dogs once they step outside of the bubble of the shelter. Rescuing and rehoming is essential, but the middle part, rehabilitation is also so important and requires time, patience and resources.

On our final day we were only 184 miles from Wichita so it was shorter day of driving. After checking in the motel we took them for a really enjoyable walk around Pawnee Prairie Park. After dinner we went back to the park to enjoy our last walk with two of our favourite dogs. Once we knew Bluebell and the girls were going to America we knew there might be a chance that we could make this trip with Buttons and Charlot. it was something we always wanted to do. After Nevis we didn't really have any concrete plans of where our travels would continue onto. This was a part of our travels, it wasn't a diversion, it was something we really wanted to do and we were really pleased that it was us who could personally deliver them to Wichita. Every night of our six month second stay on Nevis, Charlot and Buttons stayed in our room, they were the founding members of the Studio Crew so it was fitting that we all ended the journey together.

The following morning was a short drive to the Northbridge Vet practise to meet Ashley as arranged. She was lovely and confirmed to us that both Buttons and Charlot would be staying together in foster with Kansas K9 rescue's founder. It was really sad to say goodbye to the pair of them but again it was a goodbye that would hopefully lead to better lives. INSTAGRAM POST 370.

It was now time to start heading back East to Richmond. Leaving the vets at 9.30am, we managed to reach Wentzville, just west of St Louis, a total of 400 miles. That included stopping at Tallgrass Prairie National Reserve on the way for a couple of hours to see the bison. INSTAGRAM POST 371. Without needing to exercise any dogs, the next day we managed a really good driving distance covering 560 miles, arriving in Knoxville, Tennessee. That included a stop at a city called Cairo in Illinois thanks to a recommendation from a friend. INSTAGRAM POST 372 and INSTAGRAM POST 373. Cairo used to have a population of 15,000, now it is only 2,000. Economic and racial tensions in the past have almost reduced Cairo to a ghost town. Driving around the deserted city, sometimes it felt as though we were driving around an eerie apocalyptic film set as everywhere we looked there were crumbling buildings and boarded up houses. It was a fascinating hour just cruising around taking it all in.

Knoxville sat just west of the Great Smokey Mountains in the southern Appalachian Mountains and this was an area we wanted to pay a visit. Our USA guide had mentioned how stunning the scenery was here and it was right. There was a reason it appeared in the top 25 list. INSTAGRAM POST 374. The Smokey Mountains also have a famous road called the Blue Ridge Parkway, also mentioned in the book as one the most scenic drives in the US. It stretches for 470 miles through the states of North Carolina and Virginia. It was too good an opportunity not to miss so we drove about 70 miles taking in the sights of the Smokey Mountains before attempting the strenuous Mt Pisgah hike, allowing amazing 360 degree views. INSTAGRAM POST 375 and INSTAGRAM POST 376. That evening we spent the night at Mt Airy.

The next day we continued for a while on the Parkway, then after stopping for lunch we decided to find somewhere to stop off for a walk. INSTAGRAM POST 377. We had continued to read a lot of books on hiking the great trails in the US including some on the Appalachian Trail. This is one of the great long distance trails in the US. Approximately 2200 miles in length, it stretches from Georgia in the South, passing through North Carolina, Tennessee, Virginia, West Virginia, Maryland, Pennsylvania, New Jersey, New York, Connecticut, Massachusetts, Vermont and New Hampshire.

Reaching a section that crossed the parkway we parked up and decided to walk for a couple of miles on the Appalachian Trail. It wasn't long before we came across the white blazes indicating the route we had read about so many times. INSTAGRAM POST 378. On the way back to the car we met a guy who was walking the whole trail, South to North, the most popular route. I had a quick chat with him and he had loved his time so far on the trail. He declined our offer of food and water as he had only recently re stocked with supplies from a couple of zero days in town.

Having spent the night just a couple hours from Richmond we arrived back at the SPCA around lunchtime. It was great to see the girls again, and they looked pleased to see us. Jackie told us they had managed to take all of them except Saffy for a walk. Outside the SPCA there is a large pen, it is used to introduce new owners and potential dogs to each other. We carried Saffy outside and let her wander around the pen, and then we took them for a run around upstairs. In their private room, they were now joined by Pepper who had his surgery whilst we were away. Unfortunately his test came back positive for heartworm and he was undergoing treatment. The poor boy didn't look great, I remember Karen telling us all about heartworm and how the treatment for it can also be risky for the dog, but it can't be left untreated.

Heartworm is caused by the bite from an infected mosquito. The bite of just one mosquito infected with the heartworm larvae will give a dog heartworm disease. It takes about seven months, once a dog is bitten by an infected mosquito, for the larvae to mature into adult heartworms. They then lodge in the heart, lungs and surrounding blood vessels and begin reproducing. Adult worms can grow up to 12 inches in length, can live for seven years, and a dog can have as many as 250 worms in its system. It was desperately sad for him and heartworm was one thing we always had in the back of our minds about the girls. They too had spent all of their lives outside and considering it only takes one bite from an infected mosquito, we were preparing ourselves for the worst when they would be tested over the next few days.

The next day, something unbelievable happened. Saffy walked outside. On a lead. Helen and I were sat in the outside pen with her and Helen suggested we just pick her up and carry her round the corner where it is quiet and see what happens. We tried it and it worked, she just walked right alongside Helen. It was amazing to witness, the most shy out of all of the girls, we did it. For months we tried to walk Saffy and it began to seem as though we would never be able to. That was a huge step for her confidence.

We had to decide what we were going to do after Richmond. After hearing we managed to walk Saffy, Jackie was happy for us come in every day again and work with them to improve their confidence. It was agreed we would stay for a week as they would be having their operations the next day, then we would leave the girls in the capable hands of Richmond SPCA. In that week we would spend as much time as possible helping them gain confidence inside and outside of the building. Also we would help introduce volunteers to the girls so they would be more familiar with them once we had left. Amidst all this positivity it was sad to see poor Pepper not doing well, he was suffering from his heartworm treatment so we would pop into his cage and sit with him.

The 8th of May, the day the girls were going to be spayed and tested for heartworm. Helen and I arrived at the shelter early to make sure all of them had the chance to exercise and go the toilet. The shelter allowed us to sit in with the girls during their anaesthetic injections until they were asleep. The operations were so quick. Saffy was first and she was back within 15 minutes, Star, Coby and Bluebell followed soon after. Whilst they were under, the vets carried out the all-important Heartworm test, and we sat with the girls, as the results were relayed to us. Saffy's results came first, she was clear. Then Star, she was clear as well, this was great news. Coby was also clear, even better. Just Bluebell, the mum to go. Bluebell was the one we were most concerned about, we were certain that she would have heartworm. The results came in, they said all clear for Bluebell as well! We could not believe it! All four of the girls were heartworm free and wouldn't have to go through any treatment. It was such a relief and in addition it meant they were now officially up for adoption straight away. It was a stressful day but the girls did great, they were now all spayed, heartworm free and looking for their forever homes. The downside of the day was poor Pepper again, he wasn't getting any better.

The day after was another full one with the girls, but limited in exercise due to their operations yesterday, so just short toilet break walks and time sitting in the outside pen. Understandably they were more nervous because of the previous day's experiences. When we returned the next day however they were fine and the confidence was beginning to show in them. Jackie managed to take all of the dogs separately on her own to the Adoption assessment rooms and asked us to not come in until lunchtime the following day so she and the adoption team could try walking the girls on their own. This was fine by us, we wanted them to have confidence in and around other people.

The first thing we noticed when we arrived the next day was Pepper's pen. It was empty. Immediately we assumed he had passed away. It was a short while before a member of staff came in and confirmed the sad news, It was awful, poor Pepper. He was rescued from a life on the streets on Nevis where he was injured by a machete, but it was a bite from mosquito and the subsequent treatment that denied him ever having the chance to find a forever home and be treated like the pet dog he deserved. He only arrived at the shelter a couple of weeks before we left but he was such a good natured dog despite everything he went through.

The rest of the day was quite sombre even though Jackie informed us that they had managed to get all of the girls out at least once for a walk, in the playpen and upstairs in the exercise area. It was such good news. It was the first time Helen and I realised that all four of them would be ok here at Richmond and that we had done the right thing. Our big concern was that because of their nervousness, it would be difficult to get them outside walking with the staff, but they were coming on leaps and bounds here at the shelter. That evening we contacted Laura and Rich to tell them the sad news about Pepper as it was them who transferred him from Nevis.

Now the girls were all up for adoption it meant that any member of staff could enter their room, understandably they seemed a bit spooked. It was decided that Saffy would be put up for adoption first, and that Bluebell would go last after all her girls had hopefully gone. That evening Helen and I booked our flights out of the States. Central America was our next destination, but we hadn't really decided where. It was when we started looking into vaccinations that we noticed most of Central America was a malaria risk. Up until now we had not taken any malaria medication, and usually medication for malaria starts six weeks prior to arriving in the country. There are two countries that are malaria free in Central America, Costa Rica and Panama. As we had not taken any medication, we decided to miss out the northern part of Central America, that meant Belize, Guatemala, Honduras, El Salvador and Nicaragua and head straight for Costa Rica. Our flight would be leaving in three days, from Raleigh Durham airport. Belize was a country we were quite keen on visiting but it looked to be quite expensive. The other issue was that we couldn't go to Nicaragua anyway as recently as the previous month the country was protesting against the President and the country was listed as a dangerous zone for foreigners. The protests continued for over a year and resulted in 448 deaths and nearly 3,000 injured. Nicaragua bordered Costa Rica to the north, so if we did decide to visit any of those countries to the north we would then need to take a flight to bypass it. By now we had been travelling for 20 months and realized that it would have to come to end soon so it made sense to miss out a chunk of Central American countries. Costa Rica was to be our next destination and we were excited about it as it was a country we had always wanted to visit.

Our last full day with the girls was obviously full of mixed emotions. Glad that they were now finally up for adoption and improving all the time, but sad to be saying goodbye. We were there early and spent the entire day with them. Saffy walked a full lap around the neighbourhood surrounding the SPCA. We were so proud of her and how far she had come.

The next morning we only had time with the girls until 10am, but it was time well spent. We said our goodbyes to the amazing staff at the SPCA. Jackie gave us both a big hug and assured us they would be fine. It was a teary goodbye.

It had been an amazing transformation since we first met Bluebell and her girls just over a year ago. There were times when we thought that it would just not be possible to rehabilitate them, they were too feral. But in reality they were just scared and vulnerable and needed a lot of time and patience. The satisfaction from when we first walked Bluebell outside the shelter on a lead was amazing and then to have the same feeling with Star and Coby, we started to believe that it might be possible. The stress of trying to find a shelter who would take them on, and the injections required to fly them off the island, then moving them from Malabar to Richmond, it was all worth it to know that now they were up for adoption. Understandably it might seem crazy to some people how we spent so long working with the girls but to us this was part of our experience. We were doing something positive and making a difference and we were glad we did it. I certainly think the experience made us stronger as a couple. There were some really tough times but we helped each other through them. Helen amazed me through those months, her dedication to the girls was just unbelievable. Immediately she formed a bond with Bluebell and her girls and showed so much patience in developing their confidence from the outset. This determination rubbed off on me and it became our joint mission to help them.

Back at the motel, we finished packing, checked out and walked the short distance to the bus station where our Greyhound bus was late by three hours. The 15th of May, less than six weeks since we arrived in the US for the second time we were leaving again. It was a different experience to the first time, we had only returned due to the girls, we would not have done so otherwise. Nevertheless we saw some great parts of the US, covering 13 states from the Great Plains to the Smokey Mountains. So much had happened in that short time, it seemed a lot longer but this was another chapter of our travels ending, hopefully with a happy ending for Bluebell and the girls, as well as Charlot and Buttons. After a six hour layover in Atlanta we were flying over the Gulf of Mexico on our way to Central America. INSTAGRAM POST 379.

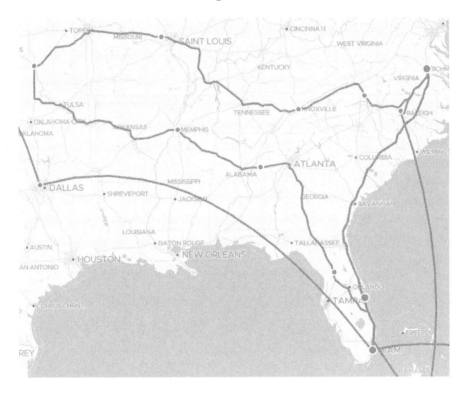

PART 5 – CENTRAL AMERICA,

A - COSTA RICA

Just two months short of two years travelling, we were now in our first country where English was not the first language. From now on it would probably be all Spanish. We hadn't learnt any Spanish during our time travelling even though we said we would. It was a big regret for us. Google translate would therefore come to our assistance many times. We had a phrase book, but it was far easier for us and whoever we were confusing to just take it in turns to type into Google Translate. As a nation we are pretty poor at other languages. As English is spoken as the secondary language in so many places, this is used as an excuse. Spanish was never an optional language when Helen and I were at school, it was either French or German. I chose French because it was more widely spoken than German. If Spanish was an option, I would have probably chosen Spanish over French.

We landed into a rainy San José, the capital of Costa Rica at 8pm and jumped in a taxi to Alajuela, just 18 km northwest of the capital. The reason we stayed at Alajuela was its proximity to the Parque Nacional Volcan Poás, the home of a 2,704m active volcano. It is possible to hike to the top and peer over the edge into the crater below. Or so we thought, as we then found out the park was closed. The volcano began rumbling in 2014, but that was the first time in 60 years, however there were significant eruptions in April and June 2017. These were serious enough for the government to close the park until further notice, much to the displeasure of the locals who relied on tourism. It was something we should have looked into before arriving in Alajuela but it was all last minute. Lesson learnt for the future. The rain continued all through the first full day so we didn't actually do anything apart from have a walk to the local supermarket and try and work out where to go next. As we only booked our flights to Costa Rica three days ago we didn't have time to research things to do and see. One thing all the guides and blogs seemed to agree on was Manuel Antonio National Park. It is Costa Rica's smallest and most popular national park so the next day, we headed back to San José to catch a bus. The park sits on the south coast, a three hour bus journey. Our accommodation was a place owned by a very friendly American, it was called Peace of Paradise and it was amazing for the price and only a short bus ride from the park entrance. The Park itself was nice but very crowded, probably due to the size. Visitors can only explore nearly 7 square km of the park. Despite the rain, it still seemed busy. The entrance fee was $16 US, even though the currency of Costa Rica is the Colón, US dollars are commonly used throughout. The whole day was spent exploring the various trails dotted around the park including the most popular, Sendero Punta Catedral or just sitting on the beach. Costa Rica is famous for its rainforests and as we know rainforests contain wildlife. This park had wildlife in abundance. We saw white faced monkeys, howler monkeys, deer and coatis. Coatis are a medium sized mammal, sort of a racoon type cute looking creature. Brightly coloured frogs, insects, crabs and birds were everywhere. The one thing we didn't see, but desperately wanted to, was a sloth. There was still time, hopefully.

As we liked our accommodation so much and the rain was eventually clearing we decided to stick around for a couple of days and chill out on some of the nearby beaches. Two days were spent on Playa Bezante where there were plenty of white faced monkeys to keep us entertained INSTAGRAM POST 380. They were also seen on the main roads but using the specially built monkey bridges, erected by local conservation groups to protect them from vehicles. INSTAGRAM POST 381. Playa Espadilla was a better beach where we spent a day, not too far from the entrance to the park. INSTAGRAM POST 382. On the first photo, Cathedral Point, part of the National Park, can be seen in the distance. The area around the park was obviously geared towards tourism but this place summed up the "Pura Vida" spirit of Costa Rica. It is impossible not to visit Costa Rica and see something for sale with Pura Vida emblazoned across it. Pura Vida is the country's motto, simply translated it means "simple life" or "pure life" Costa Ricans or "Ticos" use the term to say hello, goodbye and everything's fine. However Pura Vida is a way of life for Ticos, simple and relaxed. They are thankful for what they have and don't dwell on the negative. Our time in the south of Costa Rica had been enjoyable, and the scenery was stunning. INSTAGRAM POST 383. There were thoughts of heading further south towards the remote Corcovado National Park but we decided to miss it out and head back north of the country to La Fortuna. In order to reach La Fortuna, we had to take three different buses but it was a great way to see the how green and lush the country is. Arriving in the evening, our accommodation in La Fortuna was a hostel; this was to be a first for us. In North America, there were very few hostels and in the Caribbean we were either volunteering or house sitting. Central America does obviously have motels and hotels but they don't cater for the budget travellers so the hostels are the cheapest forms of accommodation. Hostels nowadays though are far different from those we had originally imagined before we started travelling. They cater for everyone, same sex dorms, mixed dorms, double rooms and single rooms. Helen and I agreed that hostels from now on were fine for us as long as we had our own room with our own bathroom. It was a luxury we were happy to pay a little extra for even though it wasn't that much more expensive, but we were too old to be sharing dorms with younger travellers. Dorms are great if you are travelling alone or in a larger group, but as a couple we wanted our own room and luckily most hostels offered them. Hostels come with communal kitchens, but on our first night the hostel was quite empty so no one else was using the kitchen whilst we prepared our dinner.

La Fortuna is actually quite a small town, with a population of just over 15,000, but again it was all geared to tourism. The main street was full of vendors and guides trying to sell you tours and experiences. The main draw here is the Volcan Arenal, a very active Volcano up until 2010, but the vendors also try and sell horseback riding, zip lining, visits to hot springs and various other excursions. After only a week in Costa Rica, we were surprised at the cost of doing things. A walk up the dormant volcano here cost $60 US each, and that only went part of the way up! Everything here seemed more expensive than it should be and everyone wanted to sell you something. It wasn't a case of being stingy, it was a case of being realistic as to what we could afford to do. The plan after Central America was South America and there lots of things we wanted to do and see there and we obviously couldn't afford to do them all. As nice as Costa Rica was, it was expensive. Travelindependent.info, our go-to trusted travel website was right. It had said all of the things you could do in Costa Rica, can also be done in other parts of Central and South America, but a lot cheaper. We spent four days in La Fortuna because we had accommodation booked but actually didn't do a lot, not only because of the prices but it also rained a lot whilst we were there. A couple of times we walked out of town to the Fortuna River where locals would show off by jumping off the high rocks. On the way back, as we approached town, a huge iguana caused a roadblock as it sat in the middle of the road for a couple of minutes before slowly walking off. INSTAGRAM POST 384.

Whilst we were staying down near Manuel Antonio Park we applied for a house sit in the neighbouring country of Panama. It was offered to us when we were in La Fortuna and started in just over a week's time. The house sit was situated near Torio. Our original plan after La Fortuna was to visit the Northwest of Costa Rica to Monteverde and the Nicoya Peninsula but these were in the opposite direction of where we needed to be for our house sit which was already nearly 800 km away. Weighing up our options of what to do, we decided to leave Costa Rica and spend a couple days as originally planned on the Bocas Tel Toro Islands on the north coast of Panama.

I can't say I was disappointed to leave la Fortuna, the Volcano is an awesome sight INSTAGRAM POST 385, but Costa Rica so far had been a bit of disappointment. And we never did end up seeing a sloth. Whether I had really high expectations beforehand I don't know. I'm sure Costa Rica is an amazing place but I feel it is so popular through great marketing. That was what made me want to visit Costa Rica so much in the first place. It sells itself as an amazing eco-friendly, safe, and crime free destination for travellers with a multitude of things to do whilst here. The reality is these can be done in most places in Central and South America but safety is the big draw for tourists, especially Americans. As a result Costa Rica receives more visitors than any of the other Central American countries. From La Fortuna we caught a bus back to San José as the following day we would be then travelling onto the north coast border town of Puerto Viejo de Talamanca. That evening, in the bar at our accommodation in San José, I watched Liverpool lose to Real Madrid in the Champions League Final. The journey to Puerto Viejo took four hours and after checking in at our hostel we went for a long walk along the beach to stretch our legs. On researching how to cross the land border to Panama, there was a convenient method whereby a company picked you up from the hostel and drove you to the border. They also pointed you in the right direction and instructed you where to go and what paper work you needed to fill out. And then once across the border, a minibus picked you up on the other side and drove you to where you needed to go. It was an easier option than trying to make our own way to the border. When the minibus picked us up, it seemed as though a lot of other travellers thought the same as us, the bus was full. On arrival at the border, after filling out our paperwork, we simply had to walk across a bridge into Panama. INSTAGRAM POST 386.

B - PANAMA

On the other side, as arranged, our minibus was waiting for us after we received another new stamp in our passports. The bus dropped us at the coastal town of Almirante. From here we caught a water taxi to Bocas Del Toro and finally another water taxi to the smaller island of Bastimentos. Our hostel was owned by a French couple who were still in the process of developing their dream. It was in the middle of nowhere and to reach the main part of the island you would either have to wave down a passing water taxi or walk for 15 minutes across planks of wood over the swamp. The whole area was stunning. In the afternoon we decided to make use of the kayaks and headed over to a secluded beach on the next island of Isla Solarte. Unfortunately it was pouring with rain on our first morning but we braved the slippery planks over the swamp and walked to an area called Old Bank and then up a steep hill where we had read about a coffee shop. Sure enough there was a house in the middle of nowhere and they had made a little café outside their house. By now the rain had stopped and we enjoyed a strong coffee sat outside. All around us there were birds singing and insects buzzing around. We also saw some enormous spiders just sitting in the middle of their webs hanging in the foliage. After lunch we then tried to walk to the north of the island to Wizards beach. There were reports that the only trail to the beach wasn't safe due to muggings of tourists, but supposedly there was an increased security presence on the islands to deter such activity. In the end we never actually made it to Wizards beach, we made it most of the way, but due to the amount of rain and steep sections it was impossible to walk along the trail so we just chilled out back at the hostel. Whilst sitting on the water's edge we saw a snake swimming along then reach up to a branch and pull itself out of the water. Our two days on the island were now done, it was short and sweet but a really good experience. It was amazing to see how people lived on these remote islands, but now we had to make it back to the mainland as our house sit started in two days.

At Almirante, we boarded a bus for five hours almost across to the south coast to the large city of David. In our hostel we found out we had been accepted on another house sit in Panama. This was located on the eastern side of the Azuero Peninsula, the other side of our upcoming housesit.

There was an overlap with this upcoming house sit but the couple were leaving their dog with a friend for a day or two until we arrived. Our first house sit would commence on the 1st of June until the 20th and the next one lasted until the 24th of August, just over eight weeks later on Helen's birthday. It would be a long house sit, but there was a reason we applied. As we wanted to continue down through South America we needed to make sure we travelled through it at the right time for the weather. If we arrived in June it was to be the start of winter in the southern hemisphere and as we were intending on following the Andes all the way down to Patagonia we needed to wait until the ideal time to visit. All the research had suggested spring was the best time, as not only was the weather better in order for all of the outdoor activities, but it was also cheaper in the shoulder seasons. After a night in David, another bus took us closer to our house sit in Santiago. On the bus we met an American guy called Brewster, he had not booked anywhere for that night so tried his luck at the cheap accomodation where we were staying. Brewster was fluent in Spanish but the price still seemed too much for him so he headed off in search for cheaper accommodation but we agreed to meet up with him later down the street for a beer. After Brewster had disappeared we realised we needed his help. The accommodation clearly stated that there was a fridge and freezer available so we could store Helen's insulin and ice packs overnight. However there was neither. Yet again Google translate came to our rescue. Typing our predicament in to the Ipad, I crossed the road and entered the restaurant opposite. I showed the kind owner my message and she typed a reply. She said it was no problem to use the fridge and freezer overnight and come back in the morning to collect them. All sorted, thankyou Google translate. That evening we went for a beer with Brewster, he had never heard of house sitting but loved the idea. A few days later he messaged us to say he had set up a profile and was applying for various house sits in South America.

At Santiago bus station we located the minibus that would take us to Torio and Moriato. Our backpacks were put on top of the bus and we spent an hour and a half sweating on the crowded journey south. On the way it started raining so the bus pulled over and a waterproof tarpaulin was thrown over the luggage on the roof. At our bus stop we were met by Josh who drove us the short distance back to his house, our home for the next three weeks. Josh's wife Clara, and their two rescue dogs, Dobbie and Amato were at the house to meet us. Josh and Clara were a really nice couple. They both worked on an exclusive holiday island where they spent two weeks working, followed by two weeks off at their house. They always took Amato and Dobbie with them when they worked on the island, but now they were travelling back to the US to visit relatives for their holidays, hence the need for someone to look after their dogs. Josh and Clara were leaving early the next morning and as we wouldn't have use of a car on this house sit, Josh drove us to the nearby town so as to buy some grocery essentials. It was about a 15 minute drive so over the next three weeks we would need to catch a minibus or a taxi. There was a tiny little store about a five minute walk away where we could buy some vegetables and also a bar and a small coffee shop. We spent the evening chatting after dinner and also getting to know the routines for Amato and Dobbie. It all seemed very relaxed which was good, take them out whenever and wherever we like. The house was only about 400 metres from the beach so we would probably be taking them there quite often. Our first impression of Torio was that it was very rural and very rustic, a real place to relax. The house was on two levels with the top level for living accommodation. The downstairs was fully open so it was almost like it was on stilts, and the garden was enclosed by wire fence. Josh showed us how to use the typical Latin American "suicide shower" so called as it is electric but it was very easy to get an electric shock when you altered the water temperature. One thing we hadn't known before we arrived was that there was no Wi-Fi. Even though it was expensive for us to use 4G there wasn't a decent phone reception anyway. Josh told us they used the Wi-Fi at the small coffee shop. Luckily they had a selection of DVD's for us to watch and a large selection of Jack Reacher books. The World Cup was also starting in a couple of weeks so I would be heading to the local bar to watch the games. Amato was a lovely big soft boy. Dobbie on the other hand was a lot more hesitant, she kept well away from us both all night. We would give her space and let her come to us when she was ready.

Josh and Clara left early in the morning so they were already gone as we started our first morning. After feeding the dogs we wanted to take them for a walk. Dobbie however did not want to come. Amato on the other hand was totally fine, he always wanted to be with us. In the afternoon we walked to the coffee shop to use the Wi-Fi, check our messages and let our parents know we were ok. I tried to download some films from Netflix and some books onto our Kindles but it was taking too long so gave up on that idea. We would therefore rely on the DVD collection for our evening's entertainment. It seems quite sad but it felt strange not having Wi-Fi. It is something you take for granted nowadays so when you don't have it, it really makes a difference. Each day during our stay we would walk just close enough past the coffee shop to pick up the Wi-Fi, so our phones could pick up messages and emails. On our third day we received a very sad message from my brother. Amie's mother had suddenly died the previous day. It was horrible to think what Simon, Amie and the girls were going through, also for Amie's sister Lianne who lived in London. Simon was looking after the girls whilst Amie and Lianne headed to off to be with their dad during this incredibly difficult time. With poor Wi-Fi and phone reception our contact with them was limited but we messaged them when we could to let them know we were thinking about them all.

In the knowledge that there wasn't a lot to do in Torio, we went for a walk to measure out a 5 km route we could jog. The only road was the main road but it was very quiet, and had some very steep sections. The weather wasn't helping though, it was restricting our time outside as it had rained quite a lot since we arrived. A couple of nights in our first week we went to bed early and read as the rain was so heavy on the tin roof we could hardly hear ourselves talk. Another morning we woke up without water and it eventually came back on in the afternoon. Our bed was just a mattress on the floor and it was very hot in the house. There were a lot of mosquitos and other insects inside the house so after a couple of nights of being woken by something running across my back and Helen getting bitten we decided to put up our mosquito net. The water supply for the house came through a pipe which was visible from the house. It crossed a small dyke. Whenever there was a heavy rainfall, the water level in this dyke rose considerably and all the debris that washes down from the mountains caused the join in the pipe to come apart. A number of occasions I had to wade into the dyke after a period of rain to remove the debris from around the pipe and put it back together. At least Dobbie was warming to us, after her initial nervousness with us both, she was actually an incredibly sweet dog. She started to join us for walks and even came to us for cuddles. Within a week she was laying with me in the hammock.

The days followed a similar routine of walking the dogs, walking past the coffee shop for free Wi-Fi. If it rained we would lie in the hammocks reading or sit out in the garden when the sun was out. We started running most days as well. With one big storm, the electricity went down at 3pm. By 6.45pm it was dark so we relied on candles. That meant an uncomfortable evening as the fans wouldn't work and it was really humid. The fans were also great at keeping the mosquitos away. The following morning was my brother's birthday but I wasn't able to send him a card this year, just a quick message as I walked past the coffee shop. With no electricity we decided that a trip to the supermarket would be better than just sitting around the house. The electricity eventually came back on at 6pm, 27 hours later.

During our frequent coffee shop walks, we were in regular contact with our upcoming house sit and they had asked if one of us would be able to spend a day and night with them as they would be leaving before we arrived. We had arranged that I would make the trip over to the other side of the Peninsula de Azuero to Playa El Rompio. Even though on a map, the house sit was on the opposite side of the peninsula, the only route was to head north to Santiago, then across and down due to the mountains in the middle and those roads were not used by public transport.

On the day of departure I loaded up a full backpack to make it easier for when we would both travel in a week's time. We walked the dogs in the morning then I waited on the main road for an hour for a bus to pass to take me up to Santiago. Then I caught another bus to Chitre where I was met by Ray and Kathy.

Ray and Kathy lived in a gated condo complex by the sea called Playa El Rompio. The drive to El Rompio was about 20 minutes but I was given a quick tour of Chitre to be shown which supermarkets they use and the location of the doctors. Their place was lovely and upon opening the door I

186

was met by their dog, Cairo. Cairo was huge, an enormous Doberman easily weighing over 50kgs. Like Amato he was a big softy. The whole Condo complex was virtually empty. There were over 50 units, most inhabited by Canadians but they had all gone home. The only other people left were Alan and Michelle, a French Canadian couple who would be looking after Cairo until Helen and I returned. The condo itself was fantastic, very modern and clean. Later that afternoon, we walked Cairo along the beach, this was where Ray and Kathy walked Cairo twice a day. The beach itself was ok, not the type of beach I think we would spend time sunbathing on or swimming in the sea as it was pretty rough. In the evening we had a couple of beers and pizza. I messaged Helen to tell her about my day here, the house and Cairo and then realised she wouldn't be able to read it until the following morning. Overnight I downloaded a week's worth of Netflix viewing to take back to Torio.

The next morning I was up early to walk Cairo on the beach by myself. He is big and strong but he struggles with his hips so can't walk too far. This side of the peninsula is also very warm so it is best to get him walked early in the morning before it warms up too much. After a shower and some breakfast I said goodbye to Cairo, Helen and I would be returning to look after him in a week. Instead of just taking me to Chitre, Ray and Kathy wanted to do some shopping in Santiago so they drove me all the way back there. We said our goodbyes and I would see them on their return in about nine to ten weeks at the end of August. In Santiago, I picked up some shopping before catching the bus back to Torio, getting back to Helen and the dogs at 3pm.

That evening whilst eating dinner, the house started shaking; the dogs were sleeping but quickly jumped up. Helen and I looked at each other, the shaking continued. After a couple of seconds we realised it was an earthquake. We just jumped up, grabbed the dogs and ran outside, down the stairs away from the house. It was dark, which added to our nervousness. With no phone reception or Wi-Fi we didn't have a clue what was going on. My initial fear was that we were living about 400m from the sea and we didn't know if the earthquake was inland or out at sea and there was a tsunami heading straight for us. Just to feel safe we quickly walked the dogs up the hill to the coffee shop to see if there were any reports of the earthquake on the internet. There was, and luckily the earthquake was inland and not at sea. The epicentre was just 40 km away from us and was recorded as 5.8 on the Richter scale. Ray and Kathy messaged us the next day to tell us they felt it, 100 km away on the other side of the peninsula. It was a really strange experience to have everything around you shaking, it seemed to go on for ages although it only probably lasted a few seconds, but it is certainly something Helen and I will never forget. It was lucky it had not happened 24 hours earlier when Helen would have been alone.

The next day was the start of the World Cup, after we went for a 5 km walk I watched the opening game in the local bar. Our final week in Torio after the earthquake was uneventful, walking the dogs, going for runs and watching World Cup games. Back home, sadly Amie's mother's funeral was taking place. We started packing our backpacks and I watched Panama lose their opening World Cup game to Belgium 3-0 with the locals. I returned a couple of hours later to then watch England win their opening game 2-1 against Tunisia.

On our final day, we were packed and ready to leave around lunchtime. Having already been in contact with Josh and Clara, we knew that they were due to return late afternoon and they were fine with us leaving for our next house sit. Those three weeks in Torio were like no other house sit we had experienced before, but it was fun and the dogs, Amato and Dobbie played a big part in that. INSTAGRAM POST 387. Taking the same route I took the previous week, up to Santiago and then east and south to Chitre, we were met by Alan at the bus station at 3.30pm. There was a large supermarket opposite the station so we grabbed some essentials before driving back to Playa El Rompio. The currency in Panama is the Balboa, although we only used US dollars in all our time in Panama. Alan's wife Michelle was waiting for us with Cairo when we arrived. After a quick chat she left and Helen explored the house, after the rustic accommodation we had stayed in for the previous three weeks I could tell she was pleased. After unpacking we took Cairo out for a walk along the beach.

Our first full day coincided with cleaning day, the cleaner lived in a condo a few doors down and came once a week from 8am until 4pm. Helen and I couldn't understand how it took eight hours to clean a small condo but he actually made it possible. As the cleaner was going to be around all day, it was an obvious decision to drive to Chitre and carry out a full grocery shop. Chitre was a lot larger and more modern than Torio. The supermarkets were a welcome relief to what we had on the other side of the peninsula for the past three weeks. It reminded us of when we turned up in Grenada after Bequia and were spoilt by the choice available in the large supermarkets. Two things we noticed though about supermarkets in Panama, all cheese is sold in slices and crisps are really really expensive. Instead we decided to buy a bag of popcorn kernels. Popcorn turned out to be regular snack during this house sit.

This house sit was a long one, nine weeks altogether. When I came previously I knew that the house was great, but in terms of location it was pretty isolated, so to go anywhere was going to be a drive and to be honest there was not actually a lot to do and see in this area. Cairo was a nice dog but he had hip problems so we were never going to be able to take him out on long walks.

The reason we picked this house sit in the first place was timings. It was now the end of June, we were here until the end of August. Our next destination was South America and the Andes that ran all the way down the continent to Patagonia. The Andes meant altitude and altitude and winter are not a good combination as it would restrict us on what we could do. Therefore, this house sit was an ideal time to sit back, relax, plan our route through South America, watch the World Cup and the Tour de France and enjoy the sun.

Being bored was never going to happen, we would always find something to do to occupy our time. On our second day we went out for a walk and measured out a running route. Cairo was walked early in the morning, then we would take it in turns to go for a run straight after, but even at 8 or 9 am it was already too hot. The difference in temperature over this side of the peninsula compared to Torio was amazing. We both ended up sunburnt on our third day.

The fourth day we received some fantastic news. Coby had been adopted! The first of the girls to find her forever home. We were constantly checking the website for news so it was great when Jackie contacted us directly to tell us the good news. It had taken just under six weeks, since we left Richmond, but the first of them was now in a safe home environment, it was such a good feeling. Fingers crossed now that the others would soon be rehomed as well.

That first week was capped off with England beating Panama 6-1 in the World Cup. I didn't watch it in any of the local bars as it was an early kick off local time. Four days later though England lost 1-0 to Belgium.

The days followed the same pattern, early start to walk Cairo, go for run, chill out in the sun, followed by some lunch. Most afternoons Helen and I would go for a walk on our own without Cairo as he would normally sleep. At 5pm we would take him out for his walk or a little later if it was still too warm.

One evening we were sat watching Netflix, Cairo was asleep just in front of us on the cool tiled floor. Above the TV on the ceiling there was a small square of masking tape, as though it was covering a hole. All of a sudden there was a thud of something hitting the floor, I looked down and it was a scorpion! It had fallen out of the hole in the ceiling. Now it was scuttling across the floor heading straight towards Cairo. I jumped up immediately and kicked it away. The rest of time in the house over the next few weeks, we spent way too long looking up at the patch on the ceiling, imagining there was a huge nest of scorpions up there. Fortunately that was our only meeting with a scorpion in our time there. INSTAGRAM POST 388.

Two weeks after the great news about Coby, who was now called Hero, Star was now the second of the girls to find a home. Star was now called Hannah and she was living with two other dogs. The best part was we were now able to follow the progress of both of them via Facebook and Instagram and we were talking to their new owners. INSTAGRAM POST 389. The day after England lost their World Cup Semi Final to Croatia, we heard that Star had slipped her lead and was now missing. She was gone for almost a week, but luckily she had remained in the same area and after several sightings Jackie was able to lay in wait for her one evening and managed to catch her. It was horrible not being able to do anything to help. Star's new owners were frantic with worry but fortunately Jackie saved the day and Star was back in the safety of her new home.

Four weeks later, we received another message from Jackie. More good news, well, actually unbelievable news really. Coby's new owner had also decided to adopt Bluebell, and then Saffy, the most nervous of them all, had also been taken in by a new owner. We couldn't believe it, barely eight months ago these dogs had never been walked on a lead, had no vaccinations and were looking at a very uncertain future. Now, they are all living in loving homes in the US as pets, like we always believed they could. There were never any doubts about their temperaments, they just needed to trust humans, we provided that step for them and hopefully now they will live out the rest of their lives as spoilt pets. Sadly we were not able to follow Saffy on social media but we regularly see updates of Star (Hannah) and Bluebell (now Justice) and Coby (Hero). It is amazing to see them enjoying themselves and living the lives they deserve rather than as feral strays on Nevis. Before they were all adopted, Helen and I had talked about the possibility of us adopting them if after our travels they still had not been adopted. The problem was we couldn't adopt all four as Star didn't get along with Coby and Saffy. And then it would be the difficult decision of which ones would we therefore choose? We never had to make that difficult decision. I'm positive we will one day return to Richmond to be reunited with Hannah, Justice and Hero. Would they recognise us? We would hope so but it wouldn't matter if they didn't, it would be nice just to see them again. At the same time we kept up to date with Charlot and Buttons. They seemed to be having a great time in their foster home with the owners of the dog rescue organisation but they still hadn't found a forever home. Only in late 2020 we heard the news that Charlot was recently adopted. Buttons is still a foster with the owner of the charity. It just shows how a large organisation like Richmond SPCA with all of its resources and high catchment area has such a high adoption rate, whereas Buttons and Charlot were part of a small shelter organisation where the catchment area is so much smaller. We would have never imagined that all four of the girls would have been adopted over a year before Buttons and

Charlot. At least Buttons is not living in a pen in a shelter, she is in a home environment. When all of the girls were adopted we also discussed the possibility of adopting Charlot and Buttons to the point that we sent an adoption application. Sadly we were declined as they did not want to put the dogs through the stress of flying them from the US to the UK. As a result we would start looking elsewhere to adopt a couple of dogs for our return.

With the relief that all the girls were now rehomed life was pretty good at Playa El Rompio. We were running and walking regularly, but also spending a lot of time just relaxing enjoying the sun. INSTAGRAM POST 390. I had started to pull together a plan of our route through South America. There was no way to cross from Central to South America by land as the Darian gap is dangerous due to guerrilla activity, lack of roads and treacherous jungle. That meant a flight. At the time there was unrest in Venezuela, with widespread social unrest and protests. Most of the country was living in poverty and hunger had escalated to the point that almost 75% of the population had lost an average of 8kgs in weight. The social unrest against the government resulted in the largest recorded refugee crisis in the Americas. We were now in August 2018, by the end of the year it was estimated that over 4 million Venezuelans had left the country due to the Bolivarian Revolution. Next door in Columbia, it was reported that in the first half of the year, 100,000 Venezuelans had emigrated across the border, by end of November, this had increased to over 600,000. This had reached over 1 million in early 2018. Many more were travelling through Columbia to the southern border in order to cross into Ecuador and then onto Peru or further south to Chile and Argentina. With all what was happening, the UKGov website was advising against travelling from Columbia into Ecuador via the southern land border due to the high number of Venezuelan immigrants. We therefore decided to miss out Colombia and start our South American travels from Ecuador. Columbia would have been an interesting country to visit but we would have had to use the troubled land border to then cross into Ecuador.

With our start point sorted, I then started to plan a rough route through South America, taking in Ecuador, Peru, Bolivia, Chile and Argentina, all the way down to Patagonia in the south. Our passion was hiking so the plan was to follow the spine of the Andes all of the way down taking in some of the best scenery and walks along the way. It was realistic that we were running out of time and money and had roughly estimated once we arrived in Ecuador, we would have enough money to last us up until Xmas, if we didn't take on any house sits or workaways. Planning our trip in South America really got me excited about our forthcoming travels. Central America had been a bit underwhelming, a lot of what I had read raved about South America, there was just so much to do and see, and I couldn't wait.

On our daily walks, we always used to walk past a little old lady sat outside her tiny house. Every day we would wave to each other and we noticed she also had a very small puppy. Over the next few days though we noticed she wasn't there anymore, but the puppy was still wandering around the property and the road on its own. As the days went by we noticed it was looking skinnier and skinnier, to the point that we started taking food and water for it. Each day he would come running up to us when he saw us knowing we had food, yet still there was nobody at the property. There was a German ex pat who lived just outside the complex who we regularly chatted to and we mentioned the puppy to her. She in turn then told her neighbours, an American ex pat couple. Immediately they headed over to the property without a second thought, wrapped him in a blanket and took him back to their house where they bathed him, treated him for fleas and cleared him of all the ticks that he was covered in. The US couple did a lot for stray dogs in the local area so it was a relief we had stumbled across them. George, as he had now been named loved his new foster home living with other dogs. During our remaining time we regularly popped in to see George. Again we have been in contact since our return and George is also now enjoying life in a new forever home.

In addition to the scorpion episode, we regularly came in close proximity to some large spiders. On the beach we would sometimes come across sea snakes. I had read these were poisonous but if they were on the beach they were dying. Faced with this sort of wildlife, it came as a nice surprise one day when the garden of our condo was completely full of a less harmful creature. It was really strange, a huge kaleidoscope of over a hundred butterflies. INSTAGRAM POST 391.

Our time at Playa El Rompio was now at an end. Ray and Kathy were due back on the 23rd of August, the day before Helen's birthday. We had agreed to meet them at the bus station at Chitre and we would then jump on a bus straight to Panama City for Helen's birthday. The nine weeks had been good, we relaxed, we sunbathed and we exercised. I managed to watch the World Cup, the Tour de France and we now had more of an idea of what we were planning to see and do in South America. Cairo was a good dog, very easy to look after and the Condo itself was great. The bus pulled into the large terminal early afternoon and we jumped into a taxi to our hotel.

We had a full day in Panama City for Helen's birthday. This was now her third birthday whilst travelling. The previous ones were in Montréal and Grenada. It was an overcast day and rain always seemed to threaten but we were still going to take the metro and a bus to the west of the city to view Panama City's top attraction, the Panama Canal.

The canal is one of the world's greatest shortcuts and man-made wonders of the world, it is 77 km in length, connecting the Atlantic Ocean in the North to the Pacific ocean in the South. It takes about eight hours to cross the canal and greatly reduces the time that ships have to travel between the oceans by avoiding the lengthy and hazardous Cape Horn route around the southernmost tip of South America. That is an extra 12,500 miles. The project to build the canal started in 1881, by the French, they then passed it over to the Americans in 1904 who finished it in 1914. During French construction, over 20,000 workers died, mainly as a result of infections from working in humid jungles and swamps. Between 13,000 and 14,000 ships use the canal each year and each vessel pays a toll based on its size and cargo volume. Tolls for larger ships can cost about $450,000. The smallest recorded toll was 36 cents in 1928 by a man who swam the channel. Today, some £1.8 billion in tolls are collected annually.

The Miraflores Visitor centre is where the public can watch huge ships pass through the Miraflores Locks. Instead of paying the entrance fee, I had read that you can go straight up to the bar and as long as you order a drink you can sit out on the balcony and get a decent view of the lock gates. As it was Helen's birthday, it was rude not to have a drink to celebrate so that's what we did. As luck would have it a huge ship did pass through the gates as we were enjoying a nice beer. INSTAGRAM PHOTO 392. Catching a bus outside the visitor centre we hopped off at the huge Albrook Shopping Plaza where for a change we were spoilt for choice for lunch options, before a spot of retail therapy, buying essentials for South America. Helen bought some new hiking socks and I picked up a bargain pair of trail shoes as my pair was now pretty useless.

All of the day's activities were taking place in the west of the city, and our next was immediately visible upon walking out of the plaza. Ancón Hill is the highest point in Panama City at 654ft. It offers great views of the Canal, Casco Viejo old Town and the City Centre skyline, all on the Instagram post.

There are lots of opportunities to see wildlife in this protected reserve. We didn't, although there were a couple of friendly cats at the top. It had been a really good day for Helen's birthday, proper city sightseeing. As it was late in the afternoon, we were virtually on our own at the top of Ancón hill. After walking all the way back down we caught a bus and the metro back to our hotel. Then dropping off our bags and having a quick spruce up, we headed out again into the city. When in Panama City.....go to an Irish bar and have fish and chips! And great it was too. As tempting as it was to stay out for few more drinks to celebrate Helen's birthday we had an early night as we had to be up at 3am for our shuttle to the airport. After what seemed like the blink of an eye, we were waiting in the reception of the motel for our shuttle to the airport northeast of the city. Bags checked in, through security and into the departure lounge for some breakfast, our flight to the next continent was at 9.30am. Central America was good, I don't know if we had higher expectations, but then again we only visited Costa Rica and Panama. The travel oracle, travelindependent.info, which we relied on so much for information says Central America lacks many of the "wow" factors and sights of South America that should not be missed. They had been right so many times, so we were really excited about our flight to the capital city of Quito in Ecuador.

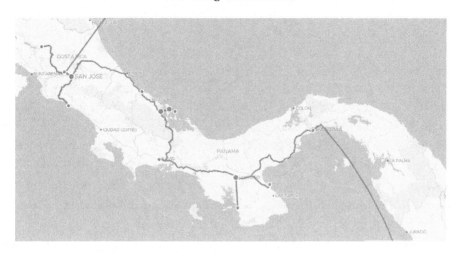

PART 6 – SOUTH AMERICA

A - ECUADOR

Our flight landed just after lunch, the airport is 30 minutes from Quito itself. We had to take a taxi as there were no buses. From our plane, we could see the Andes mountain range below us, the longest mountain range in the world. They span 5,500 miles from subtropical Venezuela down to the icy tip of Patagonia. I remember how excited I was when I first saw the Rockies to the east of Calgary. This was a similar feeling, however we sliced straight through the Rockies, this time we are following the Andes down the continent, through Ecuador, Peru, Bolivia, Chile and Argentina.

Ecuador is probably most famous for the Galápagos Islands, visited by Charles Darwin in 1835, the wildlife there inspired his theory of evolution. However we weren't planning on visiting them. Upon researching back in Panama, it seemed pretty expensive and meant we would have to sacrifice other things further on. I had a feeling this would be the case, there seemed to be so much to do and see, we might not be able to do everything we wanted. We didn't feel like doing anything though when we first arrived at Quito, the altitude hit us straight away. INSTAGRAM POST 393. Quito sits at an altitude of 9,220ft, or 2,810 metres, this was the highest altitude so far on our travels. The top of Sulphur Mountain at Banff in the Canadian Rockies was 2,450 metres. The altitude in Calgary made us feel a bit lethargic but nothing like this. Both of us felt awful that first day, we had just flown straight in from sea level and now my head was pounding. Our hostel looked out over the Plaza de Santo Domingo and the church that gave it it's name. Unfortunately our room was on the second floor and there were no lifts so it was a real struggle to reach our room. The room cost was only £13 a night, Ecuador was already great. This was a big difference to the prices we were paying in Central America. Already it felt like we were on the "Gringo Trail". Our hostel was occupied with other Europeans. Our intended route was one of the main backpacking routes so this would be a common sight now as we followed the Gringo Trail. Also we were now going to be hostelling for the foreseeable future. Breakfast here was included in the £13 cost so that was a bonus. Feeling heavy headed, we didn't do much on our first day apart from have a bit of a walk around and buy some groceries. One of the noticeable things in Ecuador, apart from the altitude, is the brightly coloured clothing prevalent amongst the locals. Most of the women tend to dress with a common theme, a Panama hat, accompanied by a brightly coloured poncho or shawl, with a skirt and tights.

In the morning we were both already feeling better so after our complimentary breakfast we used the Google Translate app to ask reception the easiest way to get to the Mitad Del Mundo. For those of you who know Spanish, that translates as "Middle of the world". Quito sits right on the equator and there is a 30 metre high monument in the San Antonio Parish of Quito which celebrates the fact. INSTAGRAM POST 394. It is a great spot for the typical tourist photos of standing either side of a line, with a foot in both hemispheres. The one slight problem with this attraction, that no one really cares about, and rightly so, is that the monument is actually in the wrong place. Using a more modern GPS, Latitude: 00°-00'-00" is actually located 250 metres further up the road. The Mitad Del Mundo is a great day out and a must do when in Quito. As well as the monument, there is a solar museum demonstrating the Coriolis Effect. There is also a living museum representing indigenous customs and traditions. To reach the Mitad Del Mundo, we took two separate buses, taking 1h 30 mins costing just 50 cents each. The currency in Ecuador is the US Dollar. It went to full dollarization in 2000 after a financial crisis saw the former currency, the sucre, collapse so badly that people started putting their holdings into dollars, the government simply followed to make it official. Back at the hostel we had some lunch and then decided to spend the afternoon at Itchimbia Park. It took about 45 mins to walk there but it was well worth it. There are great views to be had over Quito. As it was the weekend and the sun was out, the park was busy. It was a great park, kite flying seemed to be really popular and everyone just seemed to be enjoying themselves. For our first full day in Quito, we were impressed with Ecuador, everyone was really friendly. There is always a part of you that thinks South America is a bit dodgy, I don't know why, you just do, well from our first day, that couldn't be further from the truth.

Our second day, now feeling more acclimatised; we then planned on visiting another one of Quito's main attractions, the teleférico. INSTAGRAM POST 395. This takes you by cable car up the side of Mount Pichincha, an active stratovolcano, to a height of 4,000 metres, making it one of the highest aerial lifts in the world. At the top, it is possible to buy oxygen if altitude sickness becomes too much of a problem. Luckily the weather was good on the day we went to the top so the views looking back over Quito were amazing. That afternoon though we bought a woolly hat and gloves each, for the bargain price of £2.

Mindo is a small village about 90 minutes north west of Quito. Leaving our larger backpacks at the hostel, we caught a bus there as we had read about the cloud forest and the cable car that takes you across to it. The setting to the village is stunning, surrounded on all sides by forested mountains. The bus arrived just after 3pm but it turned out that it was too late to do anything that day, so cloud forest would have to wait until the morning. The morning came earlier than we hoped as outside the window at our hostel, a cockerel with no sense of timing started to crow at 1am. As a result we were waiting at the entrance gates at 9am as soon as the park opened. To reach the reserve, called Bosque Protector Mindo – Nambillo, you must board a small motor powered tarabita or cable car. INSTAGRAM POST 396. Then you are taken across a river basin 150 metres up before reaching the cloud forest on the other side. Most people have heard of rain forests but probably not so much cloud forests. One of the key differences between cloud forests and rainforests is to do with the elevation of the forest itself. Rainforests are located at lower elevations, and as a result, they tend to be much warmer, especially during the dry season. Cloud forests, on the other hand, are usually located at much higher elevations, and are much cooler. This difference in temperature contributes to the mist and fog that is often visible in cloud forests, as the milder temperatures slow the evaporation process. However, despite being a little cooler than rainforests, cloud forests are still very humid. Topography also plays a role, rainforests tend to cover large expanses of land with little change in elevation. Cloud forests, on the other hand, often feature dramatic shifts between the highest peaks and the lowest valleys. On the other side we followed the directions on our map and visited six waterfalls in total. It was very humid, and hilly, our Fitbits recorded over 200 flights of stairs that morning. It was a really enjoyable experience and we were back in Mindo to catch a bus back to Quito at 2pm, where we would be starting our journey south the following day by heading to Latacunga.

The trip to Latacunga takes you past the Parque National Cotopaxi and its namesake the Volcan Cotapaxi, a huge active volcano, the second highest summit in Ecuador at 5,897m. Latacunga was a stop off point for our next activity, the Quilotoa Loop. The Loop is a beautiful hiking area in the central highlands all at an altitude of 3,000m, with the main attraction being the Quilotoa Crater Lake. We chose to do a three-day hike, and left our main backpacks at our hostel in Latacunga. Pre booking our accommodation, the hostels on the route cater for walkers by including evening meals, breakfasts and packed lunches in their prices. However, it still meant we had to carry enough clothes, toiletries and snacks for the three days. A bus to Sigchos was our start point, from here we hiked 12 km through stunning scenery for four hours to our first hostel on the loop at the small village of Insilivi. The route was quite easy, no real issues in getting lost and we thoroughly enjoyed it. INSTAGRAM POST 398. At the hostel we met an American couple, also doing the same route, Andrew and Easter. They had arrived slightly earlier than us and were already enjoying a beer in the garden. Helen and I joined them for a chat and a few beers of our own before the four of us tucked into a delicious meal provided by the hostel.

After a good night's sleep and a lovely breakfast Helen and I enjoyed a bit of the morning sun in the garden with the resident llamas. INSTAGRAM POST 397. Andrew and Easter set off about an hour before us but we were in no hurry to start the 14 km to Chugchilán. Our second day hiking was just as good as the first, stunning scenery, great weather and really friendly locals. INSTAGRAM POST 399. Four and a half hours later we arrived at our hostel in Chugchilán, Andrew and Easter again sitting outside having a beer. As per the previous evening, after a shower we joined them for a couple of beers before we had to retreat to the warmth of the fire in the communal living room. The hostel provided a welcome hearty dinner and we continued chatting to Andrew and Easter. They were halfway through a two week vacation and told us that after the loop they were planning on hiking Volcan Cotapaxi before heading to the coast to relax on the beach. Knowing that day three was the most challenging day, we opted for an early night, barely able to move under the weight of the heavy blankets provided to keep us warm at this altitude.

We set off slightly earlier than the previous two days as the distance was 16 km, not too much further but there were more climbs and descents. As expected the hike did not disappoint, it was another glorious hike through the mountains but it was brutal. Due to the heat we were carrying a lot of water. Up and down two steep valleys, the crater at Quilotoa is visible from some distance but it never seemed to be getting closer. We finally reached the Crater Lake and it was well worth the hike to get there, we had never seen anything like it, just stunning. INSTAGRAM POST 400. Exhausted we stood at the edge admiring the view for about 30 mins before we had to make our way around to the other side where the town of Quilotoa was located. I will take the blame for what happened next, I saw some people walking along a track and assumed that was the route we should be taking. Actually we should have simply walked around the top rim of the crater. Instead we followed these people inside the crater, not realising they did not know where they were going. After a while we realised we were walking on some precarious narrow animal tracks with some very steep drops below us. We were already exhausted by this point and it was starting to get a bit scary. Fortunately some locals saw us and headed down and we all followed their safe route back up to the top of the crater where we joined the large flat wide path we should have originally taken. The whole crater episode lasted two hours. Eventually we made it to our hostel, seven hours after setting off from Chugchilán. Our altitude now was 4,000 metres and the Fitbit recorded 428 flights of stairs for the 16 km hike. Our three day Quilotoa loop was complete and it had been epic, yes it was tiring but you expect that, it makes it more rewarding. Some people choose to do the route clockwise by starting at the lake and despite my mistake at the end we were still glad we chose the counter clockwise option. We never did see anymore of Andrew or Easter so enjoyed our hostel meal on our own before having a well-deserved early night. The following morning we walked back up to the crater to admire the views again and take some more pictures before catching the bus back to Latacunga. INSTAGRAM POST 401.

Baños is a town sat in between the Andes and the Amazon and is well known as an adrenaline junkie's paradise. The river provides opportunities for water sports and the hills are ideal for hiking and mountain biking. We spent an enjoyable four days here altogether. On our first day we arrived late in the afternoon and decided to go for hike in the hills. We ending up believing we were lost and it started to get dark so we decided we should retrace our steps. The next day we decided to try the route from the other direction and it turned out if we had carried on the previous evening for another couple of hundred metres we would have been fine. INSTAGRAM POST 402. Later on we took a trip to the lookout above Baños but unfortunately it was too cloudy to give really good views of the still active nearby Volcan Tungurahua, so here are some equally poor photos I took of it on our other days in Baños. INSTAGRAM POST 403.

Bike hire is popular in Baños as a result of the popular Route of the Waterfalls. 61 km further downhill is the village of Puyo. It is possible to cycle all the way stopping along the route to admire the many waterfalls along the way plunging into the river Pastaza. INSTAGRAM POST 404. Our day included a long stop at the famous Pailon Del Diablo waterfall so we only managed 30 km. It was one of the most enjoyable bike rides ever, all downhill, amazing scenery and great weather. Instead of cycling uphill all the way back to Baños we waited at a bus stop, the driver attached our bikes to the back and drove us all the way back to Baños for $1. That evening in our hostel we felt a familiar rumble, there was a 6.2 earthquake at Alausí, just 180 km south of Baños, fortunately there were no reported casualties. A more leisurely way to see the Ruta de las Cascadas is to take a chiva bus. Although the bike ride was amazing, you can tend to keep one eye on the road, so we jumped on one of the many bus tours that travel up and down the route. Along the way to the Pallon del Diablo, it stopped at various points for photos and we also took a tarabita across the valley. The views from the small cable car were amazing looking down the valley and getting a close up view of a large waterfall tumbling over the canyon's edge into the river below. INSTAGRAM POST 405. The turning point for the tour was the famous Pailon Del Diablo (Devil's Cauldron) waterfall. Helen and I visited the falls the previous day so we treated ourselves to a drink and an ice cream at one of the local stores. During our travels we had now seen quite a few waterfalls, to the point we would, only between us, consider ourselves connoisseurs. The Devil's Cauldron waterfalls would probably make our Top 5 waterfalls, thus far, and we spent an enjoyable couple of hours admiring the views. What makes these waterfalls unique to me is the almost mystical stone staircase that takes you right underneath the falls. There are different ways to see the falls and all are well worth it. INSTAGRAM POST 406 and INSTAGRAM POST 407. One uses the staircase with the falls on your left hand side, and allows you to get absolutely soaked depending on how close you want to see the falls. Another way to see the falls takes you initially behind before appearing on the other side. There are also suspension bridges that allow you to see it again from different angles, but from here you get a really great view of the magical staircase, almost as though it should be part of a Lord of the Rings film.

Upon reading about Baños before we arrived, there was a "you'll love it and hate it" sort of review. Too touristy, too this and that. The thing is we are on the Gringo Trail now and there are going to be lots of tourists at most of the places we visit. It doesn't bother us, these people want to see the same sights as us, and they are tourist sites for a reason. Helen and I enjoyed our time in Baños but it was time to move on south to Cuenca with a six hour bus journey. It is worth mentioning the buses. To some, taking a bus in South America will conjure up images of an old American yellow school bus trundling along at 30 mph with no air conditioning, sitting next to an old man with a chicken on his lap, whilst your backpack sits precariously on top of the bus. Well this could not be further from the truth. The buses we were taking in Ecuador and the rest of our travels in South America were very high quality. I'm talking modern, comfy, reclining seats, most 160 degrees but some 180, meals included, movies, Wi-Fi and toilets. It was a great way to travel along the gringo trail and obviously it was well used by gringos, so it was easy to meet and chat to other travellers. The distance from where we started in Quito down to the tip of Patagonia, where we were planning on reaching was 8,000 km. The distance we travelled across Canada from Prince Edward Island to Victoria on Vancouver Island was only 5,700 km in comparison. Our primary mode of transport to cover this distance was going to be buses so it was a huge relief to know that they were clean, comfortable and safe. At some bus stations we even saw the drivers taking breathalysers before they boarded.

Cuenca is a large city with a population of over 330,000. Cuenca was on our stop not due to Cuenca itself but due to the Parque Nacional Cajas that was located 30 km to the west of the city. Arriving at our hostel it was evident there was no freezer to store the ice packs so I asked at the restaurant next door who said it was no problem to store them in their freezer. Our accommodation was a nightmare, it was so loud, we were next to the bathroom so there was always a lot of coming and going. Worse though was when someone drove their motorbike into the hostel and parked it outside our room at 1am. After a couple of hours sleep we caught a bus to the Cajas National Park. On the bus also heading to the park was a couple who looked familiar. I recognised them as a French couple who we shared a teleférico with on our descent whilst in Quito. Some might say it's a small world, we would say that's the Gringo Trail for you. We were now 470 km from Quito, the distance is more than London to Newcastle and it was two weeks since we shared the cable car so I suppose the odds of us bumping into each other again were quite low. The park itself strangely reminded us of Wales, wet and foggy. The park is famous for Polylepis trees than can grow at high elevations making the park one of the highest forests in the world. Altitudes within the park vary between 3,000 and 4,300m. The warden at the information centre was very helpful and suggested a walk for us, taking about three hours, also providing a map. It was an enjoyable walk and when we re-joined the main road we flagged down a bus taking us back to Cuenca. After a better night's sleep we had a day taking in some sights, mainly parks and walking along the river Tomebamba.

Back on another bus we were now heading to Zamora. Again the attraction here is another National Park, this one called Podocarpus. Our six hour bus journey didn't arrive into Zamora until 7pm so our first evening was non eventful, just a trip to the supermarket as we were staying here for two nights. One thing for certain in Zamora is you can always know what time it is. For some reason there is a hill in Zamora displaying a huge clock. Our hostel had a great rooftop terrace so we had great views of the illuminated clock at night, as well as the sounds it made every 30 minutes.

Our first morning in Zamora, it was very warm. After breakfast on the roof terrace, the reception called us a taxi for the short ride to the park entrance. Podocarpus Park is nearly 1,500 square km in size and the altitude varies greatly from 900m in the lowlands up to 3,600 in the highlands. Zamora is located near the lowlands, so the altitude was not so much of an issue for us. The Parque has some of the world's greatest plant and animal diversity with 40% of the estimated 3,000 plant species occurring nowhere else in in the world. Whilst we were at the entrance control, we saw the biggest butterfly I have ever seen; its wingspan was easily 20cm. Never ones to turn down the opportunity to hike to a waterfall, we did just that, and then followed it up with the very strenuous El Mirador trail. This was basically an hour and a half walking uphill, but it was steep, like scrambling steep and parts where you had to haul yourself up by using a rope. The view at the end was good, but it wasn't at the top, it just came to a halt with a bench and you could only see the view in one direction so after such an exhausting trek uphill it was a bit underwhelming to say the least. As it was a glorious day and we had nothing else to do we decided to walk the 8 km back to the hostel, a lot of it on the dusty track out of the park. It was here that we also saw our first stick insect. It was a great day out apart from the disappointing Mirador, but a really beautiful park.

After a big day of walking we decided to chill out the next day and Skyped our parents. It was trickier now to stay in touch with our families back home. The time difference didn't help as most of the time we were out all day doing something and it was too late to call when we returned. It wasn't like we had a good idea where we would be either from one day to the next so it was difficult to plan a specific time. Bus tickets were purchased that would take us across the border into our next country, Peru. Laundry was also done, not by us, we took it to a laundry store for a very reasonable price as everything in Ecuador is so cheap. The sun was out all day so we walked along the river and stopped for an ice cream. It was a short and sweet stay in Zamora but we were really pleased we decided to head this way instead of the more common western route. Our bus to Peru would be departing the next day at 5am so it was a very early start for our border crossing.

The destination was Jaén, as the crow flies it is about 50 miles over the border, but in reality it was a lot more due to the winding roads. The border crossing and route we were taking into Peru is the one less travelled, there were no other gringos on our bus. At a small town on the way through we picked up a young American guy called John who was also heading to Jaén. He couldn't have been older than 20 and was carrying a tent and cooking gear, he was a nice lad, and it was his first time out of the US so fair play to him, he was jumping in head first. By the time we reached the border post at La Balza, we had already been travelling for hours. The views were amazing but as expected, out in rural Ecuador, the roads were pretty bad and most of the journey was on unpaved roads so it made for slow progress. INSTAGRAM POST 408. There was a guy in a little wooden hut where we exchanged some US dollars for Peruvian Soles before John, Helen and I walked across the grass to the immigration building. The first part was easy on the Ecuador side, an exit stamp and then back on the bus to cross the bridge into Peru. At immigration the official was very friendly and everything was going smoothly, he stamped our passports, welcomed us to Peru, and then pointed in the direction of another room where some nurses were sat. This was where we had to show our vaccination cards. So far so good, we knew we had taken all the necessary vaccines, but they started talking to each other and pointing to our cards. Through Google translate we realised they were looking for proof of the measles vaccination. In the UK, we are all given this in childhood. The issue they had, was proof of this was not stated on our vaccination cards and they were adamant that we needed it. The nurses gave us the option, turn around and go back to Ecuador or roll up our sleeves and have a new jab. The choice was simple, the jab it was, and five minutes later we were back on the bus heading to Jaén. We had only spent three weeks in Ecuador but we were big fans. It was a great introduction to South America, everyone was really friendly and hospitable and genuinely happy that we had chosen to visit their country. Ecuador is a very compact country, one of the smallest in South America yet there are beaches, smouldering volcanos, rainforests, and the Galápagos islands. It was also a lot cheaper than Costa Rica.

B - *PERU*

The difference between Peru and Ecuador was visible instantly as we drove towards Jaén. It looked dirtier, dustier, more rugged and rough around the edges. At 7.30pm we pulled into a dusty bus depot in Jaén, nearly 15 hours after we left Zamora, to cover a distance of just 250 miles. It probably wasn't the best introduction to Peru, it was a bit of dump to be honest. For the traveller, this is a gateway town for further adventures, no need to hang around here. If you can, you catch the next bus out, or if like us and John, you can't, then you stay the night and get out the next morning. John was proper gung ho, he hadn't booked anywhere to stay that evening so shared a taxi with us to our hostel. Luckily they had a spare room for him and after dumping our bags, we met up in the lobby to find a place to eat. The first place we found was a little pizza shop, it was ideal after our long day. John's reason for picking this route down into Peru was the same as ours, a town called Chachapoyas and the nearby Kuelap fortress. The next morning we spent what seemed like ages trying to find the right bus but eventually we managed to book ourselves two seats. Whilst we were waiting in a café, John walked by, also looking for the bus to Chachapoyas. He joined us for something to eat, and then also booked a seat on the cramped minibus for the four hour journey to the town. In the daylight we noticed the way in which women dress in Peru was quite similar to Ecuador, the skirts though seemed to be wider, as they are layered on top of each other and called a Pollera. These are accompanied again by a shawl or a poncho and a hat.

Chachapoyas itself is at an elevation of 2,335 metres and is surrounded by cloud forest so it was no surprise when we turned up it was raining, and cloudy. Chachapoyas actually means "Cloud People" in the Quechua language. Here we said our goodbyes to John, as he went off in search of his accommodation for the night. Again, Chachapoyas, like Jaén was a dusty old rough looking town, especially away from the main square where our hostel was located. The town was just a base though to explore the region in this off the beaten track part of Northern Peru. That afternoon we booked ourselves on the tour of Kuelap.

When we were in Panama and planning out a rough journey of our trip through South America, there didn't seem to be a lot that stood out in Northern Peru. But there were a few bloggers mentioning Chachapoyas and specifically Kuelap fortress. They all seemed to say that it is hard to get to and it takes a while but if you are not in a hurry, make the trip. When most people think of Peru, Machu Picchu is the first thing that comes to mind, this is located right in the south eastern part of the country. Kuelap is located in the north and is a lot harder to reach, as we found out, therefore it is mostly ignored by tourists. INSTAGRAM POST 409.

Kuelap is the so called "Machu Picchu of the North". When compared to the more popular southern attraction it only attracts a fraction of the visitors. However, the Kuelap site and fortress is older, built between some 600 and 900 years before Machu Picchu. It is also larger and built at a higher altitude of 3,000 metres. About 1,500 years ago, Kuelap was home to, at its peak, approximately 300,000 of the Chachapoyas or "Cloud Warriors".

Over the next few years, Kuelap will undoubtedly become more popular. The reason for this is the newly installed cable car, it had only been running for a few months when we visited. The cable car covers a 4 km journey up to the mountain fortress in just 20 minutes. Before the cable car was built, a four hour uphill strenuous trek, or a one and a half hour car ride up windng mountain roads were the only ways to reach the fortress. The journey in the cable car is worth the tour cost alone, it gives a perspective of just how remote this settlement was all those years ago. At the top, it is still a trek to reach the walled city. Our guide gave a great tour of Kuelap lasting well over two hours including its history and their defeat by their southern enemy, the Incas. On the walk back down to the cable car from the fortress we bumped into John, heading in the opposite direction. He told us he was planning on staying at Kuelap overnight by camping. This was obviously not allowed, but there seemed to be plenty of places where he could hide out overnight, so we wished him all the best. Our tour included food and we arrived back in Chachapoyas at 6pm after a thoroughly enjoyable day. Machu Picchu was obviously on our list of future places to visit so we couldn't yet make a comparison. On a recent check I read that in the year since opening the cable car, Kuelap received 120,000 visitors, Machu Picchu sees approximately 5,000 per day, that's 1.8 million per year. Back in the main square we immediately booked ourselves on our next trip, tomorrow we would be visiting Gocta Falls.

I love the story about Gocta Falls. For centuries this waterfall was obviously well known locally but it was only recently that a German tourist managed to persuade the government to measure it because it was actually pretty big. It turned out that the Gocta waterfall is the 16th highest waterfall in the world at 771 metres tall. INSTAGRAM POST 410. A minibus took us to the start of the trek in Cocachimba, we shared the ride with a few other tourists and we all set off at the same time after paying our entrance fee. The trek itself to the falls was great. The falls were clearly visible in the distance from the village as we set off on the undulating path which was pretty tough in parts. You start to appreciate the size of the falls the closer you get but when you arrive you realize how big they actually are. Obviously our ponchos came in handy as we neared the falls, but the draft created was so strong we didn't stay too long. It was best to admire them from a dry safe distance and they truly are a remarkable spectacle. INSTAGRAM POST 411. In the hut where we were admiring the falls, we decided it was the ideal spot to have our lunch and stayed for about an hour before the 5 km return hike. We arrived back at the start point a little bit wet as it had started to rain. A really nice meal was waiting for us in a local restaurant, this was included in the price but afterwards we had to wait well over an hour and a half for the other people who were on our minibus to make it back. It was in Chachapoyas where I tried the infamous Inca Kola. It is like a National Symbol of Peru, a sweet yellowy gold coloured, bubble gum tasting fizzy drink that outsells Coca Cola. It was actually invented by a British immigrant in 1935. We found it way too sweet, that was to be my first and only time of drinking Inca Kola.

Instead of Inca Kola, I was a fan of another drink that seemed very popular in South America, yogurt drinks. In the UK, you are lucky to find any on the supermarket shelves. In South America they were everywhere and I loved them. I had never been a huge fan of breakfast but a strawberry yogurt drink in the morning was perfect for me and they could be found in virtually every store.

Our time in Chachapoyas was up. It was well worth the effort, and the measles jab to get here. The next place on "our list" was the Cordillera Blanca mountain range. To reach it, first we had to take a night bus west to the coastal city of Trujillo. Trujillo features in the Lonely Planet's top 20 but it was not really of any interest to us, we chose to stay in the laidback town of Huanchaco just 15 km north. Our intention was to stay here for just one night to break up the long bus journeys but as the guide book predicted we extended our stay. Huanchaco is a bit of a hippy surfer town and supposedly it is easy to lose track of time here, one traveller I met actually said that to me. Our reason was entirely different, Helen was ill and there is nothing worse than travelling on a long distance bus when feeling awful. Therefore we stayed an extra couple of days until Helen felt well enough to travel. In reality we weren't keen on the place and we would have been out the next day if we could. Each to their own but we were more interested in hiking in the Cordillera Blanca rather than yoga sessions on the roof of the beachfront hostel. Our night bus left Trujillo at 10pm but we never slept as a man was snoring so loudly, neither earplugs nor iPods were able to block out the sound. Tired and frustrated, we arrived in Caraz at 8am and didn't do much all day apart from nap and quiz the hostel owner on how and where to access the mountains. Caraz is known as "Little Huaraz". Huaraz is the main gateway to the mountains and lies about 70 km to the south, but Caraz offers easier access to some of the hikes in the northern mountains. Caraz gave us our first glimpse of the Cordilleras. This place was always on my list since I started researching places to visit in South America. The Cordillera Blanca is the second highest mountain range after the Himalayas, there are 18 summits that are above 6,000m. As well as a playground for the world's best climbers, the area has a number of stunning day hikes for us mere mortals to enjoy as well as multi day hikes such as the famous 4 day Santa Cruz Trek, giving great views of Mount Huascarán, the highest mountain in Peru and 5th highest in South America at 6,768m. Or an even longer option, the Huayhuash Circuit takes 12 days, covering 120 km and considered one of the best hikes in the world. It passes through an area made famous by the climbing survival story "Touching the Void".

The first hike we were going to try out was Lake Paron. Our hostel manager explained to us how to reach it, by directing us to a small bus and taxi depot just around the corner. After a bit of bartering, we ended up in an estate car waiting to leave, but more and more people kept getting in. In the end there were nine of us in this estate car, us the only gringos. After dropping everyone else off the driver pulled up at the Lake Paron entry point and told us where to start the walk, so we got out and started walking after signing in at the hut. The gatekeeper told us that the last collectivo would be leaving in five hours. I should have consulted my offline Google map as the Lake was still some distance away, maybe 10 km and we were constantly walking uphill, with some quite steep sections. All the time buses were driving past us with tourists so we knew we were conned and the driver only took us part of the way. After about two hours of strenuous walking we were getting tired, it was very warm and we were at an altitude of 4,000m. Thankfully a tour bus pulled alongside us and told us to jump in. After about 20 mins the bus arrived at the Lake, it would have probably taken us another two hours to reach it, so we would have never have caught the last bus back. The guide on the bus even offered us a lift back afterwards but we told her we would be fine walking back downhill. We worked out we could enjoy about an hour admiring the lake before setting off back down the hill to catch the last bus. The lake itself is simply stunning, what an introduction to the Cordilleras it was, bright blue, almost the same colour as my trail shoes. INSTAGRAM POST 412. The lake, surrounded on all sides by snow-capped peaks, all above 5,500m, seemed so tranquil, the whole place was so quiet. A rowing boat slowly went past us as we sat above the lake eating our lunch. Soon it was time to head back and catch the collectivo into town. Knowing the gradient, we knew it would be an easy downhill walk back to the signing in hut. It also gave us amazing views back down the valley which we had previously struggled to walk up. INSTAGRAM POST 413. After a really enjoyable walk, we arrived at the hut, only to be told by a different gatekeeper that there were no more collectivos today. Gutted was an understatement. There was nothing we could do, however by coincidence, the gatekeeper seemed to have a friend who would come and pick us up in his taxi for a price. We had to, there was no other option, he phoned his mate and waited for him to come and collect us. Whilst we waited, the gatekeeper and I had a game of chess but the taxi turned up before we could finish the game. Further down the road at the next village, we could see locals catching collectivos to take them into Caraz, but the gatekeeper never mentioned this to us. This was becoming a bit of a theme in Peru, that a gringo equals money. This was never the case in Ecuador at all. That aside, our day at Lake Paron was a good days hiking. The Fitbit recorded 30,000 steps and 412 floors climbed.

The next day we travelled south a short distance to another town on the edge of Cordellias, Yungay, we had found a nice cheap Airbnb to stay in for three days. At the bus stop, we jumped on the back of a moto taxi to take us to our Airbnb, before we got in we had agreed a price. However when we arrived at the Airbnb, the guy asked for double, he claimed the price he told me was for one person not two. I couldn't even be bothered to argue with him, but it was a lesson learnt. Reading through our guide books, Yungay was supposed to be a good point to be able to access some more great walks within the park. Unfortunately this was not the case. Yungay was 60 km away from Huaraz and even though the entrance to the park was here, all the bookings and pick up points were in Huaraz. In the three days we were in Yungay, we never even saw another tourist or gringo. Our Airbnb host even took photographs of us to use on their Airbnb page, presumably to attract more tourists. There wasn't a single tourist office or booking office in the whole town. Our whole experience of Yungay was ruined when we saw a poor dog, obviously poisoned and frothing at the mouth die in front of us at the side of a main road in the town centre. Hardly anyone battered an eyelid at the poor thing or tried to help it. I went looking for a vets but it was shut. I explained to a policewoman what was happening but by the time we had returned to Helen it had sadly died. Witnessing something like that is horrible to see, we witnessed plenty of sad sights when we were in Nevis but it still breaks our hearts to see any animal in pain like that especially when you can't do anything. Again we had only Ecuador to compare against but during our short time in north Peru, there were a lot more stray dogs on the streets. We were already missing Ecuador. That day I let Helen cut my hair with amusing results, after a bit of tidying up it looked more acceptable!

Before we arrived in Yungay, we knew nothing about the sad history of the town. The original town was actually located 2 km away, but is little more than a pile of rubble, except for the giant cemetery and national memorial built to remember a tragic event in 1970 and the worst natural disaster in the Andes. On the 31st of May, coinciding with the opening game at the 1970 World Cup, a huge earthquake dislodged over 50 million cubic tonnes of ice and debris from the west wall of Mt Huascarán. The original town was in the path of the resulting debris avalanche, within minutes the town was buried under eight metres of ice and granite, and 20,000 people were killed. The area is now covered in rose gardens, gravestones and monuments. INSTAGRAM POST 414. The second and third photos show the remains of a bus and the third and fourth photos show what is left of a church.

It was time to move onto Huaraz, the epicentre of all things hiking and climbing in the Cordillera. A collectivo drove us south to the busy city. With a population of over 125,000 it sits at an already high elevation of 3,100 metres. Our accommodation was simple, but it was central. It was attached to a bar and café which served great soup and chips for a very reasonable price. It was located near numerous tourist agencies offering all sorts of trips into the Cordillera Blanca. Sitting outside with a beer, it was also a great spot for people watching with everyone wearing different coloured and branded down jackets and trekking gear. Nearby tables were full of people examining maps for their next planned adventure or reliving those just experienced. Booking office workers were coiling climbing ropes and re packing hired tents. It was a real mecca for the outdoor enthusiast and we loved it, you could feel a real buzz about the area and the shops catered to everything you would ever need in the mountains.

Apart from our short time on the coast at Trujillo we had spent the past month at a decent altitude as we had been following the Andes south through Ecuador and Northern Peru. Even so, we didn't want to get ahead of ourselves, so we had heard about a hike that didn't exceed 4,000 metres, one of the few in the area, and was highly recommended as an

215

acclimatisation hike. It was called the Laguna Wilcacocha hike and it was located about 10 km from Huaraz, but was easy to reach by a collectivo that drops you right next to the start on the main highway.

For a starter hike, it was actually really tough as it was uphill the entire way until reaching Wilcacocha Lake. In all the round trip is just over 6.5 km. It took us about two hours to reach the lake and only about an hour to get back down. The Lake itself is not that impressive, instead everyone sits with their backs to the lake in order to enjoy the impressive view across the valley. The views across to the Cordillerra Blanca mountain range are just spectacular. INSTAGRAM POST 415. On the way back down, we bumped into some familiar faces, the French couple again, with whom we shared the teleférico in Quito and then saw again in Cajas National Park. The distance since we first saw them was now nearly 1,000 miles and yet we had already seen them once in that time, I found it quite amazing, Helen didn't seem to care. Back at the bottom of the hike, we treated ourselves to a bottle of beer and an ice cream and sat in the shade until we flagged down a collectivo that took us back to Huaraz. Day one in Huaraz was a good one, day two was even better.

Next door at the tourist guide shop we had been talking to the owner about what hikes she recommended, a chat she probably has numerous times a day with tourists. She therefore recommended the most famous day hike in the Cordillera Blanca, Laguna 69. This was always on our list as it features on many websites and blogs as one of the best hikes in South America. However she also recommended a hike that we had never heard of or read about. Lake Rajucolta was a hike where the only way to the start of the trail was via a taxi. With what happened at Lake Paron, we were a bit dubious about taking another taxi to the start of a hike but she assured us this would be ok. We signed up and our taxi driver picked us up on time and drove us right into the Cordillera Blanca, passing through tiny remote villages until we arrived at some gates after nearly two hours. Our driver told us just to climb the small wall to the side and then follow the trail to the lake. He reclined his seat and said he'd sleep and wait for us, saying it would normally take about four hours to complete the round trip. If he wasn't there when we got back we were in serious trouble as we were absolutely in the middle of nowhere, the last remote village we had passed was about half an hour ago. Our fate relied on the driver telling the truth and waiting for us as we climbed the wall, walked past the empty hut and followed the trail around the bend and out of sight. Overall the walk was 16 km but completely flat, although the altitude was 4,200 metres. It was one of most enjoyable hikes Helen and I had during our whole trip. That was saying something as we had walked a lot in the past two years. INSTAGRAM POST 416. During the whole walk, we never met a single person, it was so quiet. It was impossible to get lost as we followed the mountain stream in the direction of the towering Mt Huantsán in the distance. It is the 6th highest mountain in Peru and the lake was situated at its base with a glacier at the far end. Upon reaching the lake we had our lunch and then walked around the side to get a closer view of the glacier with the waterfalls running into the lake which provided the first proper sounds we had heard since setting off. Higher up we could hear some loud thundering and cracking noises from the glacier moving, we didn't hang around too long and set off back to the taxi by the same path. On the way back we could hear some avalanches behind us coming from higher up Mt Huantsán, we would turn around and see plumes of snow. We were really hoping our taxi driver would still be there waiting for us. Luckily he was, sound asleep in the driver's seat, we were safe. It had been a truly brilliant day of hiking which Helen and I still talk about today.

Back at our hostel, the convenience of a central location was great but the noise at night from other guests was annoying so we decided to move accommodation that afternoon to a quieter hostel out of the city centre. Now more familiar with the layout of the city it was only a 15 minute walk back to the centre.

The next day was supposed to the Laguna 69 hike, but unfortunately Helen wasn't feeling well again. I offered to miss the hike so we could both go when Helen felt better but she persuaded me to go on my own. My pick up was at 5am as my hostel was one of the first collections. By the time we had driven around all the other hostels and the bus was full, the darkness had cleared and it looked like it would be a fine day for a hike. Breakfast was at a roadside restaurant just before we entered the park. Back on the bus I ended up sitting next to a Brazilian guy called Henrique. He was on his own as well and spoke really good English so we enjoyed a chat until the bus pulled up at the start of the hike. Henrique and I decided we would hike together, fortunately we had a similar walking pace. The hike itself was great, starting off flat through the valley then some serious uphill sections before reaching the lake after about 7 km. INSTAGRAM POST 417. This is the most popular day hike in the area and so it can seem crowded at times especially after the secluded hike at Rajucolta. With some tourists only spending a day or two in Huaraz, this is the walk they choose, but if you've not acclimatised it can be a challenging walk. We passed a few walkers who looked like they were suffering purely because they hadn't taken the time or had the inclination to acclimatise. The Laguna 69 hike starts at 3,850 metres and finishes at the lake at 4,600m, so there is a fair bit of elevation involved. Henrique and I were feeling good and managed to reach the lake in two and a half hours. The Lake was the same vivid blue as Lake Paron, sitting at the base of Mt Chacraraju (6,112 metres). The setting is stunning but you have to share it with everyone else, I would say there were about 200 people at the lake when we arrived. After a while Henrique and I decided to head back down which only took an hour. We timed it perfectly, it started to rain just as we reached the bus, it didn't matter that we had to wait over an hour for our party to return, at least we were dry. It was a real shame Helen was unable to take part in this hike so it will always have that as a bit of negative for me, but Henrique was great company throughout the day and we chatted all the way back to Huaraz. My Fitbit recorded over 600 flights of stairs and just over 40,000 steps that day. This was on top off 35,000 steps for the Rajucolta hike the day before and 23,000 for Wilcacocha. We came to Huaraz for the hiking and it was certainly delivering.

Our next organised tour in Huaraz was to the Pastoruri Glacier. This was a rest day in terms of steps and distance covered but a new high in terms of elevation as we passed the 5,000 metre barrier. Again we were picked up a by a bus and driven the 70 km to the start point of a short hike to the glacier. There were no other Gringos on the bus and everyone else was part of the same large party, all in their senior years. The guide also didn't speak any English. Half way during the drive we stopped at a café for some food and a chance to try coca tea for the first time. It is well known that coca is used widely throughout South America as a way of preventing altitude sickness. It comes in various forms and is completely legal in Peru and Bolivia. In the supermarket you can purchase coca sweets, coca leaves and coca tea. Since arriving in Huaraz Helen and I regularly used coca sweets to help ease the effects and it did help. We had both tried the leaf method which involves folding up some leaves placing them between your gum and cheek. After a while it makes your cheek tingle, so we both preferred the hard boiled sweets method. Today as we were reaching new heights of 5,250 metres we were adding tea to the sweets and leaves. It didn't taste much different to any other herbal tea but it was drinkable. Even though we were on a bus with a bunch of older people who we didn't understand it was an enjoyable journey, whether that had something to do with coca I'm not sure but not long after the café the whole group started singing all the way until we reached the start point for the glacier.

After a 40 minute uphill hike, including a few brief stops to catch our breath, the glacier comes into view. INSTAGRAM POST 418. Sadly and predictably, the Pastoruri glacier is a shadow of its former self. It is rapidly retreating, losing a third of its size in just the last 30 years, this in turn has resulted in a decline in visitor numbers. It is expected to completely disappear in the next decade.

Our last full day in Huaraz meant another epic walk, next on the list was Laguna Churup. Another organised minibus pick up, taking us directly to the start of the walk. As expected by now in Huaraz, we knew we would be in for a tough hike, but equally the rewards of amazing views made it all worth it. The hike was pretty much uphill the entire way, about 4 km, at some points we had to use ropes as certain sections were so steep. Whether it was because we had crammed a lot of walking in over the past few days, plus Helen had been unwell, we both felt it more on this one than any other. My Fitbit recorded another epic day of over 600 flights of stairs so it was a tough one finishing at 4,450m. INSTAGRAM POST 419. On the 6th photo you can just see the trail snaking all the way back down towards the valley. The scenery at the top was now familiar; a tranquil gorgeous lake surrounded by snow-capped mountains, but it was sight we could never get bored of.

Our time in Huaraz had come to an end. Both of us had really enjoyed our time here and agreed that it was a place we would love to visit again without a shadow of doubt. If you like hiking and want the scenery to match, whilst testing yourself on some really tough walks, Huaraz and the Cordillera Blanca is the place to visit. We couldn't recommend it enough. Knowing there was so much else for us to see and do in South America, we pushed on south but we could have easily stayed another week. After Caraz and Yungay, Huaraz had improved our experience of Peru.

The next couple of days involved a lot of time on buses as we pressed on South, firstly to Lima. With no intention of staying here we continued on to Arequipa. Huaraz to Lima was eight hours and Lima to Arequipa was a further 16 hours. For that reason we opted for a full 180 degree reclining seat on our leg to Arequipa and enjoyed a really good night's sleep. Helen's insulin was also running low. The supply she returned to Grenada with from the UK was almost gone, it had lasted over a year, but we would have to purchase insulin from now on.

After another night bus we arrived in Cusco at 6.30am. Fortunately we were able to check into our hostel and then slept till midday. Cusco nowadays is famous the world over as it is seen as the gateway to Machu Picchu, the Sacred Valley and all the other archaeological remains. It was once the capital of the Inca Empire until the Spanish conquest by Francisco Pizarro in 1533. Tourism is obviously the main driver to the economy here with 1.2 million visitors per year. After our nap we walked from our hostel to the main Plaza De Armas. The 20 min walk was a bit of an eye opener, it appeared we were passing the meat and cheese vendors selling their goods on the streets. Various animals were in cages awaiting their fate including quite a lot of guinea pigs. Here in Peru, the guinea pig is a national dish. That morning I was messaged by Steve, a friend from home asking when we would be arriving in Cusco, I told him we had just arrived and he asked for a favour. An old University friend of his had supposedly settled in Cusco and owned a shop selling maps in the main Plaza de Armas called King Of Maps. Steve asked if we would we be able to check if it was true and find Olly. Locating the shop, I walked in, asked for Olly, the lady said he was due in later, maybe a couple of hours. Around the Plaza De Armas, there are dozens of tourist agencies trying to get you to buy their tours. With a couple of hours to kill we decided to see what was available. We definitely knew that we would be visiting Machu Picchu, the Sacred Valley and Rainbow Mountain. Before arriving in Cusco we had read a load of blogs and websites saying book up in advance for Machu Picchu but realised that was only if you wanted to do the Inca Trail. This may appeal to some, but to us, it is an overpriced guided hike so we weren't interested. There was so much to do in Cusco and lots of different ways to reach Machu Picchu. After a couple of hours we were armed with a load of leaflets from various agencies. Nothing purchased yet, we would think it over in the evening and return tomorrow to book our trips. I then returned to the King of Maps shop and introduced myself to Olly. He was a bit bemused that I just turned up saying we had a mutual friend who would like to reconnect. After passing on Steve's number we had a good chat and arranged to go for a beer during our time in Cusco.

Our first night's sleep in the hostel was not great as somehow a cat had managed to climb to a place where it was then unable to get down so then proceeded to let everyone know of the fact all night. When the day shift arrived in the morning, the cat was safely rescued. Bleary eyed, we walked back to the Plaza de Armas and bought ourselves a coffee. An hour later we had booked ourselves onto three tours. Tomorrow we would be setting off to Machu Picchu on a three day / two night Inca Jungle Tour. This comprised of downhill mountain biking, white water rafting and zip lining before reaching the ruins. We would also be visiting Rainbow Mountain and then two days after that we would be having a tour of the Sacred Valley. All three tours cost £300 for the pair of us, a lot cheaper than we thought it would be. Just to walk the Inca Trail, costs start at about £400 per person, and prices increase when you don't want to carry your own gear and start paying for porters. That meant in all we would be spending ten days in and around Cusco. Back at the hostel we packed what we needed for our three days away and booked the remaining nights for when we returned. The hostel was kind enough to let us leave our main backpacks whilst we were on our tour.

221

Our Jungle Inca Tour started with an 8 am pick up in a minibus where we met our fellow tourists. A three hour drive then took us to San Luis at an elevation of 4,300 metres. After a quick safety talk and a change into full protective gear, we all jumped on our bikes and cycled 60 km downhill to 1,200m. INSTAGRAM POST 420. There was no pressure to keep up with those at the front, you could go at your own pace and we all stopped a couple of times so we could regroup. As the cycling was all downhill on relatively quiet roads it was great fun, Helen and I really enjoyed it. At the bottom, with bikes loaded onto the roof we transferred to Santa Maria where we all sat down for lunch. Food and accommodation was included in the price of our Jungle Tour package. At our table we chatted to a couple of guys, both travelling alone. One was a young German guy called Tom and the other was a Turkish guy called Emré, a commercial pilot who was on a short holiday. After lunch, most of the group then went to the white water rafting leg of the tour. Helen and I weren't actually fussed about this part, so we were taken straight onto our accommodation in Santa Teresa, driving along unpaved roads with a huge drop down to the river below. It was a relief when we reached our hotel to find we had our own room with a hot shower. Toilet roll for some reason wasn't provided so that meant a trip to a small nearby store where we also stocked up on snacks and water for tomorrow. Santa Teresa was a small rural village. We had plenty of time to kill so enjoyed a few beers sitting outside a bar on the main street. It was really nice just sitting out in this tiny village in the middle of nowhere both enjoying a drink. The day after tomorrow we would be at Machu Picchu, it just seemed crazy. We never thought we would be here, it was now mid-October, so we had been travelling for two years and three months. We had only spent six weeks in South America but we couldn't believe how much we had already done in such a short space of time in this continent. And yet there was still so much more left to see and do. I remember a few times looking at where we were in Ecuador on the map and just looking at the distance all the way down to Patagonia thinking it is so far away. Thus far, we had kept an eye on workaways and house sits but there was nothing particularly appealing to us so we carried on with our rough plan south. Our group and numerous other groups all joined together later in a large restaurant, we sat with Tom and Emré listening to their stories about rafting. It turned out Tom was left behind and had to get a lift here with another group.

Our day started at 7.30am the next morning with a short walk to the same restaurant for breakfast. Afterwards we were all split into different groups again, Tom joining another group but Emré remained with Helen and me. Once we were all fitted with our harnesses and helmets we were driven the short distance up to the first zip line. It now appeared the large valley we were driving along the side of yesterday; today we would be zip lining across it! INSTAGRAM POST 421. There were five zip lines in total and it was great fun. Our party included a group from Ireland. It seemed Helen must have adapted to the conditions as some of the Irish were getting eaten by mosquitos but Helen was absolutely fine. Zip lining lasted a couple of hours, then we were transferred to Hydroelectrica for lunch. This is where our trek to Machu Picchu began. On the fourth photo, our guide told us that Machu Picchu sat on the other side of the mountain. Tom re-joined us for lunch as the larger group was back together, then it was time to hike to Aguas Calientes, the closest overnight stay to Machu Picchu. The hike was 12 km but our guide wanted to make sure we all arrived together. By now Helen and I had acclimatised pretty well and our walking speed was quicker than everyone else in the group. The guide told us to wait at a shack along the route. The hike follows the train track from Hydroelectrica and the trains give a good warning when approaching with plenty of room to stand out of the way. When we set off again, Helen and I took to the front again but once more we were told of a place where to wait. This was annoying as we could see it started to look like rain. It would have been preferable if they had given us the name and address of the hostel, we could have arrived there earlier and just grabbed a drink somewhere. Instead we ended up soaked, even though we wore ponchos, as we had to wait for everyone else but obviously we packed light for the three day tour. That evening in the hostel we desperately tried to dry all our items of clothing and shoes. Again dinner was included in the tour but the majority of the group declined and went in search of their own sustenance for the evening. The only ones who took up the offer were Helen, myself, Tom, Emré and three girls who were part of a bigger group from Israel. We soon found out that their group, about a dozen in total had all just finished their

National conscription. This is compulsory for all Israeli citizens over the age of 18 and the length of service normally lasts about two years and eight months. Having recently finished, the group were all taking a well-deserved holiday. It was an interesting chat, Emré also had to serve a year's compulsory conscription in Turkey. Obviously at present this is not something that happens in the UK, nor in Germany for Tom, but I don't think it's a bad thing and I know it's easier to say that when you are older but I think it would be beneficial to all parties. Both Emré and the three Israeli girls were in favour of it. Indeed only last year, French President Emmanuel Macron has reintroduced national service on a voluntary basis of four weeks, but it is likely to be become compulsory in the future. After dinner, our guide started handing out the tickets for entry to Machu Picchu. There are two options to get to Machu Picchu, take the bus or hike the 8 km steep winding mountain path. The site opens at 6am and we knew we had to walk back down and additionally hike 12 km along the tracks again to Hydroelectrica so we decided to go for the bus option. The guide advised us to start queuing early. Buses start leaving at 5.30am so we were told to start queueing at 4.15am. It was going to be an early start. For some reason, they didn't have a ticket for Emré, how this happened was baffling but he was left with no explanation why and there was nothing we could do to help. We felt really bad for him, there was no way he could even delay it a day, as his flight out was tomorrow evening. He had a really small window to see Machu Picchu and it had been taken away from him. The last we saw of Emré, he was trying to contact the tourist agency back in Cusco but they had closed for the day.

After a short sleep, Helen and I were up at 3.45am to start queuing for the buses. There were already about 500 people in the queue ahead of us. Whilst we were waiting, we saw the three girls from dinner last night, they were hiking the 8 km to the top, as was Tom, but we never saw him. Our bus dropped us at the entrance at 6am where we met our guide. It seemed like a good decision to take the bus after seeing all of the people covered in sweat who had attempted the hike.

Getting in was a bit of a free for all, our guide told us where to meet him. Tom appeared, it turned out he spent most of the night being sick so decided to catch a bus up rather than hike. He also told us Emré still hadn't managed to locate an entry ticket which was really unfair on him. At 6am there is not actually a lot to see, the whole site was covered in thick fog at this time of the morning. Our guide gave us a tour for approximately two hours and then we had another three hours all to ourselves. Afterwards we would have to start the descent and the walk along the tracks in order to catch our transport back to Cusco.

What can you say about Machu Picchu? Everyone knows about it, and it appears on most people's bucket list. Yes, the location is stunning. INSTAGRAM POST 422, but even with a daily limit of nearly 6,000 people it can seem crowded. The photos taken for our posts look like we are the only people there, believe us, we were not. It is one of the most famous tourist attractions in the world so don't turn up and get frustrated with the number of people, accept it and enjoy it for what it is, an Inca archaeological site dating back to the 1400's in a jaw dropping location. Although the actual function of the site is still not really known, you have to be impressed with the size of the site, the ruins themselves and the location. To be honest the location is the big draw here. Our first two photos show the classic photo of Machu Picchu with what most people are familiar with. This viewpoint is called the Hut of the Caretaker. Lush green mountains all around and high in the clouds. It wasn't until we arrived that we discovered the large peak behind the ruins in the first two photos, called Wayna Picchu, can also be climbed. Visitor numbers are limited to only 400 per day and need to booked months in advance. The main site can be walked around at your own leisure and part of the site has a one way system finishing on the lower agricultural terraces after starting at the ceremonial baths. In between you will pass through the Royal Tomb, the Temple of the Sun, Temple of the Three Windows and the Sacred Plaza. The site is actually quite large and there are other areas to explore such as the Inca Drawbridge and the Sun Gate. The Sun Gate, or Intipunkuas as is also known is where the Inca Trail ends, so it is the first viewpoint of the site for the weary hikers. We took hundreds of photos and videos, you can't help it, you want to capture as much as you can from this New Seventh Wonder of the World. Those three hours allowed us plenty of time to explore the parts we wanted and also just to sit and take it all in and admire it. At 11.30 we decided we should leave, it only took us just over 30 minutes to get back down to Aguas Calientes then another two hours to walk the 12 km along the tracks to Hydroelectrica. The last photo on the post shows the train track. Luckily it hadn't rained all day and only started once we reached the hydroelectric pick up point where there were dozens of minibuses with guides and drivers just shouting out names. When your name was called you were directed to a bus and your day was over, enjoy the sleepy journey back to Cusco. After about half an hour, sheltered under a hut, Helen and I had worked out that we had listened to every driver but we still hadn't heard our name. It was bound to happen, things happen in threes so they say, no ticket for Emré to enter Machu Picchu, Tom was ill the night before, and then us with no lift back to Cusco. I ended up talking to a guide who spoke good English, he phoned our tourist agency and he arranged for us to board another bus with a load of school kids. We didn't care, nor did we care that they stopped in a town for an hour for something to eat at a restaurant, who kindly offered us some free food. Eventually we pulled up in Cusco at 11pm, it had been a very long but memorable day. Great news was received the next day from Emré via WhatsApp, I forgot I had his number, I had taken it as I recorded a video of him the previous day on the zip lines. They managed to sort him out a ticket eventually so he made the afternoon visitors slot and still had time to catch his flight. It all ended up ok for us, presuming Tom made a full recovery; he was looking a lot better when we saw him for the last time about 10am. On reflection, the thing that Machu Picchu has over Chachapoyas is the view, the picture postcard, Instagrammable shot. Chachapoyas does not have one, it is built on the highest point, and there is nothing around it higher than the Chachapoyas fortress itself. But then that justifies why it is where it is, it was a fortress, it is supposed to be difficult to reach and attack. For that reason, and the Inca Trail hike, Machu Picchu will always be one of most wanderlusted places on the planet, but I expect Chachapoyas to gain a lot more visitors in the future.

As expected, the next day was a zero day, we Skyped our parents and stocked up on snacks for tomorrow, the trip to Rainbow mountain. I had seen photos of Rainbow Mountain before and just thought it looked amazing, as soon as I showed Helen, she was the same and it was a simple

226

day tour from Cusco with another early start for a three hour drive to Cusipata

Again like most attractions in Cusco, it was crowded, but this is quite a cheap day tour though. The hike to reach the mountain is still tough, all above 5,000 metres, the round trip is just over 10 km with a couple of steep-ish sections that really take your breath away. This hike was the first time I had felt the sensation of really being out of breath and gasping for air. The Coca sweets were needed for this hike. One of guides also had a jar of liquid that he would offer for a sniff to help with the altitude. After I sniffed it he told me it was llama urine and to this day I still don't know if he was joking. Whether it was or not it still perked me up. Unfortunately when we reached the Rainbow Mountain, the heavens opened and we were covered in a snowstorm. Eventually it all cleared and the mountain, Vinicunca revealed its striking colours of reds, greens and oranges. INSTAGRAM POST 423.

After another rest day, next on the Cusco to do list was the Sacred Valley Tour. Five tourist attractions all in one day exploring the beautiful area around the Rio Urubamba Valley. INSTAGRAM POST 424. First up was Chinchero (2nd photo). Andean mountain village, tick. Inca ruins, tick, church, tick, large market, tick. The next place we visited was Maras (1st Photo). Our guides explained to us how the bowl shaped structures were used for growing different crops, but again that hasn't been proven. One of my favourite parts of the day was a visit to the Moray Salt mines, where several hundred terraced ponds dominate the landscape, (3rd Photo). Our penultimate attraction was the impressive ruins of Ollantaytambo. (4th and 5th Photo) before finishing at Pisac. Unfortunately once we started walking around Pisac fortress it started to rain. Even though we had ponchos and brollies, our guide wasn't keen on getting wet so the tour ended rather abruptly (6th photo) which was a shame as it looked like it would have been a good tour. We would recommend the Sacred Valley Tour, it isn't expensive and you get the chance to see five sights all in one day. Back in Cusco, I got in touch with Olly and arranged to go for a beer that evening.

It was now our last full day in Cusco, when I went to make breakfast on our final morning, I opened the fridge and saw half a guinea pig on a plate sat on the bottom shelf. Worst of all, its little foot was hanging off the edge, like a miniature version of the Thing from The Adams Family. After breakfast we walked up one of the surrounding hills to get a great view of the city, INSTAGRAM POST 425. In all we had ten really enjoyable days here, there is so much you can do aside from Machu Picchu, it is easily possible to spend three weeks exploring the city and the surrounding sights. That evening I went for another drink with Olly to say goodbye as the next morning we would be catching a bus to Puno. Puno was no more than an overnight stop on our way to the border crossing at Bolivia. This border patrol was pretty straightforward compared to our crossing into Peru and we arrived at Copacabana on the Bolivian side by midday. INSTAGRAM POST 426.

C - BOLIVIA

First impressions, we couldn't tell that we had entered another country like we did when we crossed from Ecuador to Peru. The women were dressed the same, in polleras, and shawls. The only difference was the hat, here in Bolivia the hat of choice was a bowler hat. The alleged story is that when the British shipped them out to the railway workers at the end of the 19th century they were unfortunately too small. Not wanting to waste the stock, they convinced the women that all the fashionable females in Europe wore these hats. The rest as they say is history.

After checking in to our hostel, we walked back downhill to town followed by a steep walk up to the top of Cerro Calvario. Sunglasses and sun cream are essential here as lack of shade and thin air mean sunburn is a real danger throughout the region. We were rewarded with amazing views back over the town but more importantly, out as far as the eyes could see across Lake Titicaca. INSTAGRAM POST 427. Lake Titicaca is big, very big, it is the largest lake in South America and covers some 3,200 square miles. In length the lake stretches for 120 miles and 50 miles at its widest with over 40 islands spread throughout. It is also high, at an elevation of 3,812 metres. As well as its size, Lake Titicaca is well known as the birthplace of the Inca civilisation. The ancient Incas believed that the lake gave birth to the sun. Archaeological sites can be found all around the lake and these date back to 1500 BC. Even discoveries at the bottom of the Lake lead some to believe that there were inhabitants as far back as 6000 BC.

The largest island on the Lake is Isla del Sol. One of the most recommended day hikes in South America is a hike through the middle of the island, however a dispute by two communities on the island have since made this famous walk impossible. Starting in early 2017, the argument started when some guesthouses were built so as to draw visitors to the southern part of an island. Other communities in the north of the island disagreed with the idea and wrecked the guesthouses. As a result the south then blocked off the whole of the northern island from tourism and this still continues, hence the reason it is not possible to walk the length of the island. Despite this Helen and I still booked a tour that would take us to the southern part of the island as well as to the neighbouring Isla de La Luna.

To be honest, the tour was pretty disappointing. The boat was very slow, and the lake is large. It seemed to take about two hours to reach one island, another hour or so to then travel to the next and then another two hours back. If you are prepared to spend most of your day sitting inside a very cramped boat then this would be ok for you. The tour allowed us about an hour on the Isla de la Luna, so no time to explore at all. On the Isla del Sol, the boat dropped us off at one part of the island and then we walked around to be picked up from the main port. We probably had about two hours on the Isla del Sol. Our stay at Copacabana was short as we wanted to press on to La Paz. The bus journey took about four hours and included a ferry crossing across part of the lake. About half of the journey skirts around the shores of the lake offering great views.

Arriving in La Paz is a real eye opener and an assault on the senses. A population of over 1.7 million people in a city at an elevation of 3,660m, it was everything we normally hate about cities, but for some reason we really liked the urban jungle of La Paz. La Paz is not actually the capital of Bolivia and would have slipped up many a pub quiz team. Sucre is the constitutional capital but La Paz is considered the de facto capital. Our first afternoon was spent stocking up on some groceries. A bit like in Cusco, we had an idea of a couple of activities we wanted to do so we knew we would be here for a short while. It's amazing how some of the most trivial things to normal people could now excite us, but the sight of a toaster at the hostel was really welcome. It had been a long time since we had enjoyed toast.

On our first full day in La Paz, we decided to use the famous public transport system, Mi Teléferico. Due to the geography of La Paz this subway in the sky has transformed the way locals commute around the city. It is set in a canyon, created by the Choqueyapu River and located in a bowl like depression surrounded by the high mountains of the Altiplano. The first phase was completed in 2014 with three lines spread out across the city. Phase two saw the addition of a blue line and then six more were announced. The system is easily the world's longest aerial cable car and an absolute must for any visiting tourist. INSTAGRAM POST 428. Riding the teleférico gives unbeatable views of the hustle and bustle below. I thought it would make a great scene as part of a James bond film. I could just see Bond fighting a bad guy on top of a cable car above the city with the stunning backdrop of the mountains. And at 33p a ticket it is amazing value. Knowing that Chile and Argentina are a lot more expensive than Bolivia I needed to buy some clothes for our upcoming visits to the salt flats and Patagonia where the temperatures were expected to drop. The district of Irpavi is out to the east of the main city centre and about a 40 minute enjoyable trip on the cable car to reach the large Megacenter. It was here I picked up a nice warm hoody. The shops and stalls around our hostel were full of fake gear, I ended buying a thick thermal top, supposedly North Face but I wasn't convinced. My day pack was also on its last legs so a new one was purchased.

Our hostel was also located near the famed Mercado de las Brujas, or Witches Market. Not for the squeamish, the stalls have various potions and charms but it was the llama foetuses that raised our eyebrows. For the following day we booked ourselves a tour to Chacaltaya. The day was then spent planning our itinerary for Patagonia. There was always a rough outline but with so much to do and see we felt we needed to have more of a concrete route in place.

Cerro Chacaltaya is 5,421 metres in altitude, this was to be the highest we would reach on our trip, and puts it higher than Mt Everest Base Camp. With what is now becoming common along the Andes, the original glacier was once home to the world's highest ski resort, but the glacier started retreating. Scientists made the stark prediction that the glacier would disappear by 2015, sadly it had completely disappeared by 2009. The bus journey takes about 90 minutes from the buzz of La Paz to the desolate mountain resort. Once the bus pulls up to the top car park it is a relatively short but steep and tricky walk to the summit. When we exited the bus, the temperature was cold and windy, and we started the slow walk to the top. The problem wasn't the altitude, we were well acclimatised now and felt no effects of altitude sickness. The problem was the weather, as we were heading up a snow storm came in and that made it difficult with visibility. With the height, the majority of the route was covered in snow and ice and therefore it was quite slippery. We were in two minds whether we should carry on to the top but persisted. Fortunately by the time we arrived at the summit, the skies had cleared and we were awarded with some stunning views around the region. INSTAGRAM POST 429. Our day tour also included a tour of the Valle de la Luna. This is an area in eastern La Paz which has numerous hoodoos where the rock has been eroded to create spires and canyons. It was great, but having visited Bryce Canyon in the US, it was never going to quite compare in in terms of size and wow factor.

That evening Helen started feeling ill again unfortunately. Since travelling in Central and South America we were picking up more and more germs and bugs from constantly travelling on public transport and again it seemed Helen had caught another one, just recently after falling ill in Cusco. As a result we booked some extra nights in our hostel. The next day I wandered around the nearby tourist agencies and booked myself on the infamous Death Road cycle tour. Helen wasn't keen on this activity anyway so it seemed the ideal time to do it, allowing her to rest up all day in the hostel.

"The World's most dangerous road" was given its name by an inter Development Bank Report. Linking La Paz to Coroico, it was identified that on average 26 vehicles per year were disappearing off the narrow 3.2m cliffside road into the canyon some 600 metres below. The majority of the road is without safety barriers and the worst tragedy occurred in 1983 when a truck with 100 passengers plunged over the side. Thankfully a new replacement road was built in 2007 and now the Death Road is largely unused by vehicles, except those supporting tourist cycling groups who ride downhill along the 60 km route. Over the years 27 cyclists have also fallen victim to the infamous death road so this was something to take seriously. In my group there were 13 of us, I sat on the bus with a friendly girl called Noelia. The rest of the group was made up of a Scandinavian couple, a group of French friends and a small group of Irish lads. It was a really enjoyable day. The start of the road is at 4,700m altitude, and finishes at 1,200m so that is a lot of descending. Obviously we were given a full safety briefing at the start and we were wearing full body protection and helmets. Even before we started it was raining and it continued for most of the day, some points it was torrential. It was impossible to see the drop off at the sides as the valley was covered in thick cloud. The Irish guys were a really good laugh and they all went hell for leather down the road, and I joined in, despite the horrendous wet conditions. The tour leader would be up front and we would stop every so often to regroup but then myself and the Irish guys would resume our racing down the road. INSTAGRAM POST 430. At the end of the ride we were taken to a restaurant for a nice warm meal and a shower, it was 9pm when I eventually made it back to the hostel where Helen was feeling better. Our time in La Paz had come to an end, and with the exception of Helen's illness we really enjoyed our time in this city. The fact that there are loads of opportunities for excursions always helps, as it did in Cusco and Huaraz. Our way out of La Paz was another overnight bus leaving at 10pm. Deciding to give the Cordillera Real and Sucre a miss, we headed straight for Uyuni, gateway to the world famous Salt Flats.

It felt very strange arriving in Uyuni at 7.30am the following morning. It is a small desert town in the middle of nowhere, down in the south western part of Bolivia. Instantly the sun was blinding, there wasn't a cloud in the sky and the temperature was rising. However we read as soon as the sun goes down it can get extremely cold down here. Unable to check into our hostel until 11.30am, we and everyone from our bus had the same idea, head to main square for coffee. The main square is also the place where all the tour agencies are centred so there is no shortage of guides vying for attention to book a tour with them. There are numerous tours available and most people book a three day, two night tour which culminates in a border crossing into Chile. With concerns about Helen's insulin in the heat of the day and the freezing night temperatures we found a tour that only required one night out in remote desert. Day one consists of a full day on the salt flats and instead of continuing on into the remote southwest circuit we would return to Uyuni for the night and commence the tour again the next day. Tours don't run between December and March as the salt flats flood and only the edge of the flats can be visited. The whole town has the feel of a remote outpost. Most vehicles are the 4x4 jeeps covered in salt that drive tourists to and from the salt flats. There is a high turnover of tourists not spending more than a couple of nights in the town as they make their way across to Chile or vice versa. Our tour started with a very short ride out of town to the Train Cemetery with our five other co-tourists which included two really nice older guys from Chile who were on a motorcycle tour.

233

There used to be railcar factory here years ago but no longer and all that remains are the weather battered historic carriages and locomotives. Photos 7 and 8 on INSTAGRAM POST 431. After a stop off at a market place for lunch, it was then time for the salt flats. The flats are everything we expected and more, it is just so surreal. The jeep drove for about 30 mins across the flats and parked up outside the original salt hotel. The hotel no longer has overnight stays but is a place to stop for photos and admire the flag monument. Sunglasses are a must here, the glare is just so bright, and there are basically two colours, the white of the salt flats and the bright blue of the cloudless sky. The world's largest salt flats cover an area of 4,086 square miles, that is roughly the size of Cyprus, at an elevation of 3,656 meters above sea level. They are also 120 metres deep. After a look around and photo opportunities we jumped back in the jeep and headed to a dormant volcano called Tunupa about an hour's drive away. The Volcano rises out of the salt flats to a height of 5,321m. Our tour didn't venture inland, instead we were told we had about 30 minutes to take some photos of the llamas and flamingos. Back in the jeep it was another ride across the surreal world of the salt flats. In the distance we could see our destination, Cactus Island, but apart from that, the place was deserted. Once in a while you would meet another jeep transporting tourists across the flats. Cactus Island, or Isla Incahuasi to give its proper name was probably our favourite part of day. INSTAGRAM POST 432. We parked up and paid our entrance fee and then followed the marked pathway to the top of the island. Even though it wasn't a big climb to the top, it gave a new perspective to the salt flats. Tanupa Volcano can be seen in the distance on the fourth photo. There is an obvious reason the island is called Cactus Island, some of them reach 10 metres in height. There were great photo opportunities all over the island and you could spend ages just gazing out across the vast openness, occasionally seeing a jeep moving slowly across the flats in the distance. After an hour it was time to reboard and our time on the salt flats had come to an end. If you chose just a one day tour, this is the package you would get. If you chose a longer tour, the jeep would continue to drive towards some remote accommodation further into the desert. Our driver had been running tours on the flats for over 20 years. We had heard horror stories before we came of drunken tour drivers but ours was excellent. As we were approaching the edge of the flats he parked up and pulled out a toy dinosaur. He then told us to walk over to a spot in the distance and leave our phones with him. I know this sounds really dodgy, but we knew he wasn't going to shoot us all and drive off with our phones. He set the dinosaur down on the salt flat and laying down himself he directed us all into position. First of all we had to pretend the dinosaur was in front of us, and then we were running away from it. The results aren't perfect but you get the idea, the Salt Flats are great for some quirky photos. INSTAGRAM POST 433. It had been a great end to an unforgettable day. The salt flats truly are a special place and definitely worth visiting. Tomorrow we would be back in the jeep again to have a tour of the remote southwestern circuit. The next day our companions were a group of four Spanish girls and a girl travelling solo from Mexico. Day two involves a lot of basically just being driven around in a jeep which would then stop to allow you out to have a stroll and take some photos of this remote part of Bolivia called the Reserva Nacional de Fauna Andina Eduardo Avaroa . A bit of a mouthful, I know. Most of the time we stopped it was to look at a lake, normally bright turquoise. Then after a few photos it was back into the jeep to continue the bumpy ride. It did start to get a bit repetitive but there was no doubt the scenery here was simply stunning, almost Martian like. INSTAGRAM POST 434. During the day it was hot and humid, but as soon as the sun started to go down though it was cold, really cold. Day two finished at some remote accommodation in the middle of desert and we would be sharing a dorm with the five other girls. It wasn't too bad, we had gotten on really well with each other during the day. In the evening we all sat huddled together trying to keep warm as our food was prepared. Afterwards we all shared a couple bottles of wine and played some games of cards, but then it was an early night as we had to be up at 4am. We didn't manage to get much sleep and before we knew it, it was 4am and time for breakfast for our final day. INSTAGRAM POST 435. We set off in the dark and could make out the lights of all the other jeeps heading to the same destination. Sol de Mañana is a geyser field, stinking of sulphur but containing lots of bubbling mud holes. Next we visited another Laguna, this time Laguna Verde (4,400m). Most tours would then head to the Chilean border which is close by but as we were going back to Uyuni, we had an eight hour bumpy jeep ride to look forward to. On the way back we stopped for a couple of hours at Termas de Polques for a hot spring soak. It was nearly 6pm by the time we arrived back in Uyuni. The salt flats of Bolivia are famous and rightly so, they are high on the list of places to see on any trip to South America. It was an amazing experience in this harsh remote corner of Bolivia which we will never forget. INSTAGRAM POST 436.

D - CHILE AND ARGENTINA

It was now November, another month and another country. An early start again, we were waiting in the dark with the other travellers for our bus from Uyuni to Calama in Chile. After the border crossings we had experienced so far in South America, the crossing into Chile was by far the strictest. With exit stamps completed on the Bolivian side, the bus drove us through into Chile. Here our backpacks were given a full inspection. Back on the bus for a short drive of about 100m, we then had to exit again, take our packs out and put them in a large line and sit on some nearby benches. This was then the point when the sniffer dogs came out walking up and down, firstly past us travellers then up and down the line of luggage as well as on the bus. In all, the whole process took over two hours. INSTAGRAM POST 437. Once everything was ok we were moving again, Chile was a stark contrast to Bolivia. Instantly we felt we could have been in the US, it didn't feel like South America at all, the whole place was wealthier and people dressed like Americans, unlike neighbouring Bolivia which is the second poorest country in South America after Venezuela. There was no more of the traditional clothing and dress on show that we had grown so used to in Ecuador, Peru and Bolivia. So far we had been in South America for just over two months. I know it sounds bad, but it was a welcome sight when we saw there was a Walmart in Calama and we treated ourselves to some veggie burgers! We had no intention to stay in Calama, nor in Northern Chile for that matter. All our research told us there wasn't much to see in Northern Chile apart from the Atacama Desert. Chile is 4,300 km long and has an average width of just 171 km. On one side is the Pacific and on the other the Andes. Easter Island I suppose is sort of Northern Chile except it is over 3,500 km out to the west in the Pacific Ocean. Patagonia in the South was our destination though and we needed to miss out some of Chile to get there. So we decided we would be taking a flight south. It wasn't like we were in a hurry, we had now been travelling for two years and four months. But money was running low and there were lots of things we wanted to do in Patagonia, but realistically we knew we wouldn't be able to do them all. The following day we caught a bus to the coastal city of Antofagasta, Chile's second largest City. The bus stop was on the northern outskirts of the city and it seemed the only way to reach our hostel was by taxi. The taxi drivers were obviously used to overcharging travellers who exit the station laden with big backpacks. Asking how much, we were surprised with his expensive reply. Helen and I looked at each other and she asked me how far it would be to walk. After looking at Google Maps it looked like it was just over 3.5 km. This was a quite a walk with us both carrying over 20kg especially in the midday heat. But it was more an indication of how far we had come. We both felt fit and strong enough to do the walk and had no real fear of the area we had to walk through. We looked at each other and nodded, we would walk. We told the taxi driver he was charging too much, thanks, but no thanks. You could tell he was surprised. It wasn't the fact he was trying to rip us off but that didn't help, the point was we could do this and we were almost testing ourselves to do this. There was no hurry, we had nothing planned for the rest of the day. Waving to the taxi drivers we set off for the city. After about an hour and a few stops we arrived at our hostel. Nearby was another huge Walmart, we felt we had earnt some peanut butter cookies for all of our exertions. Our flight south was already booked and we had a couple of days to spare in the city. Not bothered about sightseeing we withdrew some US dollars from the bank and spent two full days at the beach. The first day I burnt my front and on the second I burnt my back.

Helen and I had talked about wanting to adopt a couple of dogs to take back to England but were unsure about the cost and practicalities of returning with some South American rescues. Helen showed me a website from a dog shelter in Spain. She had followed them on Instagram for a while. They rescued abandoned dogs known as podencos. These dogs are heavily abused in Spain, bred to hunt and not protected by law, at the end of hunting season, many are killed or abandoned by the hunters. They have a lovely temperament, are very loyal and have a distinctive look, very recognisable by their large pointed ears. Hope for Podencos does an amazing job saving the lives of hundreds of dogs. I was sold. I was more than happy to adopt two rescue dogs from Spain. The hardest decision would be deciding on which ones to adopt.

Since arriving in Chile I was suffering with a really bad cold. I remembered that one of the Spanish girls on the Salt Flat Tour in Uyuni was suffering with one, so it was inevitable after spending so much time in the confines of a jeep that we would also catch it. The next day we caught an internal flight from Antofagasta to Santiago, for a short stopover before boarding another flight down to Concepción. The distance was 1,833 km so we probably saved ourselves two or three days sat on a bus.

Not realising there are a couple of bus stations in Concepción, we almost missed our bus to Pucón. Pucón only has a population of 22,000 people but it is a common stop on the Gringo trail. It reminded me of Baños in Ecuador in that it was marketed as an activity town, with lots of activities to cater for the traveller. Sitting on the edge of Lago Villarrica, it is a picture postcard town that perfectly captures the tourist market. In between all of the various tourist agencies are numerous high end hiking shops and cute little boutiques and cafes.

One of the main draws of Pucón is the chance to climb the large active Volcano that smoulders above the town, Volcan Villarrica. After checking in at our hostel, Helen and I had a walk around the town. After leaving Bolivia we still had about £55 worth of Bolivianos. Trying our luck we popped into a currency exchange but turned down their offer of £20. It was only later that we learnt it was a closed currency. We still have them to this day so if anyone reading this plans on visiting Bolivia let us know! Having stocked up on some groceries we stopped in at one of the many agencies to book myself on the Volcano climb. I was doing this solo, Helen wouldn't be joining me. After trying on all the clothing, hiking boots and crampons, I was told to be back at the tourist agency at 5.45am the next morning. It was 7.30am by the time our minibus arrived at the bottom of the climb. INSTAGRAM POST 438. I was still suffering with a cold and the four and a half hour hike to the top and the crater rim was exhausting. The first part wasn't too steep, but then we needed to strap on our crampons and use our ice axes to trudge zig zagging up the side of the volcano. Just before we reached the crater rim, about 100m below it, we took shelter from the strong winds and put on our gas masks to protect us from the toxic fumes and left our backpacks behind. The final 100 metres were really tricky due to the wind but then the rim flattened out and we could see right inside the volcano with the magma clearly visible. Due to the strength of the wind, we probably only spent 20 minutes at the top, trying to take photos without been blown off the side. Coming down the volcano was far easier than going up. In our backpacks we had a tiny sled and this was how we descended. It probably only took 45 minutes to get back to the minibus. I was absolutely shattered when I arrived back at the hostel but it was well worth it. Later that afternoon we walked down to the lake and could see the steaming Volcano in the distance, and it seemed strange that only a few hours beforehand, I was stood at the top of it. Yet another unforgettable experience in South America.

As predicted by the tour agency, the weather changed for the worse, the next day it rained constantly. The guy in the agency had told me I only had a one day window and then they probably wouldn't be going up Villarrica for another week. Helen and I spent all day in the hostel, by the fire, planning our route and activities down through Patagonian Chile and Argentina.

Pucón was a short sweet visit, it was a shame we couldn't do anything on one of our days due to the weather but it was time to cross into the Argentinian Lake District. Geographically the Lake District is central Argentina and the region just north of what is considered Patagonia. The Andes continue to run through the Lake District and still provide all year round activities and it is obviously a trekker's paradise. Compared to the other side of the border in Chile, this area in Argentina is easily accessible due to main roads snaking up through the western part of the country. On the other side of the border in the Chilean Sur Chico region it is slightly more of a challenge to navigate and far more remote. Originally we had considered taking a boat in Chile from Puerto Montt down to Puerto Natales and then returning North through Argentina. In the end we decided to cross to Bariloche in Argentina, head south via overnight buses and cross back into Chile further down and then possibly catch a flight north. The Argentinian Lake District is a prime tourist destination and rightly so with the surrounding Parque Nacional Nahuel Huapi offering the resources for those wishing to escape to the outdoors. Central to all this is Bariloche, our destination, sitting in the middle of the park.

The border crossing was quite simple, a lot quicker than our previous one from Bolivia. All along here and further south, travellers are constantly crossing between Argentina and Chile. Yet again the bus station was on the outskirts and we decided to walk the 4 km to our hostel.

On our first full day we enjoyed a couple of hikes despite me still suffering from a heavy cold. INSTAGRAM POST 439. The first was a hike to the viewpoint at Cerro Campanario offering views over Lago Nahuel Huapi and then further along to Cerro Llao Llao. The next day we intended on attempting Cerro Catedral, a 2,388 metre peak however there were reports of deep snow still near the summit so we changed it slightly but enjoyed a full days hiking and hardly saw anyone all day. Bariloche was a great place to stay and there was a lot more to do but we wanted to press on south. Now both of us were suffering with colds.

El Bolsón is a small hippie town only 100 km south of Bariloche. Again there are numerous hikes here but actually they are more difficult to access as there is no public transport that takes tourists around as they did in Bariloche. As a result there wasn't a great deal we could do. On this occasion the bus station was in the centre of town but our accommodation was 3 km away on the outskirts, but again we walked it. With one full day in El Bolsón the guy at the hostel recommended a hike that we could do with some great lookouts. INSTAGRAM POST 440. In all, out and back it measured about 15 km. Our intention was to call in at the supermarket on the way back from our walk but I had forgotten my wallet so we had to go back to the hostel first. A quick turnaround and then we headed out back to the supermarket. Just as I was paying for our groceries, all of a sudden I felt the blood run from me and felt really faint. The checkout assistant pointed to a chair for me to sit on. After making it to the chair I felt like I was burning up and started sweating profusely. I said to Helen that I needed to get outside to cool down and get some fresh air. I was barely outside the store when I passed out. Helen caught me as I was falling. When I came around there were some locals around me who had come to help. Someone handed me a sugary drink whilst I slowly realised what was going on. One lady then said she would drive us the short distance to a pharmacy to check my blood pressure. Whilst we were inside, by chance there was a doctor there and he suggested we go to the hospital to get checked out. He drove us there. By now we realised we were not carrying our phones, or our passports and only had a small amount of cash on us, and no cash cards so we couldn't pay for anything. Everyone at the hospital was so friendly. I ended up having two bags of IV fluids before they were happy that I was well enough to leave. I had no money and no identification yet it didn't matter. It was amazing how well I was treated, from the passers-by at the supermarket, the pharmacy, the doctor who took me to the hospital then finally the medical staff who treated me. After leaving hospital, I bought another energy drink for the walk back to the hostel, getting back about three hours later than we intended. It was quite a scary experience, I had been feeling a bit rough but put that down to the cold. Were we doing too much? At the time we didn't think we were, we felt good as we were walking to hostels from the bus stations. I realised I hadn't been eating very well, not that I was eating rubbish, just that I didn't really have an appetite despite probably burning more calories than normal. I told myself to drink more fluids going forward and have an energy drink in my bag at all times.

El Bolsón was a short stop, and not what we expected. Very soon we would be down in Patagonia taking on some of the most wonderful hikes in the world. Ahead of us we had our longest bus trip, 22 hours straight down to El Chaltén, the mecca for hiking. Yet the previous night I had collapsed. I admit I was feeling a little bit nervous mainly because of the unknown. Was it a one off because I was run down, or was it something more serious and underlying? I assumed it was just the former but I had been looking forward to reaching El Chaltén for a long time and didn't want to miss out through not feeling well or worse, it happening whilst out on a hike when I am a couple of hours away from town.

Our epic long bus journey left early afternoon, in the morning Helen bought some new waterproof trail shoes with great grip. In Bariloche we were surprised at the amount of snow and snow melt knowing it could possibly be worse further south.

The 22 hour journey wasn't actually that bad, apart from me been unable to fully stretch out my legs on the reclining seat as we were seated at the front of the bus. It was actually a good opportunity for me to rest up and eat and drink more than I normally would. I was feeling a lot better and rested when we arrived at El Chaltén. Despite being the launch pad to numerous World class trails, El Chaltén only has a population of just over 1,500. The view of El Chaltén with the snowy peaks of Los Glaciares National Park in the background is just an unbelievable sight and I couldn't wait to see what it had to offer. This was something I had been looking forward to ever since I had started researching South America and Patagonia. One resource that proved very helpful was a website called worldyadventurer.com. Her website is really helpful and provides details of itineraries of what to see and do in Patagonia for trips ranging from one to four weeks.

Parque Nacional Los Glaciares geographically has two areas, the northern part which includes El Chaltén as the gateway, and the southern part where the main hub is El Calafate. We arrived in El Chaltén at lunchtime, the weather was ok. Patagonian weather can be very unpredictable, El Chaltén is known for very strong winds. Luckily it was pretty calm on the day we arrived but I had read blogs where people had to stay inside their hostels for days as the weather was too rough to attempt any hiking. This was always going to be a possibility for anything going forward now in Patagonia. But it is what it is unfortunately and if it happened to us we would have to decide at the time whether to sit it out or move on. After a long bus journey we were keen to stretch our legs, but due to the time of the day, we had to keep it quite local. For the afternoon we headed out and walked to two miradors. On the way we saw our first armadillo, INSTAGRAM POST 441. Our two lookout walks were Mirador de los Concordes and Mirador de las Aguilas. These gave great views of the park with all of the rugged peaks in the distance past El Chaltén. INSTAGRAM POST 442. Looking away from El Chaltén it was completely deserted, with just the one road in and out and the huge Lago Viedama in the distance.

El Chaltén is all about supply and demand due to the number of visitors. Hence accommodation is more expensive. Our hostel was one of the cheaper ones available but we booked our own room. Unfortunately it was next to the communal kitchen and this was where people sat to chat in the evening. There was a notice asking that the area shouldn't be used after

11pm. At 2am I couldn't take it anymore and went out and asked a group to keep quiet.

A good sleep would have been good as today we were going to hike the famous Laguna de Los Tres Trail. There was no entrance fee to the park yet it is known as one of the most famous hikes in South America as it culminates in the amazing views of Cerro Fitz Roy. INSTAGRAM POST 443, INSTAGRAM POST 444 and INSTAGRAM POST 445. The hike is pretty strenuous, I was still a bit concerned how I would fair after collapsing only two days ago. I actually felt pretty good, but I was probably on a high that I was here, in Patagonia, hiking to Fitz Roy. It is about 12 km to reach Fitz Roy with an elevation gain of about 800 metres, making it an eight hour round trip. Hopefully the posts give some justice to how awe inspiring the view was hiking the Cerro Fitz Roy Trail. The climb to reach Fitz Roy at the end was pretty tough, and obviously it is a popular hike, but for good reason. For a couple from flat south Lincolnshire these are sights we are not used to and ones I would never get bored of. We have been fortunate to see such sights in Canada, the US and South America already but these sorts of natural views of jagged peaks and rugged wilderness are just what we wanted to experience here in Patagonia. Already we could see the appeal. For the return we decided to take an alternative route past Laguna Madre e Hija and Laguna Neita that took our distance to 30 km. Back at the hostel I struggled to finish just an average sized bowl of pasta and vegetables, even after a full day of hiking so I still wasn't 100%.

For our final day in El Chaltén we would be hiking the other famous walk in this area, Laguna Torre. INSTAGRAM POST 446. This hike was shorter at 20 km and there were no steep sections either. However it was windy. This is a hike which can be dictated by the weather, the toothy peak of Cerro Torre can be virtually impossible to see some days as it is shrouded in cloud. This was unfortunately the case for us, virtually all the way to Cerro Torre it was blocked by cloud but it had been a fine walk and most of the time we were shaded from the wind. However as we rounded the final bend, the wind was insane. All of the other hikers were sheltered behind a small hill, most took this as the opportunity to have some lunch, so we did the same whilst the wind whistled over our heads. Then we braved the wind as we saw Laguna Torre for the first time. The wind was just unbelievable. Helen tried to take a video of me leaning into the wind with the Ipad but it was so strong and so cold she was unable to film anything longer than three seconds, the minimum length of a video to load on Instagram. I ended up battling the wind down to the lake to record a quick video. INSTAGRAM POST 447. Hopefully it shows the strength of the wind with the waves it was creating on the lake. As warned, Cerro Torre was hidden behind the clouds whilst we were at the lake and typically, the clouds cleared as we were returning from the hike. Our final night at the hostel predictably resulted in me asking people to keep the noise down again outside our room. Our three days in El Chaltén were fantastic. We had hiked two of the most famous day hikes in South America. There were other hikes we would have liked to have attempted but we were conscious of the places we still needed to visit. Looking back I suppose we were quite lucky with the weather in that we managed to go hiking each day we were there. Without a doubt, El Chaltén is a special place. If hiking is what you are into, this place is an absolute must.

However, our journey south continued as there were more epic sights for us to see. We took a four hour bus ride to the gateway of the southern part of Los Glaciers National Park, El Calafate. With a more upmarket feel to it compared to the rugged frontier town of El Chaltén, El Calafate is a convenient location to access some of the most popular tourist attractions in Patagonia. Both hostel and hotel accommodation proved too expensive so we opted for an Airbnb in a place about 15 minutes from the main street. We wouldn't be spending too much time there so it was no more than just a roof over our heads at night. The main draw of El Calafate is the closeness to the magnificent Perito Moreno Glacier. Calling in at one of the many tourist agencies on the main street we booked our tour to the glacier for the following day. The Glacier is located 80 km away from El Calafate and the main attraction of the southern sector. We had seen pictures of it on the internet but when seeing it in person it is just astounding. We have had the pleasure of seeing some amazing sights on our trips, including some just a couple of days earlier at El Chaltén. Perito Moreno Glacier was high on the list. INSTAGRAM POST 448, INSTAGRAM POST 449,

INSTAGRAM POST 450, INSTAGRAM POST 451. The Glacier is 30 km long and 5 km wide, in some places it is 70 metres high. In a world full of sorry stories of retreating glaciers, this one is actually advancing at two metres a day. Our tour started off with a boat ride which sailed slowly up and down the mouth of the glacier from a distance of about 100 metres. Icebergs were all around and the whole experience was strangely quiet and every so often there would be a loud crack coming from the glacier caused by the constant movement. Sadly, the weather was pretty miserable and it was raining, luckily we were wearing our ponchos. One fantastic feature of the attraction is the boardwalk that allows you to get another close up look of the glacier. Because of the rain, the boardwalks were really quiet as most people were sheltering in the visitors centre. Helen and I weren't put off, it was not going to stop us from admiring the glacier. There was a moment that we witnessed when there was no one else around us. We were stood admiring the glacier as you do and Helen saw a small piece fall off and then another. I was starting to walk away and she told me to wait and pointed to an area on the glacier wall saying that it looked unstable. Then all of a sudden an enormous chunk of ice detached itself from the glacier and crashed into the water below. This chunk of ice must have easily measured 70 x 30 metres in size. The sound was so loud and it created an enormous wave of water as a result. We just looked at each other and couldn't believe what we had just witnessed. It was just a shame we didn't capture it on video. Ponchos are only good for keeping the top half dry, our bottom halves were soaked and we were freezing cold. My hands were numb from taking photos and videos on the Ipad but none of that mattered. We were given a time to be back at the bus and it was a shame when we had to leave. In reality we could have spent hours at the glacier, that's how much we enjoyed it, easily one of the most amazing things we had seen on our travels.

The next day we took a bus south again on the famous route 40, but this time we crossed back into Chile, to Puerto Natales. The bus was full of travellers heading to the famous Torres Del Paine National Park, some were carrying tents and walking poles. Much like El Chaltén, Torres Del Paine has some well-known, world class hikes. Puerto Natales is the base to this Park even though it is 70 km away. It is also the destination we would have arrived at had we taken the boat from Puerto Montt in Chilean Northern Patagonia. Our hostel was a 30 minute walk from where the bus dropped us off and we were now in what is considered Southern Patagonia. Although we were nearing the end of November, so the end of spring down here, it was dull, it was cold and it was windy when we turned up. Our hostel was great though, the owner was really friendly and offered lots of advice and information at accessing the park. The communal kitchen was also really large and clean and luckily there weren't many guests staying here. There was a reason that we and others opt in stay in Puerto Natales rather than any of the accommodation inside the National Park. Supply and demand again, it is that simple. This place is world renowned for some of the best hiking but there are a limited number of places to stay, unless you bring your own tent. We looked at staying in some of the accommodation and were amazed to discover that a single bunk bed in an 18 bed dorm was over £100 per night. Because of the demand, people will pay this. Those who can't, stay in Puerto Natales and catch the 7am bus that takes hikers to the park. Later in the afternoon we went for a walk around the coastal part of the city which looks out onto the Señoret Channel. INSTAGRAM POST 452. This part of Patagonian Chile is quite difficult to navigate as the area is basically fjords and islands. Prior to arriving here we had already booked an online tour. Money was running low now and we had gone under the limit we wanted to return home with but we were almost at the end so it wasn't too much of a concern. Our tour was basically a one day excursion of the best sights in the Torres Del Paine National Park, so if we hadn't the time or money to do anything else, at least we had done this.

In the evening we sent an email to Hope for Podencos. Even though we were spoilt for choice with the amount of dogs available for adoption, there were some in particular we liked. We expressed an interest and asked if they needed to carry out a home check. The home check would be done with Helen's parents meeting one of the network of volunteers based in the UK. Hope for Podencos replied a day later and they were obviously pleased with our interest, a house check was organised and our home and garden were vetted and passed.

Our tour bus picked us up from the hostel at a reasonable time the following morning. After a stop at the Milodon Cave on the way, we entered via the southern Serrano entrance. After paying for our pass, which gave us admittance to the park for the next three days, the bus then proceeded to the Grey Ranger Station. The park looked stunning. I follow National Geographic UK on Facebook and not long ago saw a post. It was a picture of the Torres Del Paine National Park taken from distance much like the view we had as we approached it. Underneath it had the following quote: "My concept of grandeur and natural beauty has changed drastically after visiting Torres Del Paine National Park." I liked that. It was from a guy called Victor Lima, a professional photographer who also obviously appreciated the scenery.

The station is a 15 minute walk to the Grey Lake. INSTAGRAM POST 453. Photos 2, 3 and 4 were taken on the shore of the lake and the peninsula. In the distance on photo 3, the Grey Glacier is clearly visible. Icebergs were floating within close proximity of the shore, measuring 50 metres in length, photos 3 and 4.

This was our first experience within the park and it was just as we hoped. Icebergs, glacial lakes, glaciers and the jagged peaks of the park in the distance, little wonder this is the one of the most popular attractions in South America. After this great start the bus then drove eastwards and parked up near the Explora Hotel so we could all have some lunch, photo 1. Helen and I instead chose to hike some of the Condor lookout to get some more great views of the park. Continuing through the park the bus stopped for some more photo opportunities, photo 5. Then heading eastwards through the park towards the exit we saw the Guanacos, who are closely related to the llama, photo 6. Our final stop on our day tour was at the Laguna de los Cisnes lookout. This gave us an amazing side view of the famous granite pillars, photos 7,8 and 9. Our day tour was really enjoyable, it was ideal for those who wanted to see the highlights of the park in a day without too much exertion. For us though it whetted our appetites and made us want to get closer within the park. On the way back we decided we would return early in the morning and hike to the Torres Del Paine lookout. On the way back to the hostel we stopped at the supermarket to pick up supplies for the following day. That came around quickly as we were up at 5.30am in order to walk across town and catch the 7am bus into the park. The bus was full of other hikers eagerly waiting to do one of the most famous hikes in South America. Others were clearly heading out on longer hikes considering the size of their packs.

The two famous multi day hikes in Torres Del Paine are the W trek and the O trek. Imagine the main peaks of the park are like a piece of paper that has been scrunched and pushed up in the middle. Basically the O trek walks around the whole perimeter of the middle mass of peaks, but it also includes two trips into the middle and back to the perimeter. One of these is to the Torres del Paine lookout and the other is to the Frances lookout, through the Frances valley. The W trek doesn't go around the perimeter but instead does the two trips into the middle and the third part of the "W" takes the hiker to close proximity of the Grey Glacier. There is also a Q trek that has an additional hike on top of the O trek. Our hike today was basically one leg of the W trek that takes us deep within the park to the base of the famous towers.

After arriving at the park and signing in, we caught another bus to the Las Torres lodge that marks the start, it was now 9am. The hike started pretty flat for a couple of kilometres before rising, then it followed the course of a valley for 8 km before reaching a very tough final uphill section. INSTAGRAM POST 454. The hike reminded me very much of the Fitz Roy hike. It's a really long but enjoyable hike with a very difficult end section. However it was totally worth it for the final views, again we sat and ate our lunch whilst taking in our surroundings and just appreciating how lucky we were to be here. It was a little cloudy but the views of the famous towers were mostly unobstructed. Our 20 km round hike finished at 5pm, but we had to wait over an hour for a bus to take us back to the entrance station and then an hour again for the bus back to Puerto Natales. It was a very long day, after starting at 5:30am, eventually we arrived back at the hostel at nearly 11pm after walking back from the bus station. Our park tickets had one more day left on them, we could return to the park tomorrow but we were too tired from today's exertions. We also had no food either for the following day. Looking back we probably should have had another day in the park. We could have bought some food at the bus station, and enjoyed a final days hiking possibly getting a close up view of the Grey Glacier.

We didn't, we had already booked a flight from Punta Arenas, two hours south by bus. This would be our furthest point south, from here we took a plane north up to Puerto Montt and then a short bus journey across to Puerto Varas. As the crow flies, just 200 miles further south of Punta Arenas was the Isla Grande de Tierra del Fuego and the city of Ushuaia, the most southerly city in the Southern Hemisphere. This is the southern extreme of the Americas, past here lays Antarctica. As with all of Patagonia, there is still plenty to do and see in terms of hiking and outdoors. However a lot can depend on the weather down here, especially on the southern tip. Our weather window didn't look great hence the decision to fly back north to the Chilean Lake District.

There was an obvious realisation hanging over us that we were very near the end of our adventure. As much as we didn't want it to end, it was inevitable. Over the last couple of weeks we discussed how we would like our trip to end. The past three and a half months were a constant trip south, moving on from one amazing sight to another through long bus journeys and staying in the cheapest accommodation possible. We had talked about spending our final days in the sun on a beach. Columbia was discussed, we missed the opportunity to visit the country and thought some time on the northern Caribbean coast would be a great way to finish our trip. Wherever we chose though we would be flying from Santiago. Columbia turned out to be way too expensive. By far the cheapest destination to turned out to be Rio de Janiero in Brazil. Of course it was, it made sense, where else to finish our journey in the Americas than in one of the world's most famous cities. Our minds were made up, we booked the flights and in a week's time we would fly to Rio and spend the last few days in the Cidade Maravilhosa (Marvellous City).

Puerto Varas has been called the new Pucón. Having been in Pucón I can understand why, it has the same small town charm, perched on the edge of a lake with active snow-capped volcanos close by. Our plan was to spend a couple of days here before actually stopping in Pucón again on our way back up to Santiago. We decided to return to Pucón as we were likely to have decent weather and therefore that meant we would be able to get in some guaranteed hikes towards the end of our trip.

Having bought our groceries from the local Walmart, our first full day involved taking a bus to the outside of town in the direction of the National Park and the Osorno volcano. The journey follows the edge of Lago Llanquilue before veering off to follow the river where the road finishes at Petrohué, the river's namesake. Research had told us that we needed to sign in at the ranger's station. This was closed so we couldn't, but we started our hike anyway. The terrain proved to be really tricky, not through gradient but due to the powdery volcanic ash. It was just like walking through sand. Despite the conditions underfoot, it was a really nice hike and we hardly met anyone all day. The weather was glorious and a big difference compared to what we had further south in Patagonia. We were about a mile from the volcano, it looked stunning against the blue sky. Noted for its similarity to Mount Fuji in Japan, it is a classic conical shaped stratovolcano. INSTAGRAM POST 455. Instead of taking the trail that went left and headed towards the volcano we turned right and followed a route back along the shore of the lake, Lago Todos Los Santos. At Petrohué, we sat and had an ice cream after the 15 km hike, before catching a bus back to Puerto Varas.

That evening, we discussed the dog situation and it turned out that flights from Rio to Valencia, via a stopover in Lisbon were significantly cheaper than direct flights back to the UK. This would give us the opportunity of visiting the Hope for Podencos shelter in person and meet all the dogs. First we checked with Hope for Podencos that this would be ok, thankfully it was.

The following day we decided to get a bus back to Petrohué, but on this occasion we jumped off about halfway. The previous day when we came along this road on the bus we both commented how it would be good to just walk along the river as it looked stunning. So that's what we did, we walked 6 km to Petrohué, then turned round and came back again, choosing a great spot at the side of the river to enjoy our lunch. INSTAGRAM POST 456. Later that day, we booked our bus tickets for tomorrow to take us back to Pucón. It was late in the afternoon when the bus pulled into the now familiar bus station. Last time we stayed here our hostel was only a couple of mins walk away, not this time. It was a 20 minute walk on the outskirts, but fortunately located right next to a supermarket. The hostel was great, really clean with a good kitchen and hardy anyone else staying there. A friendly cat and dog also added to the appeal. During our previous stay in Pucón, poor weather prevented us from doing some hikes we had read about. Taking advantage of the good weather we caught the bus the following morning that took us into the Parque Nacional Huerquehue where we hiked the Tres Lagos trail. INSTAGRAM POST 457. As the name suggests, the hike took in three lakes and was a great day out. Another of our days in Pucón, we decided to visit the old Quelhue hanging bridge on the eastern outskirts of the town. Not the most scenic 10 km walk by our standards, a lot of time is spent walking along the main road, before taking a left and heading towards the Trancura River. We spent a good a few hours just sat on the side of the river in the sun. Every so often people would fly past in a canoe or a raft on their way back to Pucón. Talk obviously mentioned our impending return home. Fortunately our time in South America had been so busy with visiting attractions we were not really thinking that much about the end. But these last few days the realisation was here that this was it, it was really ending soon. The overall feeling was definitely sadness. The last two and a half years were by far and away the best times of our lives, naturally we didn't want it to end. There was also some fear. We were soon going to be back in the real world in our 40's, unemployed with a mortgage to pay. Getting back onto Civvy Street would be strange, we would have to slip back into "the normal". There was also a sense of excitement though that it wouldn't be long until we would have two new additions to our lives with our own dogs.

The weather on our final day was another bathed in sunshine. It was now the 1st of December, pretty sure the weather wouldn't be like this back home. Our bus to Santiago was a night bus . We spent the morning packing our backpacks and spent the day walking around Pucón and sitting by Lake Villarrica. Again talk inevitably would centre around us returning home. Practical issues were discussed. Very kindly, Helen's parents were

252

allowing us to live with them on our return for three months. That would allow us some breathing space in paying our mortgage as the tenants would be living there until the end of March and the rent would cover the mortgage. We already knew that whichever dogs we chose, they would be driven over from Spain mid-January. That meant Helen's parents were not only taking us in, they would also be taking in two puppies! I had said to Helen that I was happy to throw myself into finding a job and there was no rush for her to do the same. Helen could spend the first few months settling in with the new puppies. Hopefully I would have a job lined up for when we moved back into our house.

We arrived in Santiago at 7am on a Sunday morning. There were people still getting over the Saturday night so the bus stop had a bit of an edgy feeling to it with a few arguments going on around us. Our hostel was a good 20 minute walk away and check in wasn't until 2.30pm. As a precaution we put our bags in storage at the bus station and walked to the hostel. If they agreed to let us in early, fine, it would be worth the walk back to the station to pick up our bags. It was the right decision, we couldn't check in early and they didn't have anywhere to keep our bags anyway. By now we were used to killing time, so we headed to a nearby park. This was full of people walking dogs and jogging so it seemed a sensible and safe choice. I spent most of the time researching what we could do in Rio and before we knew it, it was time to check in. Our flight the following morning was at 6am, so after a Domino's pizza, we had an early night.

Although we still had time in Rio to finish our trip of a lifetime, our time following the Andes through five countries of South America far exceeded everything we ever imagined. In just over three months we crammed in so much. It seemed as though we were always doing something and barely wasted a single day. There were parts we missed out on, which would have been great to see but we couldn't do everything. Ideally we would have spent longer in El Chaltén and Puerto Natales to enjoy more hikes around Fitz Roy and Torres Del Paine and maybe reach the end of world at Ushuaia on the Tierra del Fuego. Had the funds stretched far enough, the ferry from Puerto Natales to Puerto Montt would have been an experience I am sure we would have loved. Spending more time in the remote Chilean Patagonia would have added to the already amazing experience. We particularly wanted to see the Marble Caves, these national treasures are stunningly beautiful, but difficult to reach due their isolation. The North Face clothing brand founder Douglas Tompkins sadly died in a kayaking accident whilst visiting the caves in 2015. Douglas recognised the natural beauty of Patagonia and used his fortune to purchase millions of acres of land then gifted it back to the governments for future protection as National Parks. Further north we skipped the Colca Canyon and Nazca lines in Peru and obviously we were disappointed to miss out on Columbia. But all said and done we saw the majority of the highlights of the Gringo Trail. We would recommend it to anyone. Had we started in South America it might have been a bit more of an assault on the senses but we were fine and what a continent it is. The Andes, the hikes, the world famous tourists sights, the wildlife and the people. It is a tough and hardy continent but we never faced any problems on the Gringo Trail. Don't believe the stories you hear about South America, they were probably the friendliest people we met along our trip. The bus transport system is very comfy and safe and the hostels are great for meeting other travellers. It is a continent we would certainly want to return to in the future.

E - BRAZIL

The alarm went off at 2am, the flight was on time and we landed in Rio just after 11am. The previous day we had received an email saying that we needed to confirm our credit card details at the Air Portugal Desk in departures for our onward flight to Valencia. Annoyingly the desk didn't open until 2.30pm so we wasted a couple of hours in Rio's Galeão International Airport. As it was raining outside, the pain was lessened slightly.

Our accommodation in Rio was an apartment we booked via Airbnb. It was a really good deal, located 100 metres from Copacabana beach on the northern end near to Sugar Loaf Mountain. We were here for ten days before heading back to Europe. The more I read and researched Rio, the more it appealed to me. For starters, there are world class beaches and some of the most famous tourist attractions in the world. But here in Rio the jungle is on the doorstep and that means there are mountains and some greats hikes within easy reach. To top it off, the weather was fantastic, apart from the day we arrived typically.

We woke up though to glorious sunshine. Looking out of our apartment window, people were jogging, cycling and roller blading up and down the main Copacabana Beach path. The beach was already busy with stalls being set up every 30 metres or so with groups renting out chairs and umbrellas as well as selling food and drinks. We decided to walk all the way along the beach path at Copacabana and then to the end of Ipanema Beach. Copacabana beach itself is 4 km in length and Ipanema is about another 3 km, and both were already busy. We were in no hurry, the sun was beating down, and we were in holiday mode. Rio had a real vibe about it and so far it seemed pretty safe. I had read that Rio was notoriously bad for thefts and pick pockets so we were both clinging on to our bags pretty tightly. It was a real pleasant morning though just strolling along the famous beaches with the other tourists, stopping occasionally to look at what the street vendors were selling. After lunch back at the apartment we spent the whole afternoon on Copacabana beach.

The following morning I joined all the others and jogged up and down the beach pathway of Copacabana beach. We were on the beach and sunbathing by mid-morning. In the afternoon though, that was halted by strong winds.

There is an enormous lagoon in Rio called Lago Rodrigo de Freitas, set back from Ipanema beach. It was the site for rowing in the 2016 Summer Olympics and has a 7.5 km path around the perimeter. We spent one morning walking around the lagoon and then relaxed again on the beach in the afternoon. In our short time here so far, Helen and I were really enjoying Rio.

One day we woke up and it was cloudy. It seemed the perfect opportunity for me to visit the Maracanã Football Stadium. INSTAGRAM POST 458. Refurbished for the hosting of the World Cup in 2014, the attendance is now a modest 79,000. The record attendance recorded here was back in 1950 for a decisive group match against Uruguay in which 199,854 witnessed the game. I went alone, Helen wasn't bothered about the tour, but for a football fan it is a must. I travelled there and back via Uber, it seemed the safest and easiest way as it was cashless. For me it was a great day out at this iconic stadium. The weather hadn't improved much later in the day as there was light rain. We therefore chose to walk around the Cláudio Coutinho trail at the base of Sugar Loaf Mountain. In the evening we walked across the road to the beach in order to get a closer look at a football match. INSTAGRAM POST 459.

Another cloudy day followed and we were looking up at where the Christ the Redeemer statue should be, but couldn't see it. We needed to choose our time wisely for visiting this attraction, we didn't want to get up there for the views across Rio to be hidden in cloud. The forecast for the following day looked good so that would be our window of opportunity. There are different ways to reach the famous Corcovado statue of Christ the Redeemer. Most people take the easy option and get driven up there and back in a tour bus. I had read about another route up, hiking. This appealed to us both a lot more. The start of the trail was at the rear of Parque Lage, further inland from the lagoon. There were many reports on the internet that this hike wasn't safe, with multiple reports of robberies on the trail as tourists are targeted by kids from the nearby favelas who make their way through the jungle to the trail. However our fears were eased at the lodge by the security guards who assured me that there hadn't been a robbery on the trail for over a year due to an increased police presence. That was good enough for us, tomorrow we would be returning for the hike. Whilst in the park we saw the popular cute little marmosets. INSTAGRAM POST 460. It is amazing to see these playing around in the rainforest only a short distance from the hustle and bustle of the city. Walking back around the lake, we managed to get back to the apartment before it started to rain.

The Christ the Redeemer statue is one of the most popular attractions in Rio and is recognisable around the world. We arrived at Parque Lage early to try and beat both the heat and the crowds at the top who took the easy route up via the bus or the train. Our hike started at 8.15 am and it took us just under two hours to reach the top of the 710m high Corcovado Mountain. INSTAGRAM POST 461. Near the top we had a bit of a fright. All along the trail we had not met a single person, yet as we rounded a corner I could hear some voices above us. I peered round and the only thing I could see was a gun that one of the people was holding. This is not an everyday occurrence for us so we were initially a bit worried that we were about to be robbed but fortunately they turned out to be the guards protecting the trail. Some parts of the trail were very tricky, one part required a steep ascent up a makeshift ladder built into the rock (photo 5). The Christo Redentor is 38m high and towers over Rio, in 2007 it was named as one of the New Seven Wonders of the World, attracting more than a million visitors a year. The main reason for us in reaching the top of Corcovado was not necessarily the statue itself, as impressive as it was, but for the view over Rio. If you can work your way through the crowds you are rewarded with an amazing panoramic view of Rio. The bulk of the tourists head towards the front of the attraction, this gives views out towards the sea. INSTAGRAM POST 462. From this vantage point, many of Rio's famous attractions are visible, INSTAGRAM POST 463, including Tijuca National Park, Maracanã Stadium, the Rio Niterói Bridge, Flamengo Beach, Botafogo Beach, Sugar Loaf Mountain, Copacabana Beach, Ipanema Beach, Lagoa Rodrigo de Freitas, the Jockey Club, Morro Dois Irmãos, Pedra Bonita and Pedro da Gávea. We didn't beat any of the crowds, but we knew it would be busy, in all we spent nearly an hour at the statue before we made the descent back into the park. About half way down we stopped for a snack and were joined by a few of the little monkeys, who jumped on Helen's arm and tried (successfully) to steal her biscuits. We carried on down and walked around the lake and along Copacabana beach back to the apartment in time for lunch. Today was also my Dad's birthday so we Skyped home to wish him a Happy Birthday.

After the exertions of hiking up and down Corcovado, the next day was a full beach day but we had already planned our hike for the following day. We had read about a hike to Dois Irmãos. Dois Irmãos can be seen in the distance on the final photo on INSTAGRAM POST 463 to the right and behind the track at the Jockey Club. Dois Irmãos translates as two brothers, and refers to the two peaks that rise out from near the sea at the end of Leblon beach. We had read on a blog that to reach the start of the trail, take a taxi to the bottom of the Vidigal favela. Located here is a moto taxi rank where the local guys from the favela hang around on their bikes. The blog explained that you jump on the back of a motor taxi and the locals will take you up the hill through the favela to the start of hike. They then return you back to the bottom afterwards. This seemed clear and simple enough so that was our plan. From our apartment we were picked up by our Uber driver and on the way to Leblon we chatted via Google translate. He asked what we were doing, we explained, and then he warned us against it. The driver virtually pleaded with us not to take a moto taxi and travel through the favela as he was saying it was not safe for tourists. We told him we had read on the internet that it seemed like a common thing to do, but he still advised us against it. I don't know whether we had let our guard down too much and we were now a bit complacent at this point but the way our driver was trying to get his message across, he seemed really serious. It was a real conundrum whether we should listen to his advice or just carry on regardless. He convinced us in the end to give it a miss. Even if we did decide to ignore his advice and attempt the hike, his concerns would always be in the back of our minds and ultimately we probably wouldn't enjoy it as much as we would always be on edge.

In the end our driver continued on to Pedra Bonita. Here there is an opportunity to hang glide off the mountain from 550m down to the beach below. There is also a trail that leads to the summit. The temperature was very hot at the top as we sat admiring the views. INSTAGRAM POST 464. Looking back towards the city you could see how the rainforest goes all the way down to the coast. In the other direction, Pedra da Gávea is an epic sight. INSTAGRAM POST 465. This 844 meter high mountain is one of the highest in the world that ends directly at the ocean. The hike to the top of Pedra da Gávea is supposed to be a great hike, we never did it in our time here, but we had read that it is advised to go as part of an organised hike as there is tricky vertical 30m section where you need to be harnessed. It is possible to do this part alone just using the makeshift ladders but it is not for the faint hearted. We walked all the way back down to Ipanema beach and caught a bus back near to our apartment at the far end of Copacabana beach. After lunch, we decided to spend the afternoon on the beach. Clearly I had got a little too complacent. Normally every time we went to the beach I would clip my bag to the beach chair with a carabiner. On this occasion I didn't and whilst I was sitting in the sun, someone stole my bag. Helen didn't notice anything either. Theft is a common problem on the beaches in Rio. I will never know why I didn't clip my bag to the chair on this occasion, was it complacency or did I just forget? Either way someone had noticed that I didn't and saw that I wasn't paying attention. The bag contained my phone, a second hand iPod Nano I purchased from eBay for our trip, some cheap sunglasses I bought a couple of days ago, a small amount of cash and my Kindle. I was gutted, we had read that you shouldn't take anything to the beach that you don't want to lose. Stupidly I had turned the entry lock to my phone off so all the person had to do was swipe and they could get access to everything. If they wanted to, in the notes page, was not only the address to our apartment but also the access number to the apartment itself. As a precaution we headed straight back to the apartment and contacted the owner, he headed over straight away and changed the code. Helen and I then spent the rest of the afternoon changing passwords to everything that could have been accessed on the phone. We had been travelling for nearly two and a half years and then I have some of my possessions stolen with only two days to go. I reported it to the police who were stationed on Copacabana beach but they said I would have to go a police station about an hour's walk away to fill out a report. With only two days left I didn't want to waste my time filling out a crime report in a police station so I didn't bother.

The next morning we went back to the beach and sat in the same spot for a couple of hours. I was more aware of people around me but also noticed myself how many people were also oblivious to their possessions. I watched numerous people who wouldn't have noticed that their bags could have been stolen. Late morning we took an Uber to the start of another trail at Alto de Boa Vista, a neighbourhood behind Pedra Bonita. We followed a very quiet trail through the Tijuca National Park which was part of the Transcarioca trail all the way down to the Botanical Gardens. The Transcarioca Trail is a relatively new, and at 180 km, it is Brazil's first long distance trail finishing at Sugar Loaf Mountain. It was a really nice 15 km hike, a lot warmer than we would have hoped. Towards the end as we were walking through the neighbourhoods I felt a bit nervous but that was probably because of what happened the previous day, but my guard was back up a bit more now. Later that afternoon we headed for another major tourist attraction in Rio, Sugarloaf Mountain, as tomorrow we would be flying home.

We walked up the first section. It is possible to jump on the cable car from the bottom but we had chosen to hike this part and catch the cable car to the Pão de Açúcar. We had read on the internet that before sunset is a great time to visit Sugar Loaf Mountain. I'm sure the views would be great any time of day. Like other attractions in Rio, the views of the city were stunning and looking back from Sugar Loaf Mountain they offer a different perspective from the views we had seen from Corcovado or Pedro Bonita especially when coupled with the sun setting in the distance over Pedra Da Gávea. INSTAGRAM POST 466.

Our last day in Rio, and South America, was spent on the beach, at lunchtime we printed off our boarding cards at a local internet café, then it was back to the beach until 6pm. It didn't take long to pack as there was less to put in the backpacks. The Uber picked us up at 8pm for our flight out of the Americas and back to Europe. We had spent ten days in Rio and despite having some possessions stolen we had thoroughly enjoyed our time here. There is so much to do, you can be hiking in the rainforest in the

260

morning and chilling on the beach in the afternoon. There are numerous hikes we didn't attempt and other parts of the city we didn't explore. Throw in the world class beaches and there is still plenty to tempt us back.

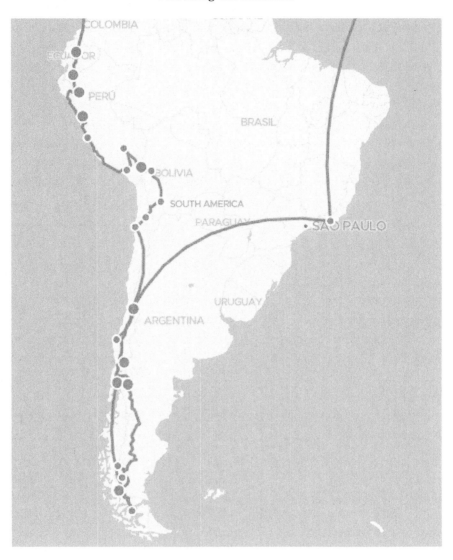

PART 7 – EUROPE

A - SPAIN

Despite it being a night flight I hardly slept and ended up watching two movies. We arrived in Lisbon at 10am, but our onward flight to Valencia wasn't until 5.30pm so there was a fair bit of hanging around for a final time. Eventually we landed in Valencia at 8pm where we picked up our hire car and drove to our motel. The following morning we left the hotel as late as possible to drive to the shelter at Albacete for our arranged time of 1pm. The owner Steve and a lovely volunteer called Iva came out to meet us. Over the past few weeks we had our eye on one dog in particular. Steve bought him out to meet us, he was very shy but seemed lovely. The only problem was that he tried to pee on both of us, lots of times, he was scent marking. This was a concern for us as for the first three months when we returned home we would be living with Helen's parents. They were doing us an enormous favour by letting us stay with them knowing full well we would end up with two dogs. Having a dog that would potentially be scent marking all over their house and us/them was a concern, so sadly we started to have a few doubts on our initial choice. There were three other puppies we were also keen on meeting, they were pointer podenco mixes and probably about six months old. They were all gorgeous, but one who stood out for us was called Adelita and we instantly fell for her. Over the course of the next couple of hours we were shown other dogs. By the time we left we were pretty certain that we wanted Adelita but there were still doubts about the other one. These were confirmed on our return the next day when he tried to pee on us again, we also tried him with Adelita but he wasn't keen on her and her boisterous puppy behaviour, so it was clear we shouldn't have them both. So our second day was just as confusing, but by the end of it we knew we absolutely wanted Adelita. That afternoon we booked our flights home for the next day, and decided we would speak to the shelter when back in the UK about who would be a good match for her.

This was it, after two and a half years of travelling it was time to face the reality that it was now over. Even towards the end of our stay in Rio, Helen and I were looking at potential house sits in Europe. After we had chosen our dogs we wouldn't be returning to the UK with them straight away.

Steve makes the drive through Spain and France in a van each month and he transports around a dozen Podencos all around the UK. Adelita, or Addie as she would now be called wasn't expected to arrive until mid-January. Therefore we looked into potential house sits. I think it was us refusing to face the inevitable and trying to string it out as long as we possibly could. We did actually apply for one in Italy and were accepted, but in the end we replied and said sorry we have changed our minds, it was just going to be too expensive. So we couldn't put if off any longer, tomorrow we would be standing on British soil again.

Over the past two and a half years Helen and I were virtually inseparable except for the week in Grenada when she returned home for medicine and a couple of times in L.A. when I was out with my brother. In all this time, Helen had less complications with her diabetes than ever before. I don't recall a time when she suffered so few hypos. It was myself who needed to visit a doctor or a hospital, Helen never required them at all. Only a few stomach bugs in South America caused the odd off day but there were never any complaints. Sourcing insulin in South America was fairly straightforward and there always was someone who would offer to keep it chilled overnight if we were struggling. Helen is a prime example that diabetes is not a hurdle to going travelling. My Fitbit recorded nearly 14 million steps in our time away and we walked, hiked or ran 11,000 kilometres, side by side for virtually all of them. Together we completed 15 house sits and 4 workaways and Helen was just amazing in all of them, physically and mentally. When I was at a low ebb she picked me up. Those times we had, and the memories we made, were very special and having her there alongside me made it the perfect adventure.

B - UK

Our flight was leaving at 11am. The previous evening Helen had spoken to her brother and he had offered to pick us up from Stansted airport. It felt strange coming back through Stansted, normally we use this airport if we are away for a weekend or a week at most. Everyone else on our flight had small carry-on bags and there was hardly any other luggage that came off the carousel. As arranged Steve was waiting for us outside, it was good to see him. After a hello and a hug we were on the M11 heading north before hitting all the new roadworks on the A14. Helen and I had decided not to tell our parents that we were arriving home today and Steve also kept it a secret. Everything looked the same on the drive home, it was the 17th Dec, soon to be the shortest day, the weather was grey and dull and we both felt strange being back, almost a sense of shock even, and the unknown, what happens now? Back home we knocked on the door of Helen's parents to surprise them. As expected, there were lots of tears and we caught up on what had happened since we last spoke via Skype and how our time at the shelter had been. We also still wanted to see my parents that evening. Helen's parents offered to drive us but it felt normal for us to walk now, so that's what we did, about 40 mins across to the other side of town. On the way we walked through the town centre and nothing had changed, but we didn't expect it would. At my parents, I rang the bell and my mum answered, she let out a yell and burst into tears. My dad soon appeared behind her as he heard Mum shout. It had been nearly two and a half years since we had seen each other. Again hugs and tears followed and we sat down and talked. There had been regular contact with both sets of parents whilst we were away via Skype but it was so good to see how happy they were that we were home and it was great for us to see them in good health.

As we were both now unemployed, there would plenty of time to catch up over Xmas. Helen and I walked back to her parents where we had a lovely home cooked meal.

This was it. We were now back home.

I found a website called Travellerspoint.com that allows you to map out your travels. Our full two and a half year journey through the Americas is seen on INSTAGRAM POST 467, and here.

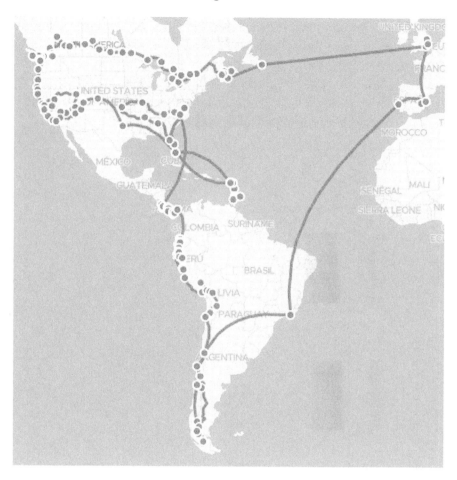

The distance we covered was roughly 73,000 km covering 14 countries. Each part of our journey is then shown in more detail. Canada INSTAGRAM POST 468. Our first time in the US, INSTAGRAM POST 469. The Caribbean, INSTAGRAM POST 470. Our second time in the US, INSTAGRAM POST 471. Central America, INSTAGRAM POST 472. And finally, South America, INSTAGRAM POST 473.

CHAPTER 3 – THE AFTER

Returning home was something we had in the back of our minds through the final part of South America. It certainly didn't detract from our amazing time but it was there. Helen and I talked about it several times, with dread. For starters there is the post-holiday blues feeling that everyone is familiar with, but this was amplified by a hundred. It wasn't a two week holiday we were returning from, it was just short of two and a half years. It will be remembered as the best two and a half years of our lives, so the prospect of returning home to carry on with life as it was before, wasn't one we were looking forward to. Returning the week before Xmas added to weirdness of it all. Everyone else was in a festive mood, but Helen and I weren't really in the spirit of it.

It was obviously great to catch up with again with family and friends. The night after we returned, we went round to my brothers for the evening. The girls had just broken up for Xmas and Emma didn't know we were back so it was nice to surprise her. It was a really enjoyable evening catching up with them for the first time since LA.

When we left, the UK had voted to leave the European Union. Two and a half years later we still hadn't! It was on the news constantly and we were fed up with hearing about it after just a few days. I couldn't imagine having to listen to it day in day out on the news for two and a half years!

That week leading up to Xmas we went up in the attic to go through our clothes. We ended up taking six bin bags to the charity shop. It was inevitable, we had relied on so little whilst we were away that we would now question why we needed so much. We drove to the storage company and took a few things out we thought we would need. I updated my CV and sent it out as much as I could but all of the recruitment agencies were shut down over the festive period. One thing we required was transport. Rather than both of us going out and buying a car straight away we thought it would be sensible if just one us of did. Depending on what job I ended up with, I may end up with a company car or a car allowance so Helen purchased one first. Time was spent that first week looking for Helen's car.

The two dogs we had adopted from Albacete would be arriving on the 18th of January so we also needed to prepare for their arrival, so dog beds, toys, food and everything else was all purchased in preparation. Yes I said two. On our return to the UK, we had only chosen Addie. There was a super cute puppy at the shelter that had jumped all over us and we really liked him, but he was already reserved. Once we were back home though, Irene from the rescue centre contacted us and said that we could have him. Iva the lovely volunteer had told Irene how much we had liked him. They had been unable to confirm his adoption so as we were in a position to make that commitment immediately, we could have him. The answer was a definite yes, so Addie would now be joined by Frodo, a little white fluffy podenco. His name would be changed to Finn, it really suited him. Third photo in INSTAGRAM POST 474.

Our first proper night out was on Xmas Eve, we went out with some of Helen's friends. The first thing I had noticed though was how uncomfortable I found jeans. I hadn't worn them for so long, I was used to walking trousers, it just didn't feel normal. The night itself was a bit overwhelming for both of us. Again it was great to see old faces and catch up with people but this was Xmas Eve, the pubs were rammed, everything and everyone was loud. I couldn't remember the last time Helen and I had a night out like this. A couple of times Helen and I both commented how it was a bit full on for us. People were interested in our travels. The main questions were "Where were your favourite and least favourite places?" and "Does it feel strange to be back?" The answers were that we loved all of it but Canada and South America were the highlights and Costa Rica didn't live up to expectations. And yes, it felt very weird to be back.

Xmas day was a lot quieter than usual. Helen's brother and his family were away so Helen and I spent Xmas Day at home with her parents, just the four of us for Xmas dinner. Later in the evening we walked round to my brother's and spent some time with them. My parents were there, my uncle, along with Amie's dad and sister so it was good to catch up with all of them.

My birthday followed three days later, coinciding with Emma's, we joined her for an enjoyable afternoon ice skating then we went to the pub in the evening for some food before my friends Matt and Dimi joined us.

New Years was a low key affair. Helen and I had a walk up town in the evening for a couple of drinks but we were back before 10pm and in bed before midnight.

In a way I was glad for the New Year to start, it meant more of a return to normality. It also meant I could speak to recruitment agencies and start the hunt for a job. We had eight weeks before we moved back into our house and needed to start paying our mortgage. The job hunt started quite positively; there seemed a decent amount of interest. I had one interview fairly quickly but knew I didn't do very well. It was a part of the experience of getting back into to it but I couldn't afford to mess up many more.

The whole job situation was something that weighed heavily on me. Through our travels when asked why now, in our forties? Our reply was that if you are young, you have the health but not the money. If you are old, you have the money but not the health. In your forties, you hopefully have both. But, and a big but, when you return, you still need to work and pay off your mortgage. I've mentioned I have always been a worrier, but back home needing to find a job I was worrying. What if I couldn't find one? Helen was always reassuring me that we came home with enough money to pay the mortgage until near the end of the year.

On a happier note, we welcomed Addie and Finn into our (and Helen's parents) lives mid-January. INSTAGRAM POST 475. They were great, they both settled in very quickly and were no trouble at all. Helen's parents really warmed to them and our days were all of a sudden a lot busier with walking them. It felt amazing to have our own dogs again, we knew it was going to be a handful having two but it was great to see them play with each other. They both have their own unique traits and were different in a lot of ways. Addie is very lean, she is a pointer cross, all bouncy, hardly any fat on her. She isn't food motivated so it's always a job just to make sure she is eating enough. She also tends to suffer from the cold more, as

271

she has very short hair. On her first day with us she was shivering due to the cold so we had to go out and buy her a jumper. Finn on the other hand is a fuzzy podenco, a lot hairier, so he is always too hot. He loves his food and would eat Addie's if we didn't pick it up. He's not as quick as Addie but has a shorter turning circle when she is chasing him. He also knows that Addie is the boss, we all learnt that very early on. If Finn has something and Addie wants it, she'll have it. He concedes and sulks by barking at us to help him out. They do get on well though and it is great to see them interacting with each other. INSTAGRAM POST 476. They missed a very important part of socialisation in those first six months. When they arrived they were scared of traffic when walking on the pavement, nervous of noises such as the kettle and the washing machine so it was and still is an ongoing process in building their confidence. After Helen had bought a car we were able to venture out further with them.

My parents had gone abroad to escape the January and February cold so they didn't meet Addie and Finn until a few weeks after they arrived. At the end of January we had a welcome visit from an old friend. Laura, who volunteered with us at the shelter in Nevis came to visit for a day. It was a short and sweet stop but it was so good to see her. Laura was looking to rekindle her love of travelling by applying for some more volunteering jobs abroad. It wouldn't be long before she would be out of the country that's for sure. We took the dogs out for a walk and spent a really enjoyable day catching up with each other.

January and February went by and I wasn't successful in finding a job so we moved back in to our house unemployed. The dogs had started to go to dog training and Addie was now coming into season, Finn was fully intact so it was a job to keep them off each other but we managed it with the help of a full body suit for Addie just in case they disappeared behind the shed when we were not looking.

After one initial online interview I was asked to go down to London for a follow up, it went well and I was then asked back again a couple of weeks later to do a presentation. The interview itself was at the factory site just inside the M25 near Dartford. The interview went well. The next day I was offered the job on a six month contract, to then be reviewed, they also wanted me to start in four days time. I had mixed emotions. I was ecstatic that I had managed to land a job, that was the main thing. Money would now be coming in and that would pay the bills and the mortgage. Big relief. But then there was the realisation that this was it, back to normal. As the time was passing with no employment I was getting more desperate. The job offer was fantastic but the site was over 100 miles away, over the Dartford tunnel. I could work from home two days a week but would need to be in the office for the other three. Due to the distance I initially would travel down on the Sunday night, stay down there for Monday and Tuesday and return home on Wednesday night after work. For the first week I borrowed Helen's car as I didn't have time to buy one at short notice. I then bought one the following weekend, it is an automatic by the way, I would never go back to a manual. I had to pay for my own accommodation so there was no way I would be spending £100 per night in a hotel. After two and a half years of travelling my standards had dropped somewhat so I stayed in the cheapest Airbnbs I could find. The night before I started, I turned up and parked up outside a block of flats and rang the bell but there was no answer. The guy wasn't there and I couldn't get hold of him as he wasn't answering his phone. By midnight I resigned myself to spending the night in my car. Not great preparation before your first day at work. Eventually he did turn up. Over those first few weeks I spent some nights in some places I would not have stayed in before travelling. But it was cheap compared to London prices.

It was that second night that I decided to write this book. I was missing Helen and the dogs massively. I was back in work, lacking self-confidence whether I could still do my job and feeling pretty low staying in an Airbnb with a shared bathroom and kitchen. On my second night I was already questioning myself if I could do this. It would have been easy to just watch Netflix or read a book when away from home, but since returning a couple of people asked me if I would write a book. It was something I had never even considered but that night I typed my first few hundred words. I didn't start writing this because I wanted people to read about our travels or thinking that I was going to be a bestselling author. I was honestly writing purely for me, it was my therapy, my escape when I was away from Helen and the dogs. When I was writing about our travels it took me back to a happy place, away from the Airbnb. So from then on I decided I would write every time I was away from home, never whilst I was at home, that time was too short and precious. I ended up changing my days and worked from home on a Monday, driving down to London in the evening arriving at an Airbnb around 10.30pm. Then in the office on Tuesday, staying down there for another two nights before I would join the rush hour traffic after work on Thursday to drive home. I would be lucky if I would walk back through my front door before 8.30pm. So in all I was away from Monday at 6.30pm until Thursday at 8.30pm. I know other people can do it no problem but for me it was tough as I had hardly spent any time away from Helen in nearly three years. I would miss her and the dogs terribly and it was getting to me more and more. I was busying myself writing whilst I was away but I wasn't right, I knew it. I was pretty depressed, I would sense myself getting emotional over stupid things and I felt I could burst into tears anytime. I don't think anyone really knew how bad I was during this time. Should I have seen someone? Yes probably. Did I? No, I did what all blokes do, I tried to knuckle down and get on with it. At the time work was heavily into mental awareness and to be honest the general manager was a real advocate and helped push lots of things to promote it. One thing was going for a walk at lunchtime. Quite a few people participated in this but I didn't, I started to go on my own after they returned. As much as it was encouraged, I wasn't going to open up to someone at work and tell them that I'm struggling after only a few weeks into my new job. I saw it as a weakness so I just bottled it up and carried on.

In June, Helen also started to look for a job and was lucky to find one straight away, an added bonus was that she would work from home for four days a week, just going into the office on a Monday, the day I worked from home. It was great to have the extra income. Helen had always said she would love to have a job working from home, especially with having the dogs and Finn was about to be neutered. The only downside was that Helen left early on a Monday morning for the office and got back about 30 mins before I had to drive down to London, so it meant we would end up seeing even less of each other. Again I know other couples have to cope with this but for us it was still strange being apart for so long during the week.

Towards the end of summer and about four months into my job I received a call out of the blue about a potential opportunity. I was interested. The factory was based up north but the role was home based with travel up to the site twice a month for a couple of days. My first phone interview went well. I was then asked to prepare a presentation for an interview four weeks later. Normally those evenings away were for writing this book but I threw everything I had into the presentation and made sure I was completely happy with it.

When the interview day came I took the train up and I thought I did a good job. It was over a week before I found out if I was successful. I was, and it was such a relief. I handed in my notice. The notice period went quite quickly and Helen and I took the dogs to a cottage in Wales for a week before I started my new role. I started in October, the job didn't turn out to be as expected and within four months the world was now a different place. Covid 19 was already in the UK. A Company restructure took place six months after Covid hit and I found myself unemployed again in September. Luckily a role came up locally so I wasn't out of work for very long. I am very grateful that I am employed and I am really enjoying my new job. The world is a crazy place at the moment and we consider ourselves lucky that we can still work.

So where does that leave us in the future. Hopefully the world returns to some sort of normality and the next 10 to 15 years we will continue to have a great time with Addie and Finn and remain fit and healthy. By then Helen will be retired and I will be nearly 60. What is important is that for now we are back home, with our dogs and our families and friends are close by. In the future we probably would go travelling again, it's something we have discussed. Hopefully we would be mortgage free by then and we could use the rent to fund our travels.

So would I recommend what we did for anyone else? Yes without a doubt and it doesn't matter what age either. Young, old or middle aged, you will never regret it. Expect to come back a different person. I personally think I have returned quite different to when I left. If you are still young it may change your perceptions on what you want to do for the rest of your life. If you are older, definitely, just go for it, life is too precious. If you are middle aged and still have a mortgage to pay, still go for it. Yes, it will still be there when you return and you may have a difficult time to start with as we did and you may end up in a different area of work than before or even earning less money. It is a risk. It was a testing few months on our return as there were so many uncertainties ahead of us. One thing for certain though is that we are so glad we took the leap of faith and did what we did. So if the opportunity arises or the curiosity is getting the better of you, take a chance and go for it.

Right now we are experiencing a third lock down due Covid-19. Hopefully this nightmare will end at some point as the vaccines are now rolling out. There are people who just want things to go back to the way they were before. Others though have seen this as an opportunity to take stock of what is really important in their lives. When all of this does hopefully subside, travel aspirations will certainly rise with a desire to escape and explore this beautiful world we live in. It completely reaffirmed to me that we made the correct decision to take the plunge when we did as life is way too short and you never know what is around the corner. If this book inspires just one person to go out and explore, then to me it has been worth writing it. Especially if you flight sponsor a dog on your return.

THE END

ACKNOWLEDGEMENTS

Obviously Helen, thank you for everything.

Thank you to our families and friends for encouraging us to take on this adventure. Especially our families who ended up storing a lot of our possessions whilst we were away. And a special mention to Helen's parents for putting up with us, and two dogs when we returned.

Thank you to all the people we met along our travels, whether hosts of workaways, co-workers, charity workers or people who trusted us to look after their pets and homes. We have made some friends for life.

Below are charities mentioned in the book. They all rely on donations to keep running and unfortunately some charities we came across are no longer operational.

www.vincentianspca.org/

www.facebook.com/wingsonwheels4dogs/

www.ksk9resq.org/

www.richmondspca.org/

www.hopeforpodencos.com/

Finally thank you to you, the reader for actually taking the time to read this book. This is the first and most likely the only book I shall ever write. Hopefully you enjoyed it. If so I would be extremely grateful if you would consider spending time to write a positive review, hopefully it may encourage other potential readers to buy it.

INDEX OF INSTAGRAM POSTS.

INSTAGRAM POST 20 – Beach time

INSTAGRAM POST 21 – Another hummingbird video

INSTAGRAM POST 22 – Picture of the farm

INSTAGRAM POST 23 – Helen picking strawberries with the dogs for company

INSTAGRAM POST 24 – Laura the cow

INSTAGRAM POST 25 – Teddy the calf

INSTAGRAM POST 26 – Helen and the farm dogs

INSTAGRAM POST 27 – Yet another hummingbird video

INSTAGRAM POST 28 – Potatoes now in season!

INSTAGRAM POST 29 – Releasing the chickens for the day

INSTAGRAM POST 30 – Confederation Bridge again

INSTAGRAM POST 31 – Confederation Bridge again

INSTAGRAM POST 32 – Confederation Bridge again

INSTAGRAM POST 33 – Confederation Bridge again

INSTAGRAM POST 34 – Confederation Bridge again

INSTAGRAM POST 35 – Stormin Norman Lane

INSTAGRAM POST 36 – Temperature rising on the thermometer

INSTAGRAM POST 37 – LAD number plate

INSTAGRAM POST 38 – Red squirrel

INSTAGRAM POST 39 – Egg cleaning

INSTAGRAM POST 40 – Moose sign

INSTAGRAM POST 41. – Baby Wendy

INSTAGRAM POST 42 – Brackley Beach, Prince Edward Island

INSTAGRAM POST 43 – Brackley Beach, Prince Edward Island

INSTAGRAM POST 44 – Hired Bikes, riding across the Island

INSTAGRAM POST 45 – Video of bike ride

INSTAGRAM POST 46 – Confederation Trail, Prince Edward Island

INSTAGRAM POST 47 – Hopewell Rocks

INSTAGRAM POST 48 – Hopewell Rocks

INSTAGRAM POST 49 – Hopewell Rocks

INSTAGRAM POST 50 – Hopewell Rocks

INSTAGRAM POST 51 – Hopewell Rocks

INSTAGRAM POST 52 – Hopewell Rocks

INSTAGRAM POST 53 – Hopewell Rocks

INSTAGRAM POST 54 – Hopewell Rocks

INSTAGRAM POST 55 – Hopewell Rocks

INSTAGRAM POST 56 – Hopewell Rocks

INSTAGRAM POST 57 – Hopewell Rocks

INSTAGRAM POST 58. – Hopewell Rocks (last one!)

INSTAGRAM POST 59 – Hire car from St John airport

INSTAGRAM POST 60 – Ville de Mont Tremblant

INSTAGRAM POST 61 – Video of Ville de Mont Tremblant

INSTAGRAM POST 62 – Another video of Ville de Mont Tremblant

INSTAGRAM POST 63 – Deer spotted on the hike up Mont Tremblant

INSTAGRAM POST 64 – Video of stream walking up Mont Tremblant

INSTAGRAM POST 65 – Arty photo attempt of broken bridge

INSTAGRAM POST 66 – Photo from the top of Mont Tremblant

INSTAGRAM POST 67 – Video from the top of Mont Tremblant

INSTAGRAM POST 68 – Another photo from the top of Mont Tremblant

INSTAGRAM POST 69 – Another video from the top of Mont Tremblant

INSTAGRAM POST 70 – Montreal City as seen from Parc du Mont Royal

INSTAGRAM POST 71 – Montreal Olympic Stadium

INSTAGRAM POST 72 – Our car!

INSTAGRAM POST 73 – Rideau Canal, Ottawa

INSTAGRAM POST 74 - Beavertail

INSTAGRAM POST 75 – Lightshow on Ottawa parliament building

INSTAGRAM POST 76 – Rideau Canal Ottawa

INSTAGRAM POST 77 – Bridal Veil Falls, Niagara

INSTAGRAM POST 78 – Horseshoe Falls, Niagara

INSTAGRAM POST 79 – Video of Horseshoe Falls, Niagara

INSTAGRAM POST 80 – Maid of the Mist boat, Niagara

INSTAGRAM POST 81 – Video of Horseshoe Falls, Niagara

INSTAGRAM POST 82 – Close up photo of Horseshoe Falls, Niagara

INSTAGRAM POST 83 – Close up photo of Horseshoe Falls, Niagara

INSTAGRAM POST 84 – Close up video of Horseshoe Falls, Niagara

INSTAGRAM POST 85 – Close up video of Horseshoe Falls, Niagara

INSTAGRAM POST 86 – Distance photo of Horseshoe Falls, Niagara

INSTAGRAM POST 87 – Distance shot of Bridal Veil and Horseshoe Falls, Niagara

INSTAGRAM POST 88 – Me at Horseshoe Falls, Niagara

INSTAGRAM POST 89 – Sunrise at Horseshoe Falls, Niagara

INSTAGRAM POST 90 – Blue Mountains

INSTAGRAM POST 91 – Lake Simcoe

INSTAGRAM POST 92 – Moose!

INSTAGRAM POST 93 – Bear!

INSTAGRAM POST 94 – Algonquin Provincial Park

INSTAGRAM POST 95 – Algonquin Provincial Park

INSTAGRAM POST 96 – Sat Nav – Long drive

INSTAGRAM POST 97 – Size comparison of Lake Superior versus England

INSTAGRAM POST 98 – Lake Superior

INSTAGRAM POST 99 – Lake Superior

INSTAGRAM POST 100 – Lake Superior

INSTAGRAM POST 101 – Lake Superior

INSTAGRAM POST 102 – Lake Superior

INSTAGRAM POST 103 – Lake Superior

INSTAGRAM POST 104 – Lake Superior

INSTAGRAM POST 105 – Thunder Bay Lake Superior

INSTAGRAM POST 106 – Terry Fox Memorial

INSTAGRAM POST 107 – Terry Fox Memorial

INSTAGRAM POST 108 – Crossing in to Central Standard Time Zone

INSTAGRAM POST 109 – Kakabeka Falls

INSTAGRAM POST 110 – Kakabeka Falls

INSTAGRAM POST 111 - Kakabeka Falls

INSTAGRAM POST 112 – Video of Kakabeka Falls

INSTAGRAM POST 113 – Manitoba landscape

INSTAGRAM POST 114 – Manitoba landscape

INSTAGRAM POST 115 – Manitoba landscape

INSTAGRAM POST 116 – Saskatchewan sunset

INSTAGRAM POST 117 – Saskatchewan sunset

INSTAGRAM POST 118 – Saskatchewan sunset

INSTAGRAM POST 119 – Glenbow Ranch Provincial Park

INSTAGRAM POST 120 – Addy and Lilly, Cochrane Housesit

INSTAGRAM POST 121 – Ferry crossing at Drumheller

INSTAGRAM POST 122 - Drumheller

INSTAGRAM POST 123 - Drumheller

INSTAGRAM POST 124 – Bow River Cochrane

INSTAGRAM POST 125 – Mt Baldy and Barrier Lake, Kananaskis Country

INSTAGRAM POST 126 – Barrier Lake, Kananaskis Country

INSTAGRAM POST 127 – Kananaskis Country

INSTAGRAM POST 128 – Kananaskis Country

INSTAGRAM POST 129 – Kananaskis Country

INSTAGRAM POST 130 – Mt Baldy and Barrier Lake

INSTAGRAM POST 131 – Grassi Lake Trail, Canmore

INSTAGRAM POST 132 – Grassi Lake Trail, Canmore

INSTAGRAM POST 133 – Bow River, Banff

INSTAGRAM POST 134 – Bow River, Banff

INSTAGRAM POST 135 – Bow River, Banff

INSTAGRAM POST 136 – Banff Scenery

INSTAGRAM POST 137 – Bow River, Banff

INSTAGRAM POST 138 – Elk strolling along the road in Banff

INSTAGRAM POST 139 – Boom Lake, Banff

INSTAGRAM POST 140 – Boom Lake, Banff

INSTAGRAM POST 141 – Lake Minnewanka, Banff

INSTAGRAM POST 142 – Lake Louise, Banff

INSTAGRAM POST 143 – Video of Lake Louise, Banff

INSTAGRAM POST 144 – Bow Lake, Icefield Parkway

INSTAGRAM POST 145 – Peyto Lake, Icefield Parkway

INSTAGRAM POST 146 – Icefield Parkway

INSTAGRAM POST 147 – Banff Falls, Banff

INSTAGRAM POST 148 – Top of Sulpher Mountain

INSTAGRAM POST 149 – Top of Sulpher Mountain

INSTAGRAM POST 150 – Banff High Street

INSTAGRAM POST 151 – Roadblock at Medicine Lake

INSTAGRAM POST 152 – Maligne Canyon

INSTAGRAM POST 153 – Athabasca Falls, Icefield Parkway

INSTAGRAM POST 154 – Sunwapta Falls, Icefields Parkway

INSTAGRAM POST 155 – Athabasca Glacier, Icefield Parkway

INSTAGRAM POST 156 – Athabasca Glacier, Icefield Parkway

INSTAGRAM POST 157 - Porcupine

INSTAGRAM POST 158 – Bloom, dog sitting in Calgary

INSTAGRAM POST 159 – Calgary Olympic Park

INSTAGRAM POST 160 – Bird feeding in Calgary

INSTAGRAM POST 161 – Glacier National Park

INSTAGRAM POST 162 - Gemma and Coco, House sit in Chilliwack

INSTAGRAM POST 163 - Linderman Lake

INSTAGRAM POST 164 – Views from Mt Thom

INSTAGRAM POST 165 – Views from Mt Thom

INSTAGRAM POST 187 – Views from the top of Giants Head Mountain

INSTAGRAM POST 188 – Frozen creek, Summerland

INSTAGRAM POST 189 – Frozen creek, Summerland

INSTAGRAM POST 190 – Frozen Okanagan Lake, Penticton

INSTAGRAM POST 191 - Ice, Penticton

INSTAGRAM POST 192 – View from Munson Mountain

INSTAGRAM POST 193 – Frozen Waterfall, Naramata Creek Trail

INSTAGRAM POST 194 – View from Kettle Valley Trail

INSTAGRAM POST 195 – Kettle Valley Trail

INSTAGRAM POST 196 – Cold enough to freeze a drink

INSTAGRAM POST 197 – Kettle Valley Trail

INSTAGRAM POST 198 – Frozen Hardy Falls, Peachland

INSTAGRAM POST 199 – Ice Hockey game

INSTAGRAM POST 200 – Lucy and Winnie, housesitting near Osoyoos

INSTAGRAM POST 201 – View from housesit vineyard

INSTAGRAM POST 202 – View from housesit vineyard

INSTAGRAM POST 203 – Golden Eagle

INSTAGRAM POST 204 – Walking Winnie and Lucy

INSTAGRAM POST 205 – Walking in mountains above the valley

INSTAGRAM POST 206 - View from Crowsnest Highway

INSTAGRAM POST 207 – Driving to Mt Baldy ski resort

INSTAGRAM POST 208 – Views of Osoyoos from Crowsnest Highway

INSTAGRAM POST 209 –Fat Biking at Mt Baldy ski resort

INSTAGRAM POST 210 – Fat Biking at Mt Baldy ski resort

INSTAGRAM POST 211 – Spotted Lake, Osoyoos

INSTAGRAM POST 212 – The Pacific Ocean

INSTAGRAM POST 213 – Wild Pacific Trail

INSTAGRAM POST 214 – Cox Bay, Vancouver Island

INSTAGRAM POST 215 – Long Beach, Tofino

INSTAGRAM POST 216 – Saying goodbye to Canada

INSTAGRAM POST 217 – Bird Rocks, Oregon Coast

INSTAGRAM POST 218 – Haystack Rock, Oregon Coast

INSTAGRAM POST 219 – Oregon Coast

INSTAGRAM POST 220 – Oregon Coastline

INSTAGRAM POST 221 – Oregon Coastline

INSTAGRAM POST 222 – Laundry day

INSTAGRAM POST 223 – Redwood National Park

INSTAGRAM POST 224 – Pier 39, San Francisco

INSTAGRAM POST 225 – Alcatraz Prison

INSTAGRAM POST 226 – Alcatraz Prison

INSTAGRAM POST 227 – Alcatraz Prison

INSTAGRAM POST 228 – Golden Gate Bridge

INSTAGRAM POST 229 – View of San Francisco from Alcatraz

INSTAGRAM POST 230 – Alcatraz Prison

INSTAGRAM POST 231 – Zoe, Prince, Blanche and Giudecca, housesit in Concord, San Francisco

INSTAGRAM POST 232 – Elephant Seals at Piedras Blancas

INSTAGRAM POST 233 – Elephant Seals at Piedras Blancas

INSTAGRAM POST 234 – Morro Rock, Morrow Bay California

INSTAGRAM POST 235 – Inca and Sydney, Ventura, California

INSTAGRAM POST 236 – Las Vegas

INSTAGRAM POST 237 – Zion National Park, Utah

INSTAGRAM POST 238 – Emerald Falls, Zion Park

INSTAGRAM POST 239 – Hiking in Zion

INSTAGRAM POST 240 – Hiking in Zion

INSTAGRAM POST 241 – Hiking in Zion

INSTAGRAM POST 242 – Hiking in Zion

INSTAGRAM POST 243 – Hiking in Zion

INSTAGRAM POST 244 – Angels Landing, Zion

INSTAGRAM POST 245 – Bryce Canyon

INSTAGRAM POST 246 – Bryce Canyon

INSTAGRAM POST 247 – Bryce Canyon

INSTAGRAM POST 248 – Bryce Canyon

INSTAGRAM POST 249 – Bryce Canyon

INSTAGRAM POST 250 – Maddie and Oreo, housesit in Salt Lake City

INSTAGRAM POST 251 – Walking Maddie and Oreo

INSTAGRAM POST 252 – Nevada Basin

INSTAGRAM POST 253 – Stanislaus Forest Range

INSTAGRAM POST 254 – Housesit Santa Cruz

INSTAGRAM POST 255 – Santa Cruz Beach

INSTAGRAM POST 256 – Santa Cruz Beach

INSTAGRAM POST 257 – Santa Cruz Beach

INSTAGRAM POST 258 – Santa Cruz Beach

INSTAGRAM POST 259 – Yosemite National Park Tunnel View

INSTAGRAM POST 260 – Bridal veil Falls, Yosemite Valley

INSTAGRAM POST 261 – El Capitan, Yosemite Valley

INSTAGRAM POST 262 – Vernal Falls, Yosemite Valley

INSTAGRAM POST 263 – Nevada Falls, Yosemite Valley

INSTAGRAM POST 264 – Nevada Falls, Yosemite Valley

INSTAGRAM POST 265 – View of Vernal Falls, from Nevada Falls

INSTAGRAM POST 266 – Upper Yosemite Falls

INSTAGRAM POST 267 – Hiking up Upper Yosemite Falls

INSTAGRAM POST 268 – Hiking up Upper Yosemite Falls

INSTAGRAM POST 269 – Top of Yosemite Falls

INSTAGRAM POST 270 – Heading back down from the Top of Yosemite Falls

INSTAGRAM POST 271 – Heading into Death Valley

INSTAGRAM POST 272 – Dante's View down to Badwater Basin

INSTAGRAM POST 273 – Sand Dunes in Death Valley

INSTAGRAM POST 274 – Badwater Basin, Death Valley

INSTAGRAM POST 275 – Badwater Basin, Death Valley

INSTAGRAM POST 276 – Family reunion in LA

INSTAGRAM POST 277 – Hollywood Walk of Fame

INSTAGRAM POST 278 – Richard Ashcroft gig

INSTAGRAM POST 279 – Richard Ashcroft gig

INSTAGRAM POST 280 – Richard Ashcroft gig

INSTAGRAM POST 281 – Santa Monica Beach

INSTAGRAM POST 282 – Venice Beach

INSTAGRAM POST 283 – Dodgers Stadium

INSTAGRAM POST 284 – Universal Studios Hollywood

INSTAGRAM POST 285 – La Galaxy

INSTAGRAM POST 286 – Hollywood sign

INSTAGRAM POST 287 – Grand Canyon

INSTAGRAM POST 288 – Grand Canyon

INSTAGRAM POST 289 – Grand Canyon

INSTAGRAM POST 290 – Grand Canyon

INSTAGRAM POST 291 – Grand Canyon

INSTAGRAM POST 292 – Grand Canyon

INSTAGRAM POST 293 – Monument Valley

INSTAGRAM POST 294 – Monument Valley

INSTAGRAM POST 295 – Monument Valley

INSTAGRAM POST 296 – Delicate Arch, Arches National Park

INSTAGRAM POST 297 – Landscape Arch, Arches National Park

INSTAGRAM POST 298 – Partition Arch, Arches National Park

INSTAGRAM POST 299 – Double Arches, Arches National Park

INSTAGRAM POST 300 – Dallas Airport

INSTAGRAM POST 301 – Arriving at Nevis

INSTAGRAM POST 302 – Beach on Nevis

INSTAGRAM POST 303 – Oscar, Dog Shelter

INSTAGRAM POST 304 – Sailing in the Booby Island Regatta

INSTAGRAM POST 305 – Monkey stealing papayas

INSTAGRAM POST 306 – Poor dog suffering from mange

INSTAGRAM POST 307 – Gigi, dog shelter

INSTAGRAM POST 308 – Front garden of the shelter

INSTAGRAM POST 309 – Sailing in the Booby Island Regatta

INSTAGRAM POST 310 – Poor puppy arrival

INSTAGRAM POST 311 – Another puppy arrival at the dog shelter

INSTAGRAM POST 312 - Trip over to St Kitts

INSTAGRAM POST 313 – Ferry over St Kitts

INSTAGRAM POST 314 – Saint Vincent and the Grenadines

INSTAGRAM POST 315 – Beautiful Bequia

INSTAGRAM POST 316 – Princess Margaret Beach

INSTAGRAM POST 317 – Red Footed Tortoise

INSTAGRAM POST 318 – Cricket at Port Elizabeth

INSTAGRAM POST 319 – Husking a coconut

INSTAGRAM POST 320 – Lower Bay Beach

INSTAGRAM POST 321 – Lower Bay Beach

INSTAGRAM POST 322 – Chill time, Friday feeling

INSTAGRAM POST 323 – Hiking to Bequia Point

INSTAGRAM POST 324 – Hiking to Bequia Point

INSTAGRAM POST 325 – Industry Bay and Crescent Beach

INSTAGRAM POST 326 - Soursop

INSTAGRAM POST 327 – Morning Beach walk

INSTAGRAM POST 328 – Molly, Maggie and Sandy, our housesit dogs on Bequia

INSTAGRAM POST 329 – View from Port Elizabeth

INSTAGRAM POST 330 – Mt Pleasant

INSTAGRAM POST 331 – Our plane to Grenada

INSTAGRAM POST 332 – Video of take off

INSTAGRAM POST 333 – Landing at Carriacou

INSTAGRAM POST 334 – La Sagesse Beach, Grenada

INSTAGRAM POST 335 – Rufus, house sit in Grenada

INSTAGRAM POST 336 – Grand Anse Beach

INSTAGRAM POST 337 – House view in Grenada

INSTAGRAM POST 338 – Bar Dominoes in Grenada

INSTAGRAM POST 339 – Lush, Green Grenada

INSTAGRAM POST 340 – Four legged friends in Grenada

INSTAGRAM POST 341 – Flights back to Saint Kitts

INSTAGRAM POST 342 – Busy first day back at the shelter

INSTAGRAM POST 343 – The Golden girls

INSTAGRAM POST 344 – Dusty, puppy arrival

INSTAGRAM POST 345 – Marathon Man and world record holder, Nick

INSTAGRAM POST 346 – Gadget Show host, Jason Bradbury

INSTAGRAM POST 347 – Lilly, absolute cutie

INSTAGRAM POST 348 – Beach on St Kitts

INSTAGRAM POST 349 – Dusty and Lilly, best of friends

INSTAGRAM POST 350 – A very rare night out for us both

INSTAGRAM POST 351 – Dusty and Charlot

INSTAGRAM POST 352 – Get me out of here!

INSTAGRAM POST 353 – Goodbye to Dusty and Charlot

INSTAGRAM POST 354 – Xmas in Charlestown

INSTAGRAM POST 355 – Xmas Dinner

INSTAGRAM POST 356 – Birthday Beer

INSTAGRAM POST 357 – Another puppy arrival

INSTAGRAM POST 358 – Lilly giving out free kisses

INSTAGRAM POST 359 – Monkey road sign

INSTAGRAM POST 360 - Tarantula

INSTAGRAM POST 361 - Views from Saddle Hill

INSTAGRAM POST 362 – Bluebell and her girls

INSTAGRAM POST 363 – Sad goodbye to Lilly

INSTAGRAM POST 364 – Bluebell and her girls arrive in Florida

INSTAGRAM POST 365 – Cape Canaveral Rocket Launch

INSTAGRAM POST 365 – Start of the road trip with Buttons and Charlot

INSTAGRAM POST 367 – Road tripping, Day 2

INSTAGRAM POST 368 – Road tripping, Day 3

INSTAGRAM POST 369 – Road tripping, Memphis

INSTAGRAM POST 370 – Sad goodbye to Buttons and Charlot at Wichita

INSTAGRAM POST 371 – Tallgrass Prairie National Reserve

INSTAGRAM POST 372 – Cairo, Illinois

INSTAGRAM POST 373 – Cairo, Illinois

INSTAGRAM POST 374 – Great Smoky Mountains

INSTAGRAM POST 375 – Mt Pisgah

INSTAGRAM POST 376 – Mt Pisgah

INSTAGRAM POST 377 – Lunch stop on the Blue Ridge Parkway

INSTAGRAM POST 378 – Appalachian Trail

INSTAGRAM POST 379 – Flying to Central America

INSTAGRAM POST 380 – Manuel Antonio Park, Costa Rica

INSTAGRAM POST 381 – Monkey crossing the road

INSTAGRAM POST 382 – Playa Espadilla

INSTAGRAM POST 383 – Quepos sunset

INSTAGRAM POST 384 – Iguana road block

INSTAGRAM POST 385 – Arenal Volcano

INSTAGRAM POST 386 – Crossing the border into Panama

INSTAGRAM POST 387 – New housesit, rural Panama

INSTAGRAM POST 388 – Scorpion

INSTAGRAM POST 389 - Great news about Bluebell and the Girls

INSTAGRAM POST 390 – New housesit, Playa El Rompio

INSTAGRAM POST 391 – Butterflies everywhere

INSTAGRAM POST 392 – Panama Canal

INSTAGRAM POST 393 – Quito, Ecuador

INSTAGRAM POST 394 – Equator line, Quito

INSTAGRAM POST 395 – Teleférico up Mount Pichincha

INSTAGRAM POST 396 – Mindo cloud forest

INSTAGRAM POST 397 –Friendly baby Llama

INSTAGRAM POST 398 – Quilotoa Loop hike

INSTAGRAM POST 399 – Quilotoa Loop hike Day 2

INSTAGRAM POST 400 – Final Day of Quilotoa Loop hike

INSTAGRAM POST 401 – Quilotoa Lake

INSTAGRAM POST 402 – Banos

INSTAGRAM POST 403 – Tungurahua Volcano

INSTAGRAM POST 404 – Route of the Waterfalls

INSTAGRAM POST 405 – Video Route of the Waterfalls

INSTAGRAM POST 406 – El Pailon Del Diablo

INSTAGRAM POST 407 – El Pailon Del Diablo

INSTAGRAM POST 408 – Border crossing into Peru

INSTAGRAM POST 409 –Kuelap Fortress, Chachapoyas

INSTAGRAM POST 410 – Gocta Falls

INSTAGRAM POST 411 – Video of Gocta Falls

INSTAGRAM POST 412 – Lake Parón

INSTAGRAM POST 413 – Lake Parón

INSTAGRAM POST 414 – Yungay

INSTAGRAM POST 415 – Lake Wilcacocha views

INSTAGRAM POST 416 – Lake Rajucolta

INSTAGRAM POST 417 – Laguna 69 hike

INSTAGRAM POST 418 – Pastoruri Glacier

INSTAGRAM POST 419 – Lake Churup hike

INSTAGRAM POST 420 – Day 1 of Jungle Inca Tour, downhill biking

INSTAGRAM POST 421 – Day 2 of Jungle Inca Tour, zip lining

INSTAGRAM POST 422 – Machu Picchu

INSTAGRAM POST 423 – Rainbow Mountain

INSTAGRAM POST 424 – Sacred Valley Tour

INSTAGRAM POST 425 – View over Cusco

INSTAGRAM POST 426 – Bolivia Border crossing

INSTAGRAM POST 427 – Lake Titicaca, Bolivia

INSTAGRAM POST 428 – La Paz

INSTAGRAM POST 429 – Mount Chacaltaya

INSTAGRAM POST 430 – Cycling on the Death Road

INSTAGRAM POST 431 – Bolivian Salt Flats

INSTAGRAM POST 432 – Bolivian Salt Flats

INSTAGRAM POST 433 – Bolivian Salt Flats

INSTAGRAM POST 434 – Remote Southwest

INSTAGRAM POST 435 – Remote Southwest

INSTAGRAM POST 436 - Bolivian Salt Flats

INSTAGRAM POST 437 – Border crossing to Chile

INSTAGRAM POST 438 - Pucón, Chile

INSTAGRAM POST 439 – Bariloche

INSTAGRAM POST 440 – El Bolsón

INSTAGRAM POST 441 - Armadillo, El Chaltén

INSTAGRAM POST 442 - Mirador de los Concordes & de las Aguilas, El Chaltén

INSTAGRAM POST 443 – Cerro Fitz Roy

INSTAGRAM POST 444 – Cerro Fitz Roy

INSTAGRAM POST 445 – Cerro Fitz Roy

INSTAGRAM POST 446 – Cerro Torre

INSTAGRAM POST 447 – Cerro Torre Video

INSTAGRAM POST 448 – Perito Moreno Glacier video

INSTAGRAM POST 449 – Perito Moreno Glacier

INSTAGRAM POST 450 - Perito Moreno Glacier video

INSTAGRAM POST 451 – Perito Moreno Glacier

INSTAGRAM POST 452 – Puerto Natales

INSTAGRAM POST 453 – Torres Del Paine

INSTAGRAM POST 454 – Torres Del Paine

INSTAGRAM POST 455 – Volcan Ozorno

INSTAGRAM POST 456 – Petrohué River

INSTAGRAM POST 457 – Pucón again

INSTAGRAM POST 458 – Maracanã Football Stadium

INSTAGRAM POST 459 – Copacabana Beach Football

INSTAGRAM POST 460 – Marmosets in Parque Lage

INSTAGRAM POST 461 – Christ the Redeemer

INSTAGRAM POST 462 – View from Corcovado

INSTAGRAM POST 463 – View from Corcovado

INSTAGRAM POST 464 – Pedra Bonita

INSTAGRAM POST 465 – Pedra Bonita

INSTAGRAM POST 466 – Sunset over Sugar Loaf Mountain

INSTAGRAM POST 467 – Our entire route through the Americas

INSTAGRAM POST 468 – Canadian Route

INSTAGRAM POST 469 – US Part 1 Route

INSTAGRAM POST 470 – Caribbean Route

INSTAGRAM POST 471 – US Part 2 Route

INSTAGRAM POST 472 – Central American Route

INSTAGRAM POST 473 – South American Route

INSTAGRAM POST 474 - Addie & Finn, our new dogs!

INSTAGRAM POST 475 – Addie & Finn arrive

INSTAGRAM POST 476 – Addie & Finn